P9-AOR-388

YOUNG STUDENTS

Learning Library

VOLUME 18

Rodent–Slavery

WEEKLY READER BOOKS
MIDDLETOWN • CONNECTICUT

PHOTO CREDITS

A-Z BOTANICAL COLLECTION page 2217(top left); GOVERNMENT OF ALBERTA page 2117(top left); ALLACTION PHOTOGRAPHY page 2118(bottom right). AUSTRALIAN NATIONAL INFORMATION BUREAU page 2201(top right). BBC HULTON PICTURE LIBRARY page 2156(top left); 2159(bottom right); 2217(bottom right). BERMUDA TOURIST OFFICE page 2233(top left). BIBLIOTEQUE NATIONALE page 2235(top right). BIOPHOTOS page 2115(top left); 2220(top left). JEAN F. BLASHFIELD page 2186(top left both pics); BRIDEN ROPES page 2136(bottom left). BRITISH MUSEUM page 2120(bottom and top right); 2121(bottom). J. ALLAN CASH page 2222(top left). CLARIT'S SHOES page 2214(top left). PETER CLAYTON page 2225(center right). COLORSPORT page 2214(bottom left); 2231(bottom right). ARMANDO CURCIO EDITORE SPA page 2117(top right); 2118(center left); 2119(center right); 2120(top left); 2125(bottom right); 2127(bottom left); 2129(top right); 2133(bottom left); 2137(bottom right); 2138(top left); 2140(bottom left); 2142(bottom right); 2143(top right); 2144(top left); 2145(bottom right); 2147(top right); 2150(top left); 2155(top right); 2157(both pics); 2170(center left); 2177(both pics); 2178(bottom left & top right); 2185(top right); 2198(both pics); 2200(bottom left); 2203(bottom right); 2204(bottom left & top right); 2205(bottom right); 2224(bottom left); 2228(bottom left); 2229(top right); 2236(top left); 2237(top). DARTMOUTH COLLEGE NEWS SERVICE page 2169(top right). DRIGGS, NEW YORK page 2227(top right). EDITORIAL PHOTOCOLOR ARCHIVES page 2171(bottom right). GIRLS SCOUTS OF AMERICA INC. page 2135(center right). GLOBTIK page 2212(top right). W.R. GRACE & COMPANY page 2174(bottom left). PHILIP GRUSHKIN page 2152(top right). SONIA HALLIDAY page 2130(bottom left); 2131(top right); 2132(bottom); 2154(top left). GERHARDS HEINHOLD page 2127(top right). RUSSEL F. HOGELAND page 2151(bottom right). THE HUTCHISON LIBRARY page 2205(top right). IMITOR page 2202(center bottom); 2225(top right). ITALIAN TOURIST OFFICE page 2122(bottom right); 2129(top left). KOBAL COLLECTION page 2175(top right). LIBRARY OF CONGRESS page 2192(bottom left); 2235(center right); 2238(both pics). THE MANSELL COLLECTION page 2121(top right); 2145(top left); 2171(top right). CHARLOTTE M. MITCHELL page 2119(top right). PAT MORRIS page 2115(bottom), 2182(top left); 2224(top right). N.B.C. page 2118(top left). NATIONAL GALLERY, LONDON page 2142(top left); 2154(bottom right). NATIONAL GALLERY OF ART, WASHINGTON, D.C. page 2117(bottom right); 2128(top & bottom left); 2162(bottom left); 2179(bottom left). NATIONAL RUBBER BOARD page 2141(bottom left). THE NATIONAL TRUST page 2195(top right). NATURE PHOTOGRAPHERS page 2116(top left); 2158(top left). NEW ZEALAND TOURIST OFFICE page 2201(bottom left). PETER NEWARK'S WESTERN AMERICANA page 2189(bottom right); 2216(center left). NOVOSTI page 2149(bottom right). OHIO DIVISION OF ECONOMIC DEVELOPMENT & PUBLICITY page 2152(top left). PHILADELPHIA CONVENTION & VISITORS BUREAU page 2138(center left). PHOTRI page 2188(bottom left). PLESSEY page 2189(top right). POPPERPHOTO page 2227(bottom left). DAVID REDFERN page 2228(top left). J. RIBIÉRE page 2122(top left); 2124(top right); 2169(bottom right); 2170(top left). SCALA page 2124(bottom left); 2131(bottom right); 2132(top left); 2179(top right). SCIENCE MUSEUM, LONDON page 2172(top left); 2210(center left). SCIENCE PHOTO LIBRARY page 2139(top left). RONALD SHERIDAN page 2125(top right); 2129(bottom right). SINGAPORE TOURIST BOARD page 2226(center left). SINGER SEWING CENTERS page 2196(both pics). HARRY SMITH COLLECTION page 2137(top right). SPECTRUM COLOUR LIBRARY page 2139(bottom right); 2163(bottom left); 2167(top right); 2224(top left). SPEEDWRITING SHORTHAND/ITT EDUCATIONAL SERVICES INC. page 2215(top right). SWISS NATIONAL TOURIST OFFICE page 2239(bottom right); 2232(top left). TATE GALLERY, LONDON page 2179(bottom right); 2180(top). TEXAS HIGHWAY DEPARTMENT page 2116(bottom left). UNITED KINGDOM ATOMIC ENERGY AUTHORITY page 2172(bottom); 2173(bottom right); 2174(top left). UNITED PRESS INTERNATIONAL page 2133(center right); 2158(top right); 2223(top right). U.S. ARMY PHOTO page 2134(top left). VICKERS page 2212(top left). V.A. page 2149(top right). WOODMASTENE page 2183(bottom left). STATE OF WISCONSIN DEPT. OF NATURAL RESOURCES page 2234(bottom left). ZEFA page 2126(top left); 2142(bottom right); 2153(top right); 2154(bottom left); 2156(top right); 2161(top right); 2168(top left); 2176(bottom left); 2195(bottom right); 2199(top right); 2219(top right); 2222(bottom left); 2231(top right).

ISBN 0-8374-6048-4

Contents

▲ *Two young gerbils peer nearsightedly at the camera.*

RODENT Rodents are gnawing animals. There are more than 1,700 different kinds of rodents in the world—in other words, about one-third of all the types of mammals in the world are rodents. Some of the best-known members of the rodent family are squirrels, guinea pigs, rats, mice, beavers, porcupines, chipmunks, hamsters, gerbils, chinchillas, prairie dogs, and gophers.

All of these animals have very sharp front teeth. These front teeth are called *incisors*. The incisors of a rodent keep on growing as long as the animal lives. The rodent is constantly gnawing on things. In this way, it keeps on wearing away the tops of its incisors. If the rodent did not keep gnawing away on things, its incisors would grow so long that it could not close its mouth or eat anything. But if the incisors did not grow, they would become worn away, and the rodent would not be able to eat properly.

The gnawing done by rodents also keeps their incisors very, very sharp. Always be very careful when you are handling pet rodents, such as hamsters. Their sharp teeth can give you a very nasty bite. If you are bitten, immediately ask an adult to treat the wound with a medical disinfectant. Some rodents can even gnaw through wire and glass if necessary.

Most rodents eat grain, seeds, and nuts, but some eat almost anything. Many rodents store away extra food for the winter. Rodents live almost everywhere throughout the world. They have many different habitats. Some live in lakes and streams, and others live in trees. Many rodents live on the ground, and some live underground, in burrows. When winter comes, many rodents *hibernate* in their burrows. That is, they go to sleep until warmer weather comes. Some rodents, like the chipmunk, sleep all winter long. Others, like the squirrel and hamster, wake up now and then to eat a bit of food. Rodents range in size from tiny mice to the South American capybara, which is about as large as a pig. Most rodents, however, are only about the size of a rat. The smallest rodent of all is the northern pygmy mouse, found in Mexico and parts of Texas and Arizona. Including its tail, it is just over four inches (10 cm) long. Another very small rodent, the mole, eats its own weight in leaves, seeds, and roots every day!

ALSO READ: ANIMAL; ANIMAL DISTRI-

▲ *Four different kinds of rodents, from the very small to the very large. Jerboas can be as tiny as 1½ inches (4 cm) long, while a capybara can be over 20 inches (50 cm) tall at the shoulder.*

Rodents are among the fastest breeding of all animals. A pair of rats, for example, can have almost a hundred offspring in one year.

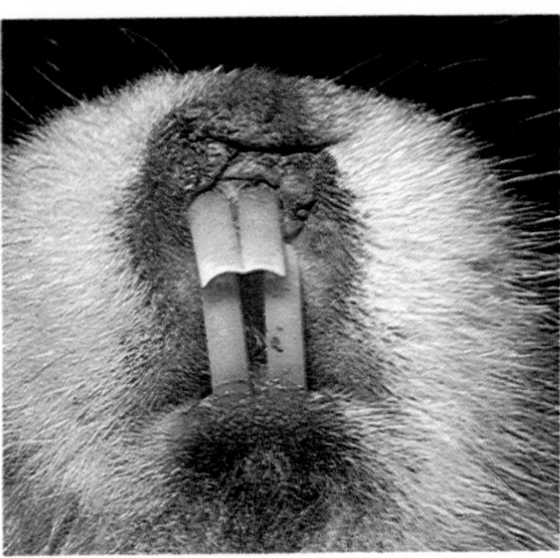

◀ *The head of an African mole rat, showing the long gnawing teeth. If rodents' teeth were not worn down as they gnawed things, they could grow to several times the animal's body-length.*

◀ *Science-fiction stories are often about voyages and exploration in spaceships and the discovery of new worlds. (See* SCIENCE FICTION.)

▲ *Dormice are very small rodents found in Europe, Asia, and Africa. They sleep during the day and feed at night, and they hibernate during the winter.*

BUTION; ANIMAL HOMES; ANIMAL KINGDOM; BEAVER; GROUNDHOG; GROUND SQUIRREL; GUINEA PIGS, HAMSTERS, AND GERBILS; LEMMING; MAMMAL; PORCUPINE; PRAIRIE DOG; RATS AND MICE; SQUIRREL.

RODEO The rodeo is an exciting spectator sport that is held in the United States, Canada, and Australia. It is a contest of skill in roping cattle and riding wild horses (called broncos or broncs) and wild bulls. Cowboys and cowgirls need strength, courage, and speed to work in a rodeo. The animals are strong and dangerous, and each event is timed.

Some professional cowboys and cowgirls travel from one rodeo to another and live on the money they earn from winning rodeo events. Most rodeo performers belong to the Rodeo Cowboys Association. They pay a fee to enter an event, but they can win a great deal of money.

Rodeo competition began in the southwestern United States about 100 years ago. The word "rodeo" comes from the Spanish word for roundup. When the hard work of rounding up, or bringing in, the cattle from the range was over, the cowhands invented racing and roping contests for fun. Soon the idea spread to towns all over the West. Before long, rodeos were a money-making business.

▲ *Bull-riding is perhaps the most dangerous of all rodeo events. Bulls are a serious danger with their sharp horns, and they can maim or even kill any rider who is thrown.*

Cheyenne, Wyoming, has a famous rodeo each year called Frontier Days. Pendleton, Oregon, has its Roundup, and Calgary, Alberta, in Canada, has the Stampede. In recent years, rodeos have been held in the eastern states as well.

Rodeo arenas have wooden passageways, called *chutes*, at one end. In the riding events, a cowboy or cowgirl climbs on a half-wild horse or bull while it is still in the chute. The door of the chute is opened and, when the animal is released, it comes leaping out. The rider tries to stay on for a certain length of time.

Saddle bronc riding is one of the oldest events. A bucking, leaping horse called a bronco must be ridden for, usually, ten seconds. The rider is allowed to hold on with only one hand and must spur the horse constantly. *Spurs* are pieces of metal worn on a rider's boot-heel to dig into the horse so it will move faster. But riders are not allowed to hurt the horses. *Bareback bronc riding* is riding a bronco without a saddle. The rider must hold onto the belt around the horse's middle with only one hand. He or she must spur the horse constantly and stay on for eight seconds. *Bull riding* is the most dangerous event. A wild bull can crush a fallen rider with its hoofs or gore him or her with its horns. The bull must be ridden bareback—just as in the bareback bronc event—for eight seconds.

Calf roping shows off the partnership of a cowboy or cowgirl and a horse. The horse and rider race after a calf. One end of the rider's rope is tied to the saddle horn. The rider throws the rope around the calf and then jumps off the horse. The well-trained horse stands still, holding the rope tight. The cowboy or cowgirl throws the calf down and ties up three of its legs. The winner of this event is the person who ropes and ties a calf in the least amount of time. *Bulldogging* is a kind of animal wrestling. The rider and horse first catch up with a running steer (an ox raised for its beef). The rider leaps from the horse, grabs the steer by its horns, and forces it to the ground. Here again, the winner is the cowboy or cowgirl who completes the event in less time than the other contestants.

Clowns are an important part of the rodeo, too. They are as funny as any circus clown, but they have the responsibility of protecting fallen riders. The clowns draw the attention of the wild bulls away from fallen riders. This allows time for the riders to get up or be rescued.

Children also compete in rodeos as

▲ *The most famous sport at the rodeo is bronco-busting. The cowboys may ride bareback or use saddles.*

amateurs. The events in these rodeos are not so dangerous. Rodeo associations for junior, high school, and college-age groups sponsor hundreds of rodeos each year.

ALSO READ: CATTLE, COWBOY, HORSEBACK RIDING.

RODGERS, RICHARD see MUSICAL COMEDY.

RODIN, AUGUSTE (1840–1917) The French sculptor, François Auguste René Rodin, has often been called the "Father of Modern Sculpture." His statues and carvings have become world famous.

Rodin was born in Paris, France, where he studied drawing and sculpture. The first exhibition of his sculpture, in 1864, was a failure. In 1875, he traveled to Italy, where he studied the sculptures of the great Renaissance artist, Michelangelo. Upon returning to Paris, Rodin set to work creating a very strong, lifelike figure of a person, entitled *The Age of Bronze*. The figure was so real-looking that many people thought Rodin had cast it from a live person, instead of from a clay model. The French government bought the statue and gave Rodin a free studio in which to work.

In 1880, Rodin did a set of sculptures for the entrance of the Museum of Decorative Arts in Paris. *The Thinker* (shown here) was one of those statues. You can see the power and energy in *The Thinker's* body. Although he is sitting quietly, his body shows that there is something on his mind. His leg and arm muscles are tense. His feet are pointed inward, and his toes are curled. His head rests on his hand, while his whole body is bent over in intense concentration. His left hand looks relaxed, but you get the feeling that any minute he may spring into action. Rodin, like Michelangelo, sculpted the human body so that the viewer could sense the thoughts and emotions that were happening *inside*.

You can see the high polish of Rodin's sculpture, *The Kiss* (shown here). The figures are smooth and even seem soft like human skin. But look at the surface that the man and woman are seated on. It is rough. The bright smoothness of the people's skin flows into a mass of dents, creases, and cut-away sections that look like ordinary, hard rock. The two completely different textures in the one sculpture make the figures come alive.

In 1900, a great exhibition of Rodin's sculpture brought him worldwide fame. Ever since then, his sculpture has had an enormous influence on artists throughout the world. People felt in Rodin's art the struggles and problems of modern people. In *The Thinker*, you see a powerful, muscular person. But he is a modern person, who must use his mind rather than his muscles if he is to figure out the rapid changes taking place in the surrounding world. *The Thinker* is

▲ *Auguste Rodin's famous sculpture,* The Kiss.

▲ *Another of Rodin's famous statues is* The Thinker, *now in the National Gallery of Art, in Washington, D.C.*

▲ *The humorist Will Rogers delighted millions of people in the United States with his radio broadcasts.*

▲ *If there were no snow one Christmas, Santa Claus might have to go on roller skates to deliver the presents!*

deep in thought with his chin resting on his hand. This pose, and his leaning position, give the sculpture a feeling of great concentration.

ALSO READ: ART, ART HISTORY, MICHELANGELO BUONARROTI, SCULPTURE.

ROGERS, WILL (1879–1935) William Penn Adair Rogers was a popular U.S. humorist. He was born in Oologah, Indian Territory, in what is now Oklahoma. He was part Cherokee Indian. Rogers was a cowboy in Texas for several years and then traveled with a Wild West show. He became a vaudeville actor in 1905. He married a schoolteacher three years later, and he and his wife had four children.

Rogers performed astonishing tricks on stage with his lariat (rope for catching animals). At the same time, he entertained the audience with short, funny comments. Rogers appeared in the musical revues called the *Ziegfeld Follies*, in motion pictures, and in plays. He wrote amusing articles for *The New York Times* and other newspapers and published several books. He also had a radio program. People loved to hear him poke fun at politicians and other well-known persons. He pretended to be a rumpled, simple, homespun kind of person. But he really had a sharp, clever mind that saw through the foolishness of others.

Rogers was killed in a plane crash in Alaska during a flight with Wiley Post, a famous aviator. One of Will Rogers's best-known comments is, "I never met a man I didn't like."

ROLLER-SKATING Roller-skating is the sport of skating on wheels instead of on a runner. (See ICE SKATING.) Roller-skating is a popular activity in the United States, Canada, and many other countries. Roller skates with steel wheels are used by some young people for outdoor skating. These skates clamp to the shoes and have straps that buckle around the ankles. Also, these skates can be adjusted to fit different-size shoes. A special skate key may loosen or tighten the clamps on the skates.

Most skaters today use roller skates that have plastic, fiber, or wooden wheels. Some of these skates are especially built for outdoor roller-skating. But most are used for skating on indoor roller rinks. The wheels are attached permanently to ankle-high shoes or boots. Rubber cushions under the soles make the wheels flexible and permit the roller skaters to turn by leaning. Indoor and outdoor roller skates usually have wheels with ball bearings inside to make less friction when the wheels turn. A drop of oil in the center of each wheel now and then helps keep the wheels turning fast. The present four-wheel type of roller skate was first patented by a New Yorker, James Plimpton, in 1867.

Indoor rinks make roller-skating a year-round pastime and sport. The rinks' floors are usually made of hardwood and are protected by a plastic finish. Often, music is played to add to the rhythm of skating.

▼ *A speed rollerskater wears protective headgear in case of a high speed tumble.*

Speed skating is a competitive sport. Contests are held outdoors or on rinks. *Roller derbies* are speed-skating contests on a circular track. You may have seen them on television. Usually, five men and five women are on each team. They take turns skating, so that men compete with men and women with women. The skaters score points by passing players on the other team. The skaters wear pads and football helmets. Roller-hockey, much like ice hockey but on roller skates, is another competitive sport.

Other roller-skating competitions are held for school figure skating, which is very much like ice skating. Dancing and free skating are judged in contests, too. Many roller skaters have created fascinating routines of spins and jumps. There are competitions for young and old.

Skateboarding is rather like roller-skating. The skater uses a board with wheels like roller-skate wheels. Skateboarding was very popular on sidewalks and on skateboard rinks a few years ago, and is still often practiced.

ROMAN ART The Romans made great advances in the field of architecture. They became skilled in the use of the arch, and of the vault and the dome that use the arch principle to cover wide areas. As the 1,900-year-old aqueduct above shows, they were good at using stone. In Rome itself, though, the Romans often used brick and concrete. These materials allowed them to create their great vaulted spaces. The dome of the Pantheon, a round temple, is 143 feet (43.5 m) in diameter inside. It was 1,300 years before such a dome could be built again, at the Cathedral of Florence.

The Greeks disliked the arch and built with columns and lintels—that is, with posts carrying beams across their tops. But their architecture was very beautiful, and the Romans used its forms to decorate their own buildings. An archway would be framed in what seemed to be two columns and a lintel that carried the sort of decoration used in a Greek temple.

▲ *The Pont du Gard, in southern France, is a Roman bridge and aqueduct built in the early* AD *100's.*

In Rome and other cities, huge buildings were erected, such as *baths* (where thousands of people came to swim and socialize), *basilicas* (where law courts and public offices were located), and *temples* (where thousands at a time met to worship). The Colosseum in the city of Rome seated about 50,000 people and contained miles of corridors and stairs to handle crowds of spectators and whole armies of performers. The aqueduct shown above is one section of thousands of miles of aqueducts erected by Roman engineers to carry water from high mountain streams to cities and towns. The water flowed along a large trough at the top. An aqueduct had to slope gradually downward so the water would keep moving and reach town before it evaporated. Using legions of soldiers as their work force, Roman engineers also built roads, fortifications, harbors, and bridges.

Roman sculptors of the 1st century A.D. were kept busy copying Greek statues. Roman citizens were very fond of Greek sculpture, and those with enough money paid high prices for copies. Eventually, this craze for Greek art died down, and Roman portrait sculpture became popular. Shown here is a sculpture of a girl. Nothing is known about her except this record of how she looked. Portrait sculptors chiseled the facial fea-

▲ *The sculptured head of a girl who lived in Rome about 2,000 years ago.*

The Roman architect Vitruvius wrote about the frescoes on the walls of Roman villas: "When the plastered walls are made solid and have been polished like white marble they will look splendid after the colors are put on. When the colors are carefully painted on wet plaster they do not fade but become permanent."

▲ *A Roman wall painting found in the ruins of Pompeii.*

▼ *The houses of wealthy Romans were richly decorated with wall paintings. This one, showing a garden, comes from the palace of Livia, the wife of the emperor Augustus. Gardens were a popular subject for these paintings; they give the impression that the solid walls of the house have melted away to reveal trees and flowers.*

tures to look exactly like the real person. They showed every detail that made a person's face individual and unique, even wrinkles, scars, baldness, or warts.

As Rome conquered more and more territory, *narrative sculpture* became popular. On long strips of stone, sculptors depicted entire histories of victorious battles, heroic deeds, and the lives of emperors.

Most Roman painting has been destroyed over the course of time, but paintings from the city of Pompeii still exist. Pompeii was a well-to-do country town that was buried under lava from Mount Vesuvius, a volcano that erupted in A.D. 79. Pompeiian wall paintings were done in fresco (painting on wet plaster). The artists are unknown, but there is a great deal of excellent art showing scenes of home life, plants and animals, landscapes, and gods and goddesses. A fine example of a Roman wall painting showing birds, trees and flowers is shown below. Artists in the 1700's imitated this art.

The floors and walls of many Roman houses and public buildings were covered with excellent mosaics that depicted scenes similar to those of the wall paintings.

▲ *A Roman altar-carving found in London. It shows the god Mithras sacrificing a bull. The cult of Mithras was popular among Roman soldiers.*

ALSO READ: BUILDING MATERIAL; GREEK ART; MOSAIC; POMPEII; ROME, ANCIENT.

ROMAN CATHOLIC CHURCH

For the first 1,000 years after the death of Jesus Christ, all Christians were members of one religion—Christianity. There were no separate sects, or branches, of Christianity as there are today. The word "catholic" means "universal," and for those first

1,000 years after the death of Jesus Christ, all Christians were members of the Catholic Church.

In 1054, however, after a long dispute between Church leaders in Rome and Constantinople (now Istanbul, Turkey), the Catholic Church split. Eastern churches under the leadership of Constantinople would not accept the bishop of Rome—the pope—as head of the entire Church. The Eastern churches became independent of the pope's rule and established the Orthodox Church. The Western church, under the leadership of the bishop of Rome, became known as the Roman Catholic Church. Except in the matter of papal authority, the beliefs of the Catholic and Orthodox churches are very much alike.

In 1517, another great split occurred in the Roman Catholic Church—the Protestant Reformation. Martin Luther and many religious leaders *protested* against the authority of the popes and the corrupt practices of many bishops, priests, and lay people (those who are not members of the clergy). The Protestants *reformed* their ways of worship and started new Christian sects, such as the Lutheran, Methodist, Presbyterian, and Episcopal churches, which have since developed beliefs and practices that differ from those of the Roman Catholic Church.

However, the popes themselves realized that changes were needed. Between 1520 and 1650 the Counter-Reformation corrected corrupt practices and strengthened the Roman Catholic Church.

In 1962, Pope John XXIII called together the Second Vatican Council, attended by bishops and Church leaders from all over the world. The Council made many new decisions about the practice of the Catholic faith. These decisions have led to hundreds of changes that are making Catholicism more understandable and more relevant to the lives of modern-day people.

Organization of the Church Roman Catholics believe that their religion was founded by Jesus Christ. The apostle Peter moved to Rome about A.D. 60, and became the first bishop there. From the time of Peter until today, there has been an almost unbroken line of bishops in Rome, who have been called pope (for about 70 years during the 1300's, the popes resided in Avignon, France). The word "pope" comes from the Greek word *pappas*, meaning "father." Roman Catholics believe the pope to be the visible human leader of the Church. He is believed to be the representative of Christ on Earth.

In charge of each local Catholic parish is a *pastor*, who may be assisted by one or more priests. An area that includes a large number of parishes is called a *diocese*. A *bishop*, appointed by the pope, heads each diocese. *Archbishops* head larger areas, called *provinces*, which contain several dioceses. *Cardinals*, who are usually bishops or archbishops, are appointed by the pope and are the pope's special advisers. When a pope dies, all the cardinals meet in Rome to elect a new pope.

▲ *Queen Mary I of England. Her father, King Henry VIII, quarreled with the pope and made Protestantism England's official religion. Mary brought back Roman Catholicism and persecuted the Protestants which is why she was given the nickname "Bloody Mary."*

Pope Pius IX had the longest papal reign. He was pope from 1846 to 1878, nearly 32 years. The shortest reign was that of Pope Stephen II. He was in office for only three or four days.

◀ *The Virgin Mary is more important to Roman Catholics than to Protestants. This jeweled cross, made in Constantinople (now Istanbul) in about A.D. 1000, shows her with Saint Basil and Saint Gregory.*

▲ *Children in France celebrating an open-air* communion solennelle *(solemn Holy Communion). Children wear white for this important day, and the girls also wear a white veil.*

Some Roman Catholics choose to serve Christ and the Church by joining religious societies. Women who become *nuns* and men who become *brothers* (or *monks*) dedicate their lives completely to the service of God by doing good works. Some of the best-known religious societies are the Society of Jesus (the Jesuits), the Franciscans (founded by St. Francis of Assisi), the Dominicans, and the Benedictines.

Roman Catholic Faith The faith of the Roman Catholic Church is based on scripture and on *tradition* (the teachings of Christ believed to have been handed down orally). Any teaching that is not in agreement with these two sources is considered *heresy* (not in keeping with God's word). When Roman Catholics have difficulty in agreeing whether a teaching is correct or not, the pope consults with his bishops, prays to God for guidance, and reaches a decision.

GOD AND HUMAN BEINGS. Catholics believe in the *Trinity*—three persons in one God—the Father, the Son (Jesus Christ), and the Holy Spirit. Catholics believe that Jesus Christ is God and that he came to free human beings from sin by offering his own life. *Sin* is doing evil by turning away from God and disobeying Christ's command to love God and all fellow human beings. Catholics believe people have a *free will*—they can make their own choices to do good or to do evil. The Old Testament tells of how Adam and Eve turned against God by disobeying God's orders. Adam and Eve's action was the first, or *original*, sin. This original sin—this tendency of a person to turn away from God—Roman Catholics believe to be part of imperfect human nature. Since people are not perfect, they sometimes choose to turn against God, just as Adam and Eve did in the Old Testament of the Bible.

By becoming human as Jesus Christ, God became one with mankind. By dying on the cross, God sacrificed life to make up for the sins of human beings. This means, according to Roman Catholic belief, that God now shares divine life with human beings, just as God once shared human life on Earth. God lives in all men and women through the Holy Spirit, and all people live in God through the same spirit. Each person has a personal relationship with God. And God shares life through a person's faith and actions, prayer, and the sacraments.

▼ *Inside the richly decorated St. Peter's, the center of the Roman Catholic Church. The pope celebrates mass here.*

SACRAMENTS. The Roman Catholic Church has seven sacraments—baptism, confirmation, penance, Holy Eucharist, matrimony, holy orders, and the anointing of the sick. The sacraments are visible ways in which God continues to share life with human beings. The sacraments are a source of strength to help people do God's will. This spiritual strength is called *grace*. The sacraments are also visible signs of God's presence and action in the world. Roman Catholics believe that the sacraments are actions of God working through the faith and actions of the people.

The central sacrament of the Church is the *Eucharist*, a remembering of the Last Supper, during which Christ told his Apostles to continue to consecrate (make holy) bread and wine in his memory. Catholics believe that at consecration the bread and wine become Christ's body and blood, even though they appear to be bread and wine. By taking part in the Eucharist, Catholics believe that they join their own lives with that of Christ.

ALSO READ: BIBLE, CHRISTIANITY, CLERGY, FRANCIS OF ASSISI, JESUS CHRIST, MISSIONARY, MONASTIC LIFE, ORTHODOX CHURCH, POPE, PROTESTANT CHURCHES, PROTESTANT REFORMATION, RELIGION, SAINT, VATICAN CITY.

ROMANCE LANGUAGES The languages of southern Europe—French, Italian, Portuguese, and Spanish—have been grouped by linguists into a category called Romance languages. This name was given to them because they developed directly from Latin—the language spoken by the Roman people. The Roman Empire covered large areas of Europe, which included modern-day France, Italy, Portugal, and Spain.

There were two major kinds of Latin—the Latin spoken by educated people (now called Classic Latin) and the less formal Latin spoken by the common people (now called Vulgar Latin). The people of conquered countries learned the Vulgar Latin spoken by the Romans with whom they were most in contact—soldiers and traders. The Romance languages come from this Vulgar Latin. For example, although the Latin word for a horse is *equus*, the soldiers called an army horse *caballus*. In French, the general word for horse became *cheval*; in Italian, it became *cavallo*; and in Spanish, it became *caballo*.

French is the language of France, Haiti, and parts of Canada, Belgium, and Switzerland. It is also spoken in French colonies and former French colonies in Africa and the Pacific islands. The great influence of French culture in the world means that French is widely spoken in diplomatic and cultural circles. To greet someone in French you would say, *Comment allez-vous?* (KOH-mawn-tahl-lay VOO? How are you?)

Italian is more like Latin than other Romance languages because Rome, Italy, was the capital of the Roman Empire. Many dialects, or variations, of Latin were spoken in Italy during the Roman Empire and after. It was not until the Renaissance that the Italian dialect of the city of Florence became accepted as the national language of Italy. To greet someone in Italian, you would say, *Comé sta?* (koh-may STAH? How are you?)

Portuguese is spoken not only in Portugal but also in the large South American nation of Brazil, which was colonized by the Portuguese. To greet someone in Portuguese, you would say, *Como está?* (koh-moh ay-ZHTAH? How are you?)

Spanish is the national language of Spain and all the Latin American countries colonized by the Spaniards. To greet someone in Spanish you would say, *Cómo está?* (koh-moh ay-STAH? How are you?)

Other Romance, or Latinian, lan-

One of the oldest Romance languages is Provençal, spoken in parts of southern France. It was in this language that the poet-musicians called troubadours entertained kings and courtiers with their love songs in the 12th and 13th centuries.

guages are Romanian, Catalan, Sardinian, Provençal, Romansh, Friulian, and Haitian Creole.

ALSO READ: LANGUAGES; LATIN; ROME, ANCIENT.

ROMAN EMPIRE see ROME, ANCIENT.

ROMANESQUE ART By A.D. 1000, Christianity was the religion of most of western Europe. Villages of humble wooden houses dotted the countryside. Among these poor homes arose magnificent stone churches and cathedrals. The townspeople built their churches as monuments to God. The church was the pride of the community—its towers soaring high in the air toward heaven.

The architects of the Romanesque period (A.D. 800–1200) left no written record of themselves. We do not even know their names. But we do know of their magnificent stone churches. When a church was built, villagers helped quarry the stone and transport it to the building site. Traveling craftworkers cut and shaped the stones. Stonemasons put the stones in place, and traveling sculptors carved religious figures used for decoration. The building of a church took 30 to 50 years or more, depending on the size of the structure.

▲ *The Cathedral of St. Blasius in Brunswick, West Germany, an impressive Romanesque structure completed in 1194.*

▼ *This mosaic in the Monreale Abbey Church in Sicily is an example of Romanesque art.*

The word "Romanesque" means "like Roman art." Although the art does not look at all Roman, architects did pattern their first churches according to the floor plans of Roman buildings called *basilicas* that were used as places for transacting business. Church basilicas of the Romanesque period were rectangular in shape, with a central aisle leading to the altar. On each side of the center aisle were rows of columns and one or two side aisles. Later churches were built in the shape of a cross. The church was usually built with the altar end facing east, toward the Holy Land where Christ had lived.

Roman basilicas had flat wooden roofs that were dangerous because they burned easily. Romanesque architects built fireproof stone vaults for ceilings instead. The *barrel vault* was like a tunnel. It was easy to build, but it had to be supported by heavy walls, so churches were very dark. The *groin vault* was like a barrel vault intersected by other barrel vaults. It allowed windows to be put high in the church, because now the weight of the vaulting fell on isolated points. In place of a heavy wall, *piers* (thick columns of masonry) and *buttresses* (masonry masses that resisted sideward thrusts) took the weight of the vault. But the groin vault was complicated to build.

The Cathedral of St. Blasius (in the picture on the left) shows the buttresses of the wall and the high *clerestory* windows, under the roof, that they make possible. The tile roof you see is a protection for the stone vault inside, which could be damaged by the weather.

The Cathedral of Durham, shown on this page, is a work of Norman (English) Romanesque. Here you see how a groin vault allows light to come through the clerestory windows, since the vaults rest on the great piers that rise from the floor in the form of clustered *shafts*.

Romanesque churches usually contained painting and sculpture. Church sculpture was not just for decoration. It was meant to remind people of God's greatness. Every piece of sculpture had a religious meaning. The figures were carved directly onto the stones that were to be used in building the church. Craftworkers called stonecutters shaped each stone to fit a certain place on the building. Sculptors then carved the figures to fit the shape of the stone and the area of the building where the stone would be laid. For this reason, Romanesque sculpture does not look realistic.

In Italy, Romanesque churches did not have much sculpture. The Italians decorated the inside walls with frescoes (pictures painted on wet plaster) and mosaics. All the paintings and mosaics had a religious meaning, just as the sculpture did. The fresco shown here depicts a scene from the Book of Revelation in the New Testament. The 12 old men represent the elders, or wise men, of the Church. They are raising gold cups that contain the wine used at Mass. (Wine is a symbol of Christ's blood, which was shed when he died on the cross.) Above the elders is a winged ox with a book and halo. The book represents the Bible, and the ox represents St. Luke, the gospel writer. Near the top you can see part of a circle. This circle contains a lamb, which is one of the symbols of Christ. The whole scene represents the Church's adoration of Christ.

The windows of Romanesque churches were made of stained glass, in which religious scenes and people were depicted. Such things as candlesticks, altars, chairs, and priests' clothing were all decorated with symbolic figures and objects. Most people of the Romanesque period did not know how to read or write. But almost everyone knew how to "read" religious painting and sculpture. Romanesque artists did not try to portray things as they look in real life. They tried to portray the spiritual things of heaven.

Among the famous Romanesque cathedrals are those at Pisa in Italy, Cluny and Poitiers in France, and Santiago de Compostela in Spain.

ALSO READ: CATHEDRAL, MIDDLE AGES, MOSAIC.

▲ *The interior of Durham Cathedral completed in 1133, one of Britain's best examples of Romanesque architecture.*

▼ *This Romanesque fresco adorns the domed ceiling over the altar of the cathedral in Anagni, Italy.*

▲ *A farm in Romania. One of Romania's national heroes was Vlad the Impaler, who lived in the 1400's. The fictional character Dracula was based on Vlad.*

Most of the oil used by the German forces in World War II came from the oil fields around Ploesti in Romania. Because of this, Ploesti was one of the targets most heavily bombed by Allied planes.

ROMAN GODS see GODS AND GODDESSES.

ROMANIA Romania is a country on the Balkan Peninsula of southeastern Europe, where the Danube River divides into several branches and then flows into the Black Sea. The river goes along Romania's western border with Yugoslavia and its southern border with Bulgaria. Hungary lies west of Romania, and the Soviet Union is north and east. (See the map with the article on EUROPE.)

The highlands of the area called Transylvania in northwestern Romania are surrounded by the beautiful Transylvanian and Carpathian mountains. Thick forests cover the mountain slopes. Between the forests, farmers tend their livestock on green pastures. The soil in the Danube River valley is among the richest in Europe. Golden fields of corn and wheat stretch from the Danube valley to the mountains. To the east are Romania's sunny beaches along the Black Sea.

Winters are cold and summers are warm in Romania. Some lowland areas (although not the seacoast and the Danube River swamps) receive little rainfall and sometimes suffer drought (prolonged dryness).

Bucharest is the capital city. It was a glamorous city before World War II, with many palaces, theaters, and luxury hotels. Today it is the country's business and industrial center.

Romania has valuable mineral resources. It is an important producer of oil and natural gas in Europe. Coal, bauxite, iron ore, manganese, lead, and other minerals are mined. Modern factories make steel and heavy machinery. But despite all the industry in Romania, about three out of every ten Romanians are farmers.

Romanians are friendly, hospitable people. Many of them belong to the Orthodox Church. Many Romanians are descended from the Romans who once settled this land and called it the province of Dacia. The name Romania comes from the Romans. Sometimes it is spelled "Rumania." Modern Romania was formed in 1859 when the old principalities of Moldavia and Walachia were joined. The country's size increased after World War I when Transylvania, which had been part of Austria-Hungary, was added to Romania.

Romania was a socialist republic controlled by the Communist Party. At the end of World War II, Russian troops occupied Romania. In 1947, the Communist Party took over the government. Romania showed some independence from the Soviet Union. In 1989, the people overthrew the corrupt communist government of Nicolae Ceausescu. They demanded and obtained democratic reforms and free elections. Ceausescu and his wife were executed.

ALSO READ: BLACK SEA, DANUBE RIVER.

ROMANIA

Capital City: Bucharest (1,900,000 people).

Area: 91,699 square miles (237,500 sq. km).

Population: 23,000,000.

Government: Communist republic.

Natural Resources: Oil and natural gas, chromium, copper, bauxite, iron ore, manganese, uranium.

Export Products: Petroleum products, industrial equipment, cement, cereals.

Unit of Money: Leu.

Official Language: Romanian.

ROMAN NUMERAL see NUMBER.

ROMANTIC PERIOD Romantic art, or Romanticism, has been popular in many ages throughout history. There have been Romantic literature, music, visual art, and architecture. The time known as the Romantic Period occurred mainly between the late 1700's and the mid-1800's. It started in Europe, but its influence spread to the United States, where Romanticism became important as the first U.S. artform that did not copy the European.

What is Romanticism? It is a certain style in the arts—be it literature, painting, sculpture, or architecture. It shows great use of the imagination. Sometimes Romantic artists put mystery and wonder into their work. They often paint subjects from nature. Painting trees and mountains, sunsets and rivers, they can often express infinite distance, solitude, and a sense of tragedy.

The British artist Joseph M. W. Turner (1775–1851) was one of the leading Romantic painters. He was apprenticed to an engraver. Turner would study the geological elements of a scene in detail, but in painting it, he used the picture in his mind rather than the facts. Turner's influence on Romanticism was very great. His powerful imagination changed the places he saw into a fantasy world on canvas. He did historical and mythological scenes. Also, he liked to paint sunsets and seascapes. The picture you see below combines the two types of scenes he liked.

▼ The Fighting Téméraire *by J.M.W. Turner—one of the finest works of the Romantic Period.*

▲ Two Men Gazing at the Moon *by Caspar David Friedrich.*

A later Romantic painting trend in England was the Pre-Raphaelite Brotherhood of the mid-1800's. They supported a movement to emphasize arts and crafts, and like the Romantics they longed for the past.

Romanticism spread through the countries of Europe. In Germany, Romantic painters and Romantic philosophers worked together very closely. One of the greatest German landscape painters was Caspar David Friedrich (1774–1840). Look at his picture above of *Two Men Gazing at the Moon.* Notice how the tree seems to have a personality of its own. It looks almost human. The mysterious feeling of the painting fits into the Romantic idea of mood setting. See how the hazy moonlight casts a ghostly light on the scene. Don't you get the feeling that magic is brewing?

George Catlin (1796–1872) was the first Romantic painter in the United States. He painted pictures of the American Indians and made heroes of

The Romantic period in literature produced the *Gothic novel.* In these novels the heroine was often imprisoned in a gloomy castle and had to experience mysterious voices, ghosts, bleeding statues, and other supernatural events. It was the Gothic novel that influenced the U.S. writers Edgar Allan Poe and Nathaniel Hawthorne.

▲ White Cloud, Head Chief of the Iowas *by George Catlin. This painting is now in the Paul Mellon Collection of the National Gallery of Art, Washington, D.C.*

them. He went West and lived among the Indians for five years, before returning East with many paintings and drawings. He wanted to portray the Indians before they all disappeared from the frontier.

Shown here is a portrait called *White Cloud, Head Chief of the Iowas.* As a Romantic, Catlin shows the Indian in a rather mysterious, wondrous way. Europeans particularly loved Catlin's way of depicting the Indian. (His fellow U.S. citizens were still shooting them on the frontier.) Some U.S. writers got their romantic notions of the Indian from Catlin's research.

The vast, untouched beauty of the North American wilderness appealed to U.S. Romantic painters. They felt that a landscape should be transfigured and lit up by the spirit of the painter. This was true of the work of Thomas Cole (1801–1848). His *The Notch of the White Mountains* (Crawford Notch) is shown here. Cole studied three years in Europe and most likely saw the work of Friedrich, the German Romanticist. Cole came back and introduced the symbolic landscape to the United States. He loved the wild, primitive character of the U.S. countryside and tried to show it in his pictures. He felt that people in Europe had tamed the countryside too much, but the United States was still untouched. A whole group of U.S. Romantics, known as the Hudson River School, became prominent painters in the mid-1800's. Some art critics today say that some of the finest Romantic paintings of the 1800's were done by U.S. painters.

▼ The Notch of the White Mountains *by Thomas Cole. (National Gallery of Art, Washington, D.C. Gift of the Andrew Mellon Fund.)*

ALSO READ: ART HISTORY.

ROME Rome, as the capital of the Roman Empire, was for five centuries the center of the Western world. Rome has been one of the major centers of civilization for over 2,000 years. For this reason, it is often called the Eternal City.

According to legend, Rome was founded by twins named Romulus and Remus in about 750 B.C. The city was built on the banks of the Tiber River in central Italy. It grew to become the center of the vast Roman Empire. The Romans built many magnificent buildings on the seven hills that made up the ancient city. The ruins of some of these are still standing. The *Colosseum* is a huge arena where Roman gladiators once fought, and where early Christians were killed because of their religion. The *catacombs* are underground caves and tunnels where these early Christians hid and practiced their religion. The caves contain chapels, meeting halls, and burial grounds. The *Forum* was the center of government and business life.

After the collapse of the Roman Empire, many of the Roman buildings were taken apart to use for building material. Wild Germanic tribes occupied Rome, and it became an area of ruined buildings and unhealthy swamps. The bishops of Rome (later called the popes) became the leaders of the city during this unsettled time. The popes built many churches in the city in the 1500's and 1600's. In 1929, the Italian government gave an area in the city to the pope. This area, called Vatican City, is actually an independent state.

Today, many visitors come to

▲ *A market square with food stalls in Rome, the capital of Italy. In the distance you can just see the white dome of St. Peter's Basilica.*

Rome to see the ancient ruins and the beautiful churches. But the city is also important for its modern achievements. It is the capital of Italy and the home of almost 3 million people. It is also an international center for motion-picture production and fashion design.

ALSO READ: CHRISTIANITY; ITALIAN HISTORY; ITALY; POPE; ROMAN CATHOLIC CHURCH; ROME, ANCIENT; VATICAN CITY.

ROME, ANCIENT In its earliest days, Rome was a small town built upon seven hills. It lay near the mouth of the Tiber River in Italy. Rome later grew into a mighty city, which ruled an empire. The Roman Empire, at its largest size, covered more than 2 million square miles (5 million sq. km). Over 50 million people lived in it.

A Time of Legend (700–509 B.C.) The first Romans were probably made up of three different peoples—the Latins, the Sabines, and the Etruscans. A well-known legend tells how twin boys named Romulus and Remus were born in Italy in the 700's B.C. Their mother was a Latin princess, descended from a mighty warrior, Aeneas. Their father was Mars, god of war. The boys were abandoned as infants. A she-wolf nursed them, and a farmer raised them. When they were grown, the twins founded the city of Rome on the Palatine Hill—one of the seven hills of Rome. Romulus became Rome's first king in 753 B.C. and gave his name to the city. According to tradition, six other kings ruled after Romulus. The last of these was Tarquinius Superbus (often called "Tarquin the Proud"). He was a harsh, cruel tyrant and was overthrown in 509 B.C.

The Roman Republic (509–27 B.C.) Rome then became a *republic*. In a republic, citizens may vote for the governors of their choice. The Romans chose two persons called *consuls* to rule the republic. Consuls could remain in office for only one year. An assembly, called the *senate*, was made up of people who acted as advisers to the consuls. Throughout much of Rome's history, the Roman people were divided into two main classes, *patricians* and *plebeians*. The patricians were members of noble Roman families. The plebeians were the com-

▲ *Augustus Caesar, the first Roman emperor. Before he became emperor, he was called Octavian.*

▼ *The symbol of Rome was the she-wolf which, according to legend, adopted the twin brothers Romulus and Remus. When the boys grew up, they decided to found a city, but they quarreled. Romulus killed Remus and founded the city later named "Rome" for himself.*

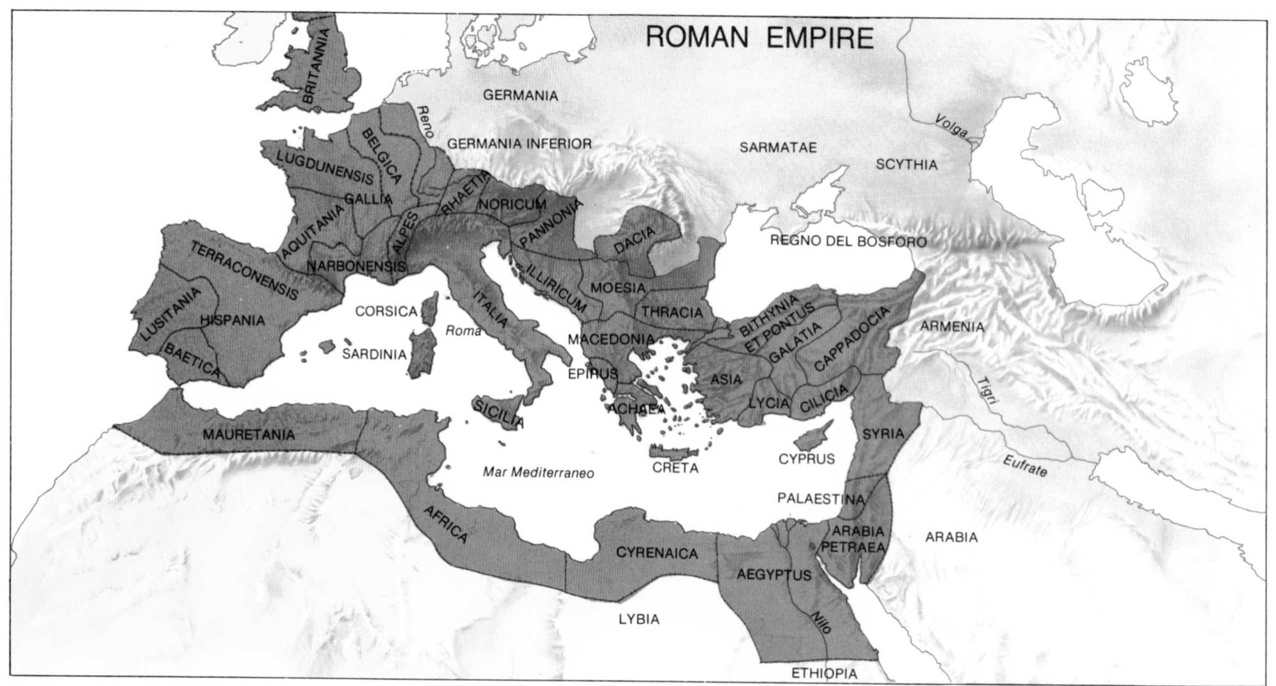

◀ *A statue of Hadrian, Roman emperor from 138 to 117* B.C. *He traveled through all parts of his empire. Here he is shown trampling a woman (representing a conquered province).*

mon people—most of the population. After a long struggle, the plebeians gained equal power in the government.

By the middle of the 200's B.C., the Romans had taken over most of Italy. In 264 B.C., Rome went to war with the powerful city of Carthage, in North Africa. Rome fought three wars with Carthage, known as the *Punic Wars*. By 146 B.C., Carthage had been totally destroyed. The Romans conquered Spain, Macedonia, Greece, and much of the Middle East. They later moved into Gaul (now France).

In 70 B.C., Pompey the Great was made consul. He formed a *triumvirate* (three-person government) with two other Roman statesmen, Julius Caesar and Crassus. After the deaths of Crassus and Pompey, Julius Caesar ruled alone. He was a brilliant leader, both in war and at home. But some people feared that he would become too powerful. In 44 B.C., he was

THE ROMAN EMPIRE—KEY DATES

B.C.	
900's	Rise of Etruscans in northern Italy.
753	According to legend, the year in which Romulus founded the city of Rome.
509	Founding of the Roman Republic.
264–201	Rome defeats Carthage (a city in North Africa) in the first two Punic Wars and gains its first overseas territories.
149–146	The Third Punic War, which ended with the destruction of Carthage.
133–60	Aristocratic (patrician) and popular (plebeian) parties struggle for power.
59–52	Julius Caesar conquers Gaul.
49–44	Julius Caesar is Rome's dictator.
44	Julius Caesar is assassinated and Rome is ruled by three men together—Lepidus, Mark Antony, and Octavian (Caesar's great-nephew).
27	Octavian becomes the first emperor and is named Augustus.
A.D.	
293	Diocletian divides the empire into two sections, east and west.
313	The emperors Constantine the Great and Licinius declare that Christianity should be tolerated throughout the empire.
324	Constantine puts Licinius to death and reunites the empire.
476	After barbarians overrun France, Spain, and Italy, the last western emperor (Romulus Augustulus) is deposed.
1453	Constantinople falls to the Ottoman Turks, signifying the end of the Eastern Empire.

stabbed to death in Rome.

Another triumvirate was formed by Caesar's grandnephew Octavian (also called Augustus), a commander named Lepidus, and Mark Antony, a young politician and general. Lepidus soon fell from power, and the rule was divided between Antony and Octavian. Antony was married to Octavian's sister, but he divorced his wife to marry Cleopatra, queen of Egypt. Octavian declared war on both of them. Cleopatra and Antony were defeated and killed themselves in 31 B.C. Octavian then became supreme ruler of Rome and its territories.

Rome Becomes an Empire (27 B.C.–A.D. 180) Octavian was the first Roman emperor. He had earlier taken the name of his great uncle, and *Caesar* became a Roman word for "emperor." Octavian was also named Augustus, meaning "revered one." In A.D. 14, his stepson, Tiberius, became emperor. The next emperor, Caligula, was insane and was killed by his own guards. Nero, also probably insane, was condemned to death by the senate for his cruel ways and killed himself in A.D. 68. Vespasian and his two sons followed one another as emperors from A.D. 69 to 96. The age of the "five good emperors" came next. They were Nerva, Trajan, Hadrian, Antoninus Pius, and Marcus Aurelius. During their reigns, the Roman Empire reached its greatest size. In A.D. 117, the boundaries of the empire stretched north and south from Britain to Egypt, and east and west from Spain to Armenia. It included 43 *provinces*, or districts under Roman rule.

The End of the Empire (A.D. 180–476) Marcus Aurelius died in A.D. 180, and his son Commodus was named emperor. Like Caligula and Nero, Commodus was insane. He was murdered. The office of emperor had been dragged so low that it was even auctioned off to the highest bidder. Barbarian tribes were attacking the Roman borders. A large and costly army was needed to defend the enormous empire. Roman citizens were forced to pay higher and higher taxes. Prices rose so much that few people could buy bread. The Romans suffered from plagues and began to die of starvation. In the A.D. 200's, many emperors came to power, but most were either weak or vicious. Several more emperors were murdered. In A.D. 284, Diocletian became emperor. His efforts to protect the borders from the barbarians saved the empire for a few more years.

Constantine, whose reign began in A.D. 312, was the last of the great Roman emperors. Constantine was the first Christian emperor. He made Christianity the official religion of the Roman Empire. Before this time, the Romans had worshiped many gods. In A.D. 330, Constantine founded a new capital city of Byzantium, later renamed Constantinople (now Istanbul, Turkey). The empire had been divided into two parts. Rome remained the center of the Western Empire. But the Eastern Empire, with its capital at Constantinople, became much more powerful. For 1,100 more years, Eastern Roman, or Byzantine, emperors ruled from Constantinople.

▲ *A coin of Constantine the Great, who became emperor of Rome in the early 300's. Constantinople (now Istanbul) was named for him.*

▼ *A model of Rome at the time of the empire. The Circus Maximus is in the center, and the Colosseum is above and to the left. In between the two is the Palatine Hill with the complex of buildings that made up the emperor's palace.*

▲ *A woman of Palmyra, Syria, during the time of the Roman Empire. Syria was one of several wealthy eastern provinces of the empire.*

▼ *The ruins of the Forum in Rome. The Forum, an open marketplace surrounded by temples and monuments, was the center of social life in the ancient city.*

The city of Rome, left almost deserted, was attacked again and again by invading barbarians. In A.D. 410, Visigoths captured and sacked Rome. The last Western Roman emperor was Romulus Augustulus. A barbarian leader, Odoacer, overthrew him in A.D. 476. Odoacer then became king of Italy. The end of the Roman Empire had come.

The Roman People What were they like, those long-ago Romans? They built magnificent government buildings, temples, bridges, roads, and aqueducts (waterways). They invented a very strong type of concrete, which they used to build impressive arches and domes. More than 50,000 miles (80,000 km) of Roman roads carried traders and armies throughout the empire. The Romans developed a system of law on which many of our own modern laws are based. They believed that laws were made for the good of the people, and that all individuals had rights—unless they were slaves.

Loose robes called *togas* were worn by Roman men. Women wore long, straight dresses called *stolas*, and both men and women wore sandals. The men spent many hours at the *baths*. The famed Roman baths had hot and cold bath areas, steam rooms, dining rooms, music rooms, rooms for playing games, and even libraries.

The Romans celebrated many holidays during the year. Free entertainment was provided for everyone on these days. In Rome, a huge arena called the Colosseum held about 50,000 people. Men called *gladiators* fought with one another or with wild animals in the arena. Criminals were sometimes fed to lions. Thoughtful people were horrified at the brutal spectacles, and in A.D. 404 the bloodthirsty entertainment was stopped. Another favorite amusement was the circus. The Circus Maximus in Rome seated almost 260,000 people. It offered animal acts, acrobats, clowns, and exciting, dangerous chariot races. *Chariots* were two-wheeled carts drawn by two to eight horses.

Roman soldiers were almost unbeatable professional fighters. They invented many new ways of winning battles. When the Romans took over a country, they sent a Roman *governor* to rule the people. They usually allowed the people of the conquered country to keep their own religion and speak their own language. But most people in the empire learned the Roman language, Latin.

Rome produced many fine writers. Livy wrote a history of Rome. Virgil, Horace, and Ovid were three of the ancient world's greatest poets. Pliny the Elder wrote a 37-volume work on natural history. The Romans often copied the best of what they found in the lands they conquered. They adopted many ideas from the Greeks, whom they greatly admired. The Romans helped to keep alive these ideas by carrying them all over the world.

ALSO READ: ANTONY, MARK; BYZANTINE EMPIRE; CAESAR, JULIUS; CARTHAGE; CHARIOT; CHRISTIANITY; CIRCUS; CLEOPATRA; GLADIATOR; GREECE, ANCIENT; ITALIAN HISTORY; LATIN; LAW; NERO; ROMAN ART; ROMANCE LANGUAGES; ROME.

The Romans were the greatest road builders of the ancient world. They laid out more than 50,000 miles (80,000 km) of road across their huge empire. The best roads were wonderful feats of engineering. They had thick beds over 3 feet (1 m) deep, made of rock slabs, stones, gravel, and sand layers.

ROOSEVELT, ELEANOR (1884–1962) Eleanor Roosevelt, wife of President Franklin D. Roosevelt, became one of the world's most admired women. She had a long career of public service as a champion of human rights, a writer, and a delegate to the United Nations.

Anna Eleanor Roosevelt was born to Elliot and Anna (Hall) Roosevelt in New York City on October 11, 1884. President Theodore Roosevelt was her uncle. She married her fifth cousin, Franklin D. Roosevelt, in 1905. They had six children, but one child died in infancy.

During her husband's recovery from polio, Eleanor began to participate actively in public affairs. With his wife's help, Roosevelt soon returned to politics. After her husband became President in 1933, Mrs. Roosevelt worked actively for many humanitarian causes, such as slum clearance, better schooling, and civil rights for minority groups.

Mrs. Roosevelt became well known as a speaker and writer. She wrote newspaper columns, magazine articles, and many books, including *This Is My Story* (1937) and *On My Own* (1958). She served as a delegate to the United Nations from 1945 to 1953 and as head of the U.N. Commission on Human Rights from 1946 to 1953. In 1948, Mrs. Roosevelt was voted "most admired woman living today in any part of the world."

ALSO READ: ROOSEVELT, FRANKLIN D.; ROOSEVELT, THEODORE.

▲ *Eleanor Roosevelt, the wife of Franklin Delano Roosevelt, was one of the most important and influential of all our First Ladies.*

ROOSEVELT, FRANKLIN D. (1882–1945) Franklin Delano Roosevelt was the only President to serve more than two terms. He served three full terms and part of a fourth—from 1933 to 1945.

The thirty-second President was

FRANKLIN DELANO ROOSEVELT
THIRTY-SECOND PRESIDENT MARCH 4, 1933–APRIL 12, 1945

Born: January 30, 1882, Hyde Park, New York
Parents: James and Sara Delano Roosevelt
Education: Harvard University, Cambridge, Massachusetts; Columbia University Law School, New York, New York
Religion: Episcopalian
Occupation: Lawyer
Political Party: Democratic
Married: 1905 to (Anna) Eleanor Roosevelt (1884–1962)
Children: 1 daughter, 5 sons (one died in infancy)
Died: April 12, 1945, Warm Springs, Georgia
Buried: Rose garden of family estate, Hyde Park, New York

▲ *President Franklin Delano Roosevelt met with Britain's Prime Minister, Winston Churchill, in January 1943 in Casablanca, Morocco. The two Allied leaders and their high-ranking military officers discussed how they could win World War II.*

The Roosevelts entertained a great deal at the White House. In 1939, King George VI and Queen Elizabeth became the first British monarchs to visit the United States and stay at the White House. British Prime Minister Churchill was a frequent wartime visitor. A map room was set aside for him on the second floor of the White House.

the son of wealthy parents. He grew up on his family's estate in Hyde Park, New York. Roosevelt had private tutors until, as a teenager, he attended Groton School in Massachusetts. He then studied at Harvard College. In 1905, Roosevelt married his fifth cousin, Eleanor Roosevelt. He attended the Columbia University Law School and afterward began practicing law.

Roosevelt entered politics in 1910, when he was elected to the New York state senate. As a state senator, Roosevelt took a firm stand against the Democratic political "machine" in New York, a position that earned him some enemies within his own party. During Woodrow Wilson's term as President (1913–1920), Roosevelt was Assistant Secretary of the Navy through World War I. He was defeated when he was a candidate for Vice-President in 1920.

Roosevelt was stricken with polio during the summer of 1921, while he and his family were at their summer cottage at Campobello Island in Canada. His legs were left paralyzed from the illness. Roosevelt tried various treatments and finally regained limited use of his legs. But for the rest of his life, he needed help to walk at all.

In 1928, Roosevelt was elected governor of New York. He held this post until 1932, when he was elected President.

When Roosevelt first took office as President (in 1933), the country was passing through the period of hard times known as the Great Depression. Businesses were failing. Many people were unemployed and poverty-stricken. In accepting his party's nomination, Roosevelt had promised the U.S. people a "new deal." This became his campaign slogan, and, after his election, the laws that Congress passed on his recommendation were known as New Deal laws.

Immediately after his first inauguration, Roosevelt began his New Deal—new laws and special executive orders aimed at bringing stability to the nation's economy and work to the nation's unemployed. He closed all banks until government controls could be established, so that people would feel that their money was safe in a bank. The Works Progress Administration (WPA) and the Public Works Administration (PWA) provided jobs for thousands of people. Bridges, dams, government buildings, and other public works were constructed under these programs. The National Recovery Administration (NRA) was established to help businesses recover from the Depression. Under the Tennessee Valley Authority (TVA), established in 1933, a series of dams was built in the Tennessee River to help control floods. The dams also furnished cheap electric power and light to a large, undeveloped area. Among other laws passed were the Social Security Acts of 1935 and 1939. These laws provided for monthly payments to retired workers over a certain age, based on their average earnings before that time. Benefits also were provided for persons out of work, widows, and dependent children.

Roosevelt established the Good Neighbor policy of noninterference in the affairs of Latin American countries. He officially recognized the Soviet Union. During Roosevelt's second administration, foreign-policy problems became increasingly important. Germany's attacks on other nations resulted in the outbreak of war in Europe. Roosevelt asked Congress for laws enabling the United States to sell military equipment to nations resisting these attacks. Although many people felt that the United States should concentrate on its own problems, his request was granted. He also persuaded Congress to build up defenses in our own country. In 1941, after World War II had already begun in Europe, Congress passed the Lend-Lease Act at the President's request. This act allowed the Allies to borrow military equipment from the United States. Lend-lease was continued even after the United States entered World War II in December of 1941. During the war, Roosevelt worked with Winston Churchill of Great Britain and Joseph Stalin of the Soviet Union in deciding wartime strategy and in making plans for dealing with the defeated nations at the end of the war. The atomic bomb was developed under his direction by a large team of scientists. It was used in 1945 after Roosevelt's death.

During Roosevelt's administration, television had not come into general use, but he made frequent use of the radio. In his "Fireside Chats," he kept the public informed of what he was trying to do. Most U.S. citizens responded to the friendly warmth of his voice. The President's unfailing optimism caused millions of discouraged citizens to take heart again. They never forgot the words in his first inaugural address: "The only thing we have to fear is fear itself."

But although Roosevelt was greatly loved by many, he was also bitterly disliked by some. A number of wealthy business executives were concerned about New Deal spending. The government had gone into debt for huge amounts of money to finance the new programs. Many of Roosevelt's critics accused him of bringing socialism to the United States because his New Deal programs emphasized government help for the poor.

Roosevelt died less than three months after he began his fourth term. One of his dreams had been to found the organization that today is called the United Nations. Roosevelt firmly believed that the nations of the world would have to learn to live together in peace to survive.

ALSO READ: FOUR FREEDOMS; PRESIDENCY; SOCIAL SECURITY; ROOSEVELT, ELEANOR; WORLD WAR II.

President Franklin Roosevelt liked to swim to exercise his crippled legs. He had an indoor swimming pool installed in the White House.

ROOSEVELT, THEODORE

(1858–1919) Few people have had a greater variety of interests than Theodore Roosevelt did. As a boy, he wanted to be a naturalist. While still in college, he began to write a book, *The Naval War of 1812*. Years later he became the first U.S. President to emphasize the conservation of the

▲ *President Theodore Roosevelt was an active man who loved to be outdoors. Here, he meets with a group of Girl Scouts.*

THEODORE ROOSEVELT

TWENTY-SIXTH PRESIDENT SEPTEMBER 14, 1901–MARCH 3, 1909

Born: October 27, 1858, New York City
Parents: Theodore and Martha Bulloch Roosevelt
Education: Harvard University, Cambridge, Massachusetts
Religion: Dutch Reformed Church
Occupation: Lawyer, soldier, naturalist, rancher, writer, explorer, public official
Political Party: Republican
Married: 1880 to Alice Lee (1861–1884); 1886 to Edith Carow (1861–1948)
Children: 1 daughter by first wife; 4 sons, 1 daughter by second wife
Died: January 6, 1919, Oyster Bay, New York
Buried: Sagamore Hill, Oyster Bay, New York

In a cartoon in 1902, Teddy Roosevelt was shown refusing to shoot a bear cub on a hunting trip. After that, "Teddy" bears became associated with Roosevelt, and toy makers began making teddy bears for children.

The thickest rope ever made was used on the liner *Great Eastern* in 1858. It was 47 inches (119 cm) thick and had four strands, each strand being made up of nearly 4,000 yarns.

▼ *This picture shows how a large piece of rope is woven together by machine.*

country's natural resources.

This popular President, who once said, "I wish to preach, not the doctrine of ignoble ease, but the doctrine of the strenuous life, the life of toil and effort . . . ," had suffered from asthma while growing up in New York City, where he was born. But he gradually built up his strength with exercise and determination. After his graduation from Harvard University in 1880, he studied law and, at the age of 23, was elected to the New York legislature.

For about three years, Roosevelt spent a great deal of time on his ranch in the Dakota territory to build up his health. At Sagamore Hill, a big rambling house that he had purchased at Oyster Bay on Long Island, he began to write his four-volume history, *The Winning of the West.*

After the death of his first wife, Alice Lee, Roosevelt married his childhood friend, Edith Carow. T.R., or Teddy, as he was often called, served as a member of the United States Civil Service Commission (1889–1895) and as president of the New York City Police Board (1895–1897). He also served as assistant secretary of the Navy (1897–1898). During the Spanish-American War, he was colonel of the regiment known as the Rough Riders. In the Battle of San Juan Hill near Santiago, Cuba, he led the Rough Riders in an attack up nearby Kettle Hill.

In 1898, he was elected governor of New York State. A Republican, he became Vice-President of the United States in 1901. When President William McKinley died, on September 14, 1901, Theodore Roosevelt succeeded him as President. In 1904, he was elected to that office.

As President, Theodore Roosevelt's motto was a "square deal" for everyone. He was convinced that "big business" was destroying free competition. Among the laws that Congress passed at his recommendation were the Meat Inspection Act and the Pure Food and Drug Act (1906) to protect the public. During the Roosevelt administration, a number of important steps were taken to conserve the nation's natural resources. In 1903, a treaty was made with the Republic of Panama. This treaty granted the United States the right to construct a canal through the Isthmus of Panama.

After leaving the White House, Roosevelt went to Africa to hunt for big game (1909–1910). At the Republican Convention in 1912, he again was a candidate for his party's nomination. But his successor, President William Howard Taft, was nominated for reelection. Roosevelt then organized a third party, the Progressive, or Bull Moose, Party, and became its Presidential candidate, but he was not elected. He often publicly disagreed with the policies of both President Taft and Taft's successor, Woodrow Wilson. Roosevelt favored entering World War I long before the United States actually did. In 1917, even though he was in failing health, he offered to raise and lead a division of troops, but President Wilson did not accept his offer. Three years later, Roosevelt died in his sleep.

ALSO READ: CONSERVATION; PANAMA; PANAMA CANAL; SPANISH-AMERICAN WAR; TAFT, WILLIAM HOWARD; WILSON, WOODROW.

ROPE Tough cord made of twisted fibers or strands is called rope. Rope that is less than a quarter of an inch (6 mm) thick is usually referred to as *twine*. The general term for rope, twine, and cord is *cordage*.

Since ancient times, people have made and used rope. *Hemp*, a tall plant grown in many parts of the world, produces a natural fiber that can be made into rope and twine. *Jute* is another plant whose fibers are made into rope.

Natural-fiber rope is made from

the stems of the abacá plant, which is widely grown in the Philippines. The hard fiber of the abacá is known as *manila* or *manila hemp*. When the abacá plant is fully grown, it is cut down. Long, strong fibers are taken from the leaf stems at the base of the plant. The coarser fibers are woven together to make rope that is very durable and weather-resistant. The finer fibers are used to make hats and fabrics.

Another important natural fiber used to make rope comes from the *sisal* plant, which is widely cultivated in eastern Africa and Haiti. Sisal hemp is not as strong as manila hemp (the word "hemp" is often used for various plant fibers). Another tough fiber, *henequen*, comes from a plant of the same name grown mainly on the Yucatán Peninsula in Mexico.

Stronger and more long-lasting than the natural-fiber ropes are those made from synthetic fibers, such as *nylon*. Nylon rope is used for parachute cords, mooring lines, and towlines; it has great elasticity—that is, it returns quickly to its original shape after being stretched. Rope woven from *polyester* fiber is extremely strong, too. Probably the strongest synthetic-fiber rope is made from *aramid* fibers, which resist intense heat and stretching. Wire rope (*cable*) is made by twisting steel wires together. It is much heavier but not as flexible as natural-fiber or synthetic-fiber rope is. Wire rope has great strength and is used in elevators, cranes, and oil-well derricks.

ALSO READ: KNOT, PLANT PRODUCTS.

ROSE In 1986, the House of Representatives voted to adopt the rose as the "national floral emblem" of the United States. Roses are grown in every one of the 50 states, including Alaska.

Roses have been grown for thousands of years. Roses grow in temperate and tropical climates all over the world. There are hundreds of different species of roses, and every year rose growers breed new varieties. Most roses grow on bushes four to eight feet (1.2–2.4 m) high. If *climbing*, or *rambler*, roses are given a support to grow on, they may grow much higher. Rose bushes are *brambles*, which means that they have thorns along the stems.

▲ *Roses are among the most loved flowers.*

In ancient times, roses bloomed only once a year. Rose growers then found some that bloomed in the spring and autumn. Using these, plant breeders produced rose bushes that keep on having blooms all summer long. These are called *everblooming*, or *perpetual*, roses. Most of them are *hybrid tea* roses. They are called hybrid because they were bred from perpetual roses and tea roses. Tea roses got their name because they smell like tea.

▲ *A yellow rose.*

The three main colors of roses are red, white, and yellow. From these colors, roses with a large number of other colors have been bred. The other colors include orange, pink,

▲ *The Rosetta Stone, now in the British Museum in London. When Young and, more important, Champollion managed to decipher the writing on this stone, they opened the way for us to find out about the history of ancient Egypt.*

▲ *The Betsy Ross House on Arch Street, in Philadelphia, Pennsylvania. Here, Betsy Ross is said to have made the first U.S. flag. The 13 stars of the flag represented the 13 original colonies.*

coral, and lavender.

In ancient times, people believed that roses could cure some diseases. Rose petals are made into preserves or eaten in salads. The seed pods of roses, *rose hips*, also are made into preserves. Rose hips are used in some products found in health-food stores, such as vitamin-C tablets and rose-hip tea. An oil, *attar of roses*, taken from rose petals, is used in perfumes.

Other plants of the rose family produce important edible fruits. Did you know that apples, cherries, plums, raspberries, blackberries, strawberries, apricots, peaches, and almonds are all in the rose family?

ALSO READ: FLOWER FAMILIES, GARDEN FLOWER.

ROSETTA STONE Scientists have known for a long time that the priests of ancient Egypt used a type of picture, or symbol, writing called *hieroglyphics*. For many years, no one was able to read this forgotten language. In 1799, a soldier in Napoleon's army was helping to repair a fort near the Egyptian town of Rosetta. He discovered a slab of stone inscribed in three languages—hieroglyphics, demotic (the common language of ancient Egypt), and Greek.

Scholars guessed that the three languages were repeating the same message. The Greek version showed that the stone had been inscribed in 196 B.C., in praise of the Egyptian king, Ptolemy V. The British scientist Thomas Young (1773–1829) recognized certain groups of symbols in the hieroglyphic inscription as the names of ancient Egyptian kings. The same names appeared in the Greek inscription. After Young's death, a French scholar named Jean-François Champollion took up Young's work. He painstakingly deciphered (made out the meaning of) all the symbols. The discovery and translation of the Rosetta Stone meant that scholars could read other hieroglyphic inscriptions and find out much more about ancient Egypt. The Rosetta Stone can be seen today in the British Museum in London.

ALSO READ: EGYPT, ANCIENT; HIEROGLYPHICS; PICTURE WRITING.

ROSS, BETSY (1752–1836) According to legend, Betsy Ross was the woman who made the first American stars and stripes flag. She is said to have stitched the flag at the request of a secret committee headed by George Washington.

Elizabeth (Betsy) Ross was born in Philadelphia, Pennsylvania. She was the eighth of 17 children. Her first husband, John Ross, opened an upholsterer's shop in Philadelphia. He was killed in battle during the American Revolution, but Mrs. Ross continued to run the upholstery business. As part of the work in the shop, she sewed flags.

George Washington and Robert Morris reportedly visited Betsy Ross early in June 1776. They asked her to design and sew an American flag. She made a rough sketch of a flag that Washington liked. No written record of an order for making a flag has been found. But some people like to believe that the flag Betsy Ross sewed was the first American stars and stripes flag. This flag was adopted as the national flag on June 14, 1777, by the Continental Congress.

Betsy Ross married three times and had seven daughters.

ALSO READ: AMERICAN REVOLUTION; FLAG; STAR-SPANGLED BANNER; WASHINGTON, GEORGE.

ROTIFER Rotifers are a type of animal so small they must be studied under a microscope. They live wherever water collects, whether in ponds, puddles, gutters, or oceans. Most

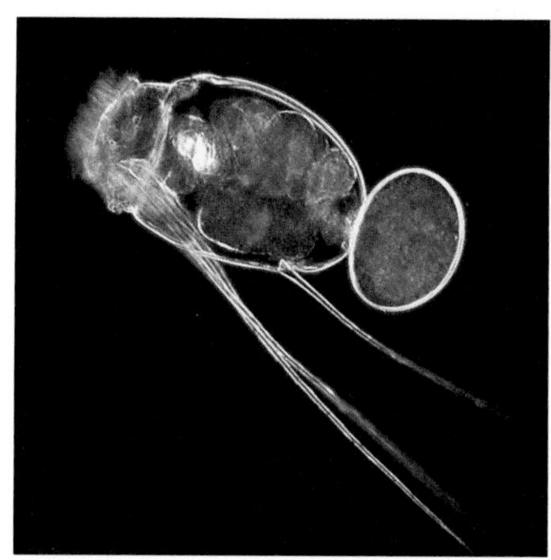

▲ *This female rotifer has three long trailers which are used to flip over backwards if suddenly disturbed. The red eye spot is visible, as is the single egg sac attached to the rear.*

kinds live in fresh water. There are many kinds, sizes, and shapes of rotifers. All are transparent, so their inside workings can be seen as if they were glass models.

Most rotifers are constantly in motion as they crawl, feed, or dart from place to place in the water. Some swim. Some creep on the bottom or on plant stems. Other rotifers spend their lives attached by stalks to plants or other surfaces. Like all animals, they must have food. They eat microscopic specks of living matter. They trap food with *cilia*, which look like tiny hairs arranged in a fringe. The word rotifer means "wheel bearer." This is because the cilia in most rotifers are arranged on one or two disks at the front end of the body. The cilia constantly beat the water in search of food or to move the animal about. The beating of the cilia makes the disks look like rotating wheels.

ALSO READ: ANIMAL KINGDOM.

ROUGH RIDERS see ROOSEVELT, THEODORE.

ROUNDHEAD see CROMWELL, OLIVER; ENGLISH HISTORY; PURITAN.

ROWING One of the most strenuous and exciting sports is rowing, driving a small boat though the water with oars. People have rowed boats for thousands of years, and until the 1700's they even rowed large warships known as *galleys*. A galley had hundreds of slaves to drive it along. Today, rowing is mainly a sport or a leisure activity. As a sport, rowing began in the 1500's on the Thames River in London, England.

There are two main forms of using oars to drive a boat, *sculling* and *rowing*. In sculling, each oarsman uses a pair of lightweight oars, known as sculls. The boats used for racing are also called sculls. They are built to take one or two scullers.

In rowing, each oarsman has a single oar, which is longer and heavier than a scull. Boats are built to take eight, four, or a pair of oarsmen. A boat for eight is always steered by a ninth member of the crew, known as the *coxswain*—pronounced "cox'n"—or *cox*, for short. The cox is generally a very small, light person. There are races for fours and pairs with or without a cox. Rowboats for racing are very light and are known as *shells*. Rowboats for leisure use are more robust.

Large knockout competitions for rowers are known as *regattas*. The

Ancient Greek triremes (galleys with three decks) were big rowboats. As many as seven men pulled on a single oar.

▼ *Rowing is both good exercise and a fun recreational pursuit. Rowers can enjoy scenic river views and keep fit at the same time.*

most famous races in the world include the annual Yale–Harvard university boat race in the United States, and the Oxford and Cambridge university boat race in Britain.

ALSO READ: BOATS AND BOATING, OLYMPIC GAMES.

ROYAL CANADIAN MOUNTED POLICE The "Mounties" are Canada's national police force. They were established in 1873 as the North-West Mounted Police. Their job was to patrol the Northwest Territories and the Yukon on horseback and by dogsled.

Canada's wild northwestern regions were a haven for smugglers and outlaws in the 1800's. Many exciting stories are told about the days when the Mounties rode through the vast wilderness tracking down criminals and keeping order. They gained the confidence of the Indians, and soon their scarlet jackets were a familiar and respected sight.

"Royal" was added to the name of the Mounted Police in 1904, in honor of their outstanding record of service. In 1920, they became known as the Royal Canadian Mounted Police. Their authority was extended to cover the whole nation of Canada.

▼ *Officers of the Royal Canadian Mounted Police in full dress uniform, outside the Parliament buildings in Ottawa.*

The headquarters of the Mounted Police is in Ottawa. The Mounties now number about 18,000 men and women. They act as local police in many areas of Canada. They are a modern police force with up-to-date crime laboratories. The Mounties now wear brown jackets and travel in automobiles, boats, airplanes, and snowmobiles. Their horses and scarlet jackets are now kept only for parades.

ALSO READ: CANADA, NORTHWEST TERRITORIES, YUKON TERRITORY.

ROYALTY see KINGS AND QUEENS.

RUBBER Balloons, golf balls, automobile tires, pencil erasers, and nursing-bottle nipples are a few of the thousands of things made of rubber. Rubber is an elastic substance made from the juice of certain plants or by chemical processes. If you squeeze or stretch an elastic substance and then release it, it will spring back to its original shape.

Natural rubber is made from *latex*, a milky liquid secreted by several kinds of plants. More than nine-tenths of all natural rubber comes from rubber trees that originally grew in the jungles of South America. Later, rubber trees were grown on large plantations in the East Indies, Southeast Asia, and the African countries of Liberia and Nigeria. Latex comes also from Siberian dandelions and from guayule bushes that grow in Mexico and the southwestern United States.

Pull a dandelion stem in half, and you can see the milky latex ooze out. To get latex from a rubber tree, several cuts are made in the bark two to five feet (60–150 cm) above the ground. The bark between cuts is removed so that the latex can run down to the end of the lowest cut and drip into a cup. The latex is then taken to a collecting station where it is mixed with acid to form rubber.

Rubber was being used by the peoples of South America before Columbus sailed to the New World. They made rubber balls, shoes, and containers, and they used rubber for making fabric waterproof. When rubber was brought to Europe, it was used for making garments such as garters. The English chemist, Joseph Priestley, discovered that the material could be used for rubbing out pencil marks. Because of this use, the material came to be called "rubber."

Pure rubber becomes sticky and melts in hot weather, and it is brittle in cold weather. In 1839, a U.S. inventor, Charles Goodyear, accidentally discovered that heating sulfur with rubber would cure most of rubber's faults. He called this process "vulcanization." Later, it was found that adding carbon in the form of lampblack would further improve rubber.

In the 1920's, chemists learned to make rubber from chemicals. This kind of rubber is *synthetic rubber*. But only natural rubber was widely used until World War II stopped the supply of latex from the East. Chemists improved synthetic rubber so that it could be used to make tires, tank treads, and many other items. Chemists have continued to make better and better synthetic rubbers with many properties. Synthetic rubber can stand much hotter and colder temperatures than natural rubber can. Synthetic rubber is not harmed by oils and greases. Most rubber articles are now made from synthetic rubber.

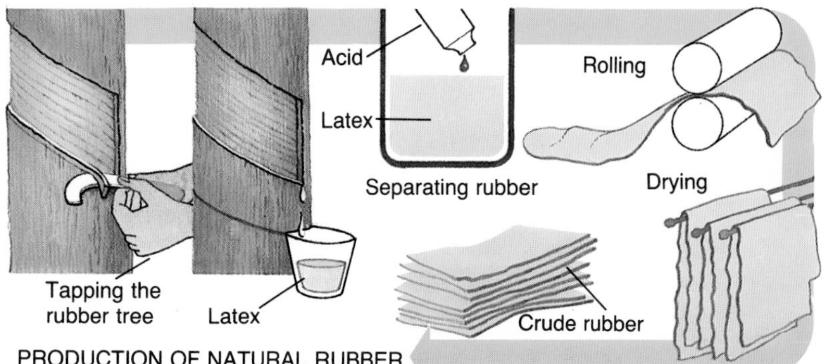

▲ *Natural rubber is made from latex, the sap of the rubber tree. The crude rubber is mixed with coloring materials and with chemicals to make it last longer and be stronger. Then machines shape it into various products, such as car tires and hoses.*

▼ *Latex being tapped in Malaya. The rubber tree came originally from Brazil.*

ALSO READ: CHEMISTRY, SYNTHETIC.

RUBENS, PETER PAUL (1577–1640) One of the greatest artists of northern Europe was Peter Paul Rubens, who was born in Flanders (now part of Belgium). At the age of 23, Rubens went to Italy, where he studied for eight years the works of the master artists. He learned the techniques of painters in Rome, Mantua, and Genoa. But he still remained a Flemish painter. Like the other Flemish painters, he faithfully painted the people and life around him. He was not like the Italian painters—more interested in creating beautiful paintings than in depicting the lives of ordinary people.

Rubens returned to his home city of Antwerp at the age of 31, having gained greater skill than possibly any other northern European painter of

▲ Saint Paul *by the great painter Peter Paul Rubens.*

▲ The Château de Steen *by Peter Paul Rubens. Obviously Rubens became very involved in this painting while he was working on it, because he had to expand its planned area by adding a further 16 wooden boards.*

that time. He had become expert at creating large paintings for churches and palaces. He could plan and execute huge paintings involving several figures in a complicated composition. But he kept the Flemish love for painting the textures of skin and the look of fine clothing.

Rubens often began a huge canvas by putting on the first brush strokes to sketch out the composition and important details. Then he would turn the canvas over to his assistants, who would paint in some of the lesser details. Then Rubens would apply the finishing touches. He produced a tremendous number of works in this manner. Rubens's greatest skill can be seen in his portraits, such as the one of Saint Paul shown on the previous page. Notice Paul's face. Rubens has made it very alive and strong-looking. The Saint's eyes are alert as he sits with sword in hand—a symbol of his readiness to die for the faith. And how like Rubens it was to show the fiery-tempered Paul as a redhead! With one hand Paul grasps the Bible. (Can you think why?) See the beautiful way in which Paul's cloak is draped over his arm. You can feel the strength of the man under the soft, silken cloak.

Europe was in the midst of religious wars during Rubens's lifetime. Much of the continent of Europe was split between Protestants and Catholics. Rubens followed the faith of Catholic Flanders. He traveled frequently to various countries, painting large, important canvases for rulers in Spain, France, and England. Charles I of England even made him a knight.

The sparkle and warmth of Rubens's canvases live on, even after 300 years of hanging in chilly palaces and museums. The painter from Flanders used his brush to give an almost magical life to the people he chose to depict in paint.

ALSO READ: ART HISTORY; DUTCH ART; PAUL, SAINT; RENAISSANCE.

RUMANIA see ROMANIA.

RUNNING see MARATHON RACE, TRACK AND FIELD.

RUSHMORE, MOUNT The noble faces of four U.S. Presidents are carved on a high granite cliff located in the Black Hills of South Dakota. The faces are those of George Washington, Thomas Jefferson, Theodore Roosevelt, and Abraham Lincoln. This huge sculpture is called Mount Rushmore National Memorial. Mount Rushmore is nearly 6,000 feet (1,830 m) high. Each face is about 60 feet (18.3 m) high.

A U.S. sculptor, Gutzon Borglum,

▼ *The faces carved on Mount Rushmore are (from left to right) Presidents Washington, Jefferson, Theodore Roosevelt and Lincoln. They were carved between 1927–1941 by Gutzon Borglum.*

designed and directed the carving of Mount Rushmore. Work on the memorial began in 1927 and lasted 14 years. Borglum first made a small model of each of the faces to use as a guide in carving the large heads. Many workers helped Borglum carve the four faces from the hard stone. They used drilling machines and dynamite. When Borglum died in 1941, before the memorial was finished, his son completed it for him.

Near Mount Rushmore, another large sculpture is being created. Since 1948, Korczak Ziolkowski has blasted tons of granite from the side of Thunderhead Mountain in the Black Hills. With the help of his family, Ziolkowski is carving a likeness of Chief Crazy Horse, the famous Sioux Indian warrior, astride a stallion. If finished, the sculpture will be 563 feet (172 m) high, the largest in the world.

ALSO READ: SCULPTURE, SOUTH DAKOTA, STONE MOUNTAIN.

RUSSIA see SOVIET UNION.

RUSSIAN The Soviet Union, also called Russia, is the largest country in land area, extending from Europe to the Pacific Ocean. Over 260 million people live in the Soviet Union. They come from many different backgrounds and nationalities. In various regions of the country, the people have their own languages. More than 100 different languages and dialects (local variations of a language) are spoken in the Soviet Union.

Russian, one of the Soviet languages, is the official language of the Soviet Union. All Soviet children must learn to speak, read, and write it. Russian is also the native language of more than 5 million people living in Czechoslovakia, Romania, and Poland. Russian belongs to the group of Slavic languages that includes Polish, Bulgarian, Slovak, Czech, Slovenian, Serbian, Croatian, Romanian, Ukrainian, and Byelorussian. All Slavic languages are similar to each other.

Здра̂вствуйте
Меня́ зову́ Пётр
Ивановице

▲ *The writing shown here is Russian for "Hello. My name is Peter Ivanovich." The words are pronounced ZDRAHV-stvoo-ee-tye. Meen-YAAH zah-VOOT PYAW-tr ee-VAHN-ah-veech.*

One important difference between Russian and Western European languages is the alphabet. English is written with the Roman alphabet of 26 letters based on the alphabet used in ancient Rome. Russian (as well as Bulgarian, Ukrainian, Byelorussian, and Serbian) is written with the Cyrillic alphabet. Cyrillic is based on the Greek alphabet. It was invented by two Greek bishops, Cyril and Methodius, who are said to have created the alphabet so that people in Slavic countries could read. Before about A.D. 900, most Slavic languages had never been written down. The full Cyrillic alphabet today has 36 letters. The Russian version uses only 33 letters.

Russia did not have much contact with western Europe until the middle 1500's. For this reason, very few Russian words have been adopted into the English language. About the only widely known Russian words are *czar*, *vodka*, *babushka* (which also means "grandmother" in Russian), *sputnik*, *bolshevik*, and *cosmonaut*. Several names for people are almost the same in both Russian and English.

Russian is the third most spoken language in the world, after Chinese and English. An estimated 250 million people speak or understand Russian.

■ LEARN BY DOING

See if you can recognize some of these common Russian names: *Ivan*, *Olga*, *Mariya*, *Irina*, *Pyotr*, *Mikhail*, *Vyera*, *Aleksandr*, *Natalya*, *Ekaterina*, *Nikolai*, *Timofei*. The Russian language has borrowed many words

▲ *This decorated clay mask from Siberia dates back to the Neolithic (New Stone Age) in Russian history.*

from European languages. The Russian word for "car" is *avtomobil.* See if you can guess what these Russian words mean: *studyent, Amyerika, avtobus, prezidyent, fotograf, orkestr, taksi, dramatika, armiya, futbol, tsigaret, dzhazz.* ■

ALSO READ: ALPHABET, LANGUAGES, SOVIET UNION.

RUSSIAN HISTORY Russia began as a tiny principality in eastern Europe, and grew into a great empire that stretched from Europe to the Pacific Ocean. After 1922, the Russian Empire and several smaller countries became the Union of Soviet Socialist Republics (U.S.S.R., or Soviet Union), which today has the largest land area of any nation in the world. The Soviet Union is still popularly called Russia.

The Earliest Russians In the A.D. 600's and before, a farming people called the Slavs lived in the northern forests of the Great European Plain. To the south lay flat, treeless grasslands, or *steppes*, traveled by roving bands of herders. To the north lay Scandinavia, home of the Vikings. Several great rivers flowed through the lands of the Slavs. Traders sailed up and down these rivers between Scandinavia and the Byzantine Empire, south of the Black Sea. The Slavs began to take part in this trade. Viking traders had settled along the rivers by the A.D. 800's. The Slavs called these Vikings *Rus*, from which has come the name "Russia." The word *Rus* comes from an old Norse term *Rothsmenn*, meaning "seamen." The Rus married into Slavic families. These people were the earliest Russians.

The strongest Russian tribes established towns along the trade routes. The two most powerful towns were Novgorod and Kiev. According to legend, the Viking chieftain Rurik settled in Novgorod in A.D. 862. The rulers of Russia for the next 700 years claimed to be descended from Rurik. This claim gave them the right to leadership.

The city of Kiev was closer than Novgorod to the rich trade routes of the Middle East. In A.D. 869, Rurik sent two of his followers to Kiev. Ten years later, Rurik's successor, Oleg, came to Kiev and took the city by force. Oleg now had control of both Kiev in the south and Novgorod in the north. He defeated local tribes around the area of Kiev and began business dealings with the Khazars (traders who controlled ports on the Caspian and Black seas).

Grand Princes of Kiev and Vladimir Eventually the rulers of Kiev gave themselves the title of *grand prince.* The rulers of smaller areas within the Kievan state were known simply as princes. The Kievan grand prince chose the princes who ruled smaller Russian territories in both the north and south. In return, the princes owed the grand prince taxes and military support.

There was no rule as to who would become grand prince after one of them died. Civil wars always followed the death of a grand prince, and these wars left the Russians weak and open to attack. The first Christian ruler of Russia was Grand Prince Vladimir I, who founded the Russian Orthodox Church at Kiev.

In the 1000's, the friendly Khazars were defeated by nomadic tribes called the Cumans. The Kievan state remained the only defender of the trade routes. In the 1100's, after a short period of strength, the Kievan princes began to fight each other for control over the Kievan state. While they were fighting among themselves, Andrew Bogoliubsky, prince of Rostov-Suzdal (an area east and slightly north of Moscow), attacked and conquered the Kievan principalities. Rostov-Suzdal became the new

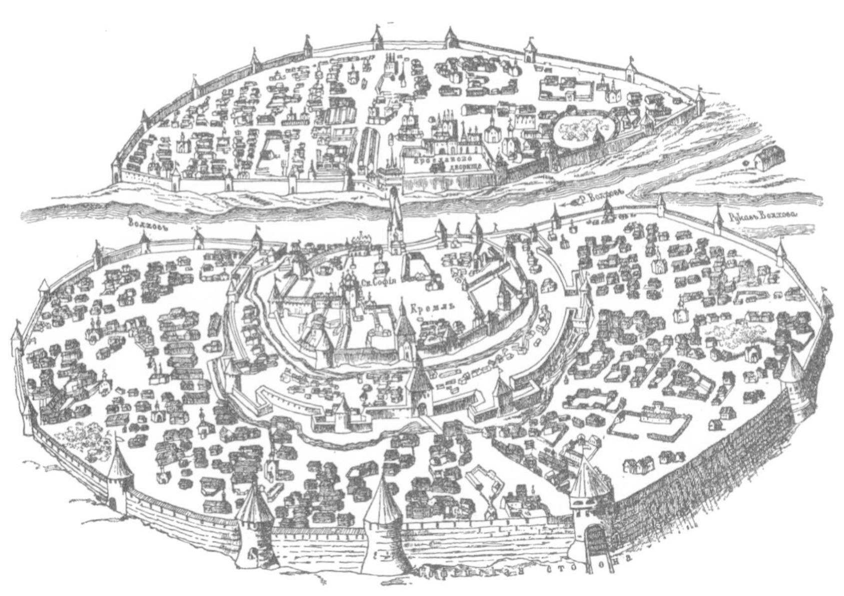

◀ *Novgorod, Russia, in the 15th century. The city was an important center of trade in amber, furs, and wax. It is usually regarded as the cradle of Russian civilization.*

grand principality, with the city of Vladimir as the new capital.

In 1237, a great army of nomadic warriors, called the Tatars or Mongols, invaded Russia from the east. They were led by Batu Khan, grandson of the Mongol emperor, Genghis Khan. The Russians, weakened by civil war, were easily conquered. For the next 200 years, the Russians were ruled by the Tatars, who settled on the southern steppes north of the Caspian Sea. The Tatar capital became known as Sarai.

Alexander Nevsky, the grand prince of Vladimir from 1252 to 1263, instructed his people not to fight against the Tatar rulers and to agree to the Tatar commands. Nevsky and all the other princes had to journey to Sarai to get permission from the Tatar Khan to rule their principalities. This shift of power from Vladimir to Sarai, and the ending of trade that resulted from the Tatar invasion, weakened the grand prince of Vladimir's control over other princes.

The Grand Principality of Moscow In 1328, Ivan I, prince of Moscow, conquered the Rostov-Suzdal capital of Vladimir. With the Tatar Khan's permission, Ivan took over the title of grand prince. The Russian capital and the headquarters of the Russian Church were moved to Moscow. Ivan I was also known as Ivan Kalita ("Moneybags") because he taxed his people heavily in order to pay money to the Tatar Khan. In return, the Khan helped Ivan take over more territory. Dmitri Donskoi, the Muscovite grand prince from 1359 to 1389, defeated an army of Tatars at the Battle of Kulikovo.

Ivan III (also called Ivan the Great) continued expanding Muscovite territory. Each time Ivan conquered a principality, he exiled or killed its rulers. The *boyars* (wealthy landowners) had their lands taken away and given to supporters of Moscow. The Tatars had become very weak because of fighting among themselves. The Tatar empire in Russia ended when Tatar territory was split into several small khanates to the south and southwest of Russia. Vasily III, son of Ivan III, conquered the last of the Russian princes. The Muscovite grand prince was the only ruling power in Russia by 1533.

In 1533, Ivan IV became grand prince of Moscow. Since he was only a child at the time of his coronation, Russian princes and boyars plotted ways to get rid of Ivan and take power themselves. When Ivan grew up, he severely crushed the power of these nobles and took complete control of

Czar Peter the Great of Russia was intensely interested in all things Western, especially shipbuilding. In 1697, he disguised himself as a ship's carpenter and went to England to study shipbuilding. He worked in both English and Dutch shipyards.

▲ *Ivan the Terrible ruled Russia harshly, executing thousands. In 1581, in a fit of rage, he murdered his son.*

▲ *Peter the Great, czar of Russia from 1682 to 1725. Under his rule, Russia rose to be a greater power in Europe.*

Tsar Peter the Great was a huge man, nearly seven feet tall, with enormous strength and energy. He died at the age of 52 when he caught a chill through diving into icy water to save some soldiers from drowning. It is said that he drove the Russians so hard that when he died a great sigh of relief could be heard all over the country.

the government. At age 17, Ivan had himself crowned *czar*. The word *czar* (also spelled *tsar*) comes from the Latin word *Caesar*, meaning "emperor." Ivan IV became known as Ivan the Terrible because of the ruthless ways he used to stop those who opposed him. Ivan created his own private army, the *Oprichniki*, which would follow only his personal commands. The Oprichniki took over newly conquered lands and killed any of the nobles or boyars whom Ivan suspected of treason. Ivan engaged in several battles with the remaining Tatar tribes, whom he finally defeated.

Ivan IV was the first Russian ruler to organize a national assembly, the *Zemsky Sobor*. It was made up of representatives of the clergy, the boyars, and important business leaders. Ivan called the assembly together in order to get money and support for his battles against Poland and Sweden. But the assembly itself had no power of its own. Ivan believed that God had given him the right to rule, and so he would allow no limits on his own power.

Fyodor II, son of Ivan the Terrible, was crowned czar in 1584. He was a weak ruler. The boyars struggled among themselves for power over the czar. The boyar Boris Godunov, who had been a close adviser to Ivan the Terrible, won out. He took charge of the czar and continued Ivan's policy of gaining more territory. Boris, who was not so cruel as Ivan, became very popular.

In 1598, Fyodor died. He had had no children, which meant that the line of rulers who could claim descent from the Viking Rurik had ended. Fyodor's death marked the beginning of a confusing 15-year period known as the "Time of Troubles." The Zemsky Sobor elected Boris Godunov as czar. Several other boyars, especially Fyodor Romanov, had also wanted to be czar. Romanov became a monk, and Boris's other opponents were either killed or deported.

Among the common people there was great dissatisfaction. Heavy taxes had left the peasants poverty-stricken. Many peasants escaped to the dense forests of the north or moved into southern territories that were not under the control of Moscow. The *Cossacks*, groups of freedom-loving but violent warriors, grew strong and raided the boyar estates. A great famine began in 1601, and no one could get enough to eat.

In 1604, a man appeared claiming that he was Dmitri, the supposedly murdered son of Ivan the Terrible. Many people believed his claim; although he has become known in history as the "False Dmitri." He got aid from Poland, and, with the support of Russian peasants and Cossacks, Dmitri took Moscow in 1605. Dmitri was murdered a few months later by jealous boyars, and the Cossacks revolted. Two czars were elected and eliminated during the next seven years, and a second False Dmitri appeared and was murdered.

The Time of Troubles ended in 1613 when the Zemsky Sobor elected Michael Romanov (son of the Fyodor Romanov whom Boris Godunov had defeated) as czar. This was the beginning of the great Romanov dynasty of czars that lasted until the February Revolution of 1917. The early Romanovs continued to gain land for Russia, but they did nothing about the terrible problems of the common people. Peasants continued to migrate out of the country. If they could not leave, many sold themselves as slaves, because slaves did not have to pay the heavy taxes. The Law Code of 1649 was an attempt to keep the peasants at home. The code forbade peasants to leave the lands or cities in which they worked. Although the code also forbade cruel treatment of peasants, this was usually ignored. A master could treat a peasant in any way he chose.

Russia Begins to Change Peter I (called Peter the Great), who ruled from 1682 to 1725, was the first czar to build Russia into an important European power. During the rule of the Tatars, Russia had been cut off from western Europe. The Russian people were superstitious and distrusted foreigners. Russian economy was based on primitive farming, and the army was still using old-fashioned methods of warfare. Peter forced the Russian people to accept the new ideas, fashions of dress, and business methods of the West. He gave women the right to go places alone in public. He changed the calendar, and he brought in European craftworkers and merchants.

Russian explorers had claimed Siberia, as far as the Pacific Ocean. A large part of the Ukraine, southwest of Russia, had been taken. Peter also captured lands on the Black Sea in 1696, after he had built ships and organized the first Russian navy. Peter had himself crowned emperor of all territories under Russian control. He founded a Western-style capital city, St. Petersburg (now Leningrad), on the Baltic coast.

Peter believed that all Russians should work for the state. He limited the independence of the nobility by making everyone who reached a certain rank work for the government. He also placed the Russian church under government control. In spite of these reforms, the peasants were no better off. Serfdom and slavery continued. Peter created his own army, the Palace Guards, to make sure people obeyed his commands.

The rulers who followed Peter continued his policies. Catherine II (called Catherine the Great), who ruled from 1762 to 1796, kept contact with the West and brought many great Western scholars to her court. During Catherine's reign, the Russians captured a large area of the steppe north of the Black Sea and conquered two regions to the west, Lithuania and Byelorussia.

To ease the hardships of the common people, Catherine herself wrote a series of laws against serfdom. However, these laws were never put into action because the landowners persuaded her that the serfs might use their new-found freedom to revolt. Between 1773 and 1774, a peasant revolt, led by a Cossack named Emelyan Pugachev, swept through Russia. Peasant groups burned and looted villages and farms and refused to work. Catherine's troops crushed the revolt, and the empress tightened the landowners' control over the serfs.

The Growth of Discontent By the early 1800's, most of western Europe had been conquered by the French emperor, Napoleon I. In 1812, during the reign of Alexander I, Napoleon invaded Russia. He marched in to conquer Moscow, but he found the city deserted. A great fire broke out in the city, probably started by a few remaining Russians. Lack of supplies forced Napoleon to retreat. But before his troops could reach the border, the terrible Russian winter had set in. Most of the French army froze to death. Many others were killed by small bands of Russians who harried the retreating columns. Alexander's troops formed part of a European army that invaded Paris in 1814 and forced Napoleon into exile.

By 1820, Russia was one of the strongest powers in Europe, but the

▲ *Catherine the Great, empress of Russia in the late 1700's when the country was rising to prominence as a great power.*

▼ *The port of Archangel, on the White Sea northeast of Karelia, was the only Russian seaport before the building of St. Petersburg (now Leningrad).*

Until 1918 Leningrad (formerly St. Petersburg) was the capital of Russia. The city was built with splendid palaces and huge squares by Peter the Great in 1703. Peter's wooden house still stands there. During World War II Leningrad was besieged for 900 days by the German armies, but the city never fell. Leningrad's cemeteries hold the graves of some 600,000 people who died in the siege.

Russian people were still suffering under the unfair treatment of the czars, the nobility, and the landowners. Because the czar was an absolute monarch, all power was in his hands. People who wanted to improve things had no power to do so unless the czar agreed. The czars were afraid that the common people would become unmanageable if given too much freedom. At Alexander's death in December of 1825, a small group of army officers revolted against the new czar, Nicholas I. These officers, called the Decembrists, hated the absolute power of the czar. They knew that governments in which the people were represented worked in other European countries. They felt such a government could work in Russia. The Decembrist rebellion was put down by the czar's army, but the Decembrists' ideas of reform had begun to spread.

Alexander II, who reigned from 1855 to 1894, decided to start some reforms in order to prevent a revolution. In 1861, he freed the serfs and gave each male serf a plot of land of his own. He also reformed the army, the court system, the educational system, and the system of local government. These were good reforms, but it took a long time to put most of them into action. Government officials were often corrupt—they would accept money for not enforcing reforms. But even honest officials could not act without the consent of the czar himself. The czar's absolute power delayed all attempts at reform.

By the late 1800's, many secret revolutionary organizations had been formed in Russia by people who wanted to improve living conditions and limit the power of the czars. In 1905, the Russians went to war with the Japanese. The war was expensive and food became scarce in Russia. Riots broke out among workers in the cities, who could not make enough money to buy food. In the factories of St. Petersburg, most workers went on strike. In January 1905, a priest named Father Gapon led a peaceful march to Czar Nicholas II's palace. The marchers intended to ask the czar to improve conditions under which the Russian people were forced to live. The day of the march became known as "Bloody Sunday," because the czar's troops fired into the crowd, killing hundreds of people. In October 1905, a general strike of workers and peasants stopped all production throughout the entire country. Czar

▼ *Napoleon's greatest mistake was to invade Russia. His retreating army was defeated by Cossack raiders and by severe weather. As they marched home they died by the thousand. Over a century later Adolf Hitler made the same mistake.*

Nicholas drew up the October Manifesto, in which he granted civil rights for all and established the *Duma*—a council of people's representatives. However, the czar had not really given up his power. He strengthened his secret police and dissolved the first two Dumas. The third Duma was made up almost entirely of wealthy landowners, and all representatives of the common people were shut out of the government.

When World War I broke out in 1914, Czar Nicholas II sent an army to fight against Germany and Austria. The sufferings of the Russian people grew worse, and many Russian soldiers refused to fight. In March 1917, a major revolution broke out in St. Petersburg. The czar was forced to give up his throne, and a provisional government was set up by two liberal politicians, Prince Lvov and Alexander Kerensky. But the war with Germany continued.

▲ *In 1905, the Russian fleet was surprisingly and humiliatingly defeated by the Japanese near Tsushima, an island between Japan and South Korea. This defeat was one of the causes of the revolution in Russia later that year.*

The Beginnings of the Soviet Union Since the late 1800's, a revolutionary organization, the Communist Party, had been gaining support among the people. In November 1917, the Communists, led by Leon Trotsky and V. I. Lenin, overthrew the provisional government. Lenin became head of the new Communist government. He immediately made peace with Germany. All Russian land was taken over by the government and distributed equally among the people. The capital was moved back to Moscow. In 1918, Czar Nicholas II and his family were executed. The czar's death and the rise of Communist control ended once and for all the Imperial Russian State. By 1922, the empire of the Russian czars had become the Union of Soviet Socialist Republics.

▲ *Bolshevik revolutionaries fighting in Petrograd (formerly St. Petersburg and now Leningrad). They forced the czar to step down from power.*

ALSO READ: CATHERINE THE GREAT; COMMUNISM; CRIMEAN WAR; GENGHIS KHAN; LENIN, VLADIMIR ILICH; MOSCOW; NAPOLEON BONAPARTE; NICHOLAS, CZARS OF RUSSIA; ORTHODOX CHURCH; PETER THE GREAT; RUSSIAN; SOVIET UNION; VIKINGS.

▲ *Babe Ruth, one of the most famous players in baseball history.*

RUTH, BABE (1895–1948) Babe Ruth was born George Herman Ruth in Baltimore, Maryland. He was one of the greatest U.S. baseball players. He was known as the "Sultan of Swat."

In 1914, Ruth was signed by the Baltimore Orioles, but later that year he was sold to the Boston Red Sox. Ruth was a successful left-handed pitcher with the Red Sox, winning 87 games and losing 44. He pitched 29 consecutive scoreless innings in the 1916 and 1918 World Series. However, his hitting ability was greater, so he was shifted to the outfield. In 1920, the Red Sox sold Ruth to the New York Yankees, for whom he played until 1934. Ruth's home runs at bat became legendary. Yankee Stadium, which opened in 1923, was nicknamed the "House that Ruth Built" because of the fans he attracted. During a 154-game season in 1927, Ruth hit 60 home runs. Ruth's lifetime record of 714 home runs stayed unbeaten until 1974 when Hank Aaron beat it.

ALSO READ: BASEBALL, SPORTS.

RWANDA Rwanda, a tiny but densely populated country south of the Sahara Desert in central Africa, is bounded by Uganda on the north, Tanzania on the east, Burundi on the south, and Zaire on the west. Kigali is its capital. (See the map with the article on AFRICA.)

Rwanda is close to the source of the Nile River. It is a country of grassy uplands, lakes, and mountains. Although it lies just below the equator, it has a temperate climate because of its high elevation.

The people farm and raise cattle. Coffee, corn, beans, cassava, tea, tobacco, and cotton are the chief crops. Cassiterite, wolframite, and other minerals are mined. Rwanda's main industries are textiles, chemicals, food processing, and tourism.

The Tutsis, the tallest people in the world—often 7 feet (2.1 m) tall—and the Pygmies, averaging no more than 4½ feet (1.4 m) in height, both live in this area. Rwandans speak French, Kinyarwanda, and Kiswahili. Over 50 percent of the Rwandan people are Christians. Others are Muslims or follow local religions.

Europeans first visited Rwanda in the late 1800's. In the 1890's, the Germans began to extend their control over the territory, and it became part of German East Africa. During World War I, Belgian troops from the Congo occupied the country. After the war was over, Belgium claimed Rwanda and Burundi as a Belgian mandate known as Ruanda-Urundi. It became a United Nations trust territory in 1946 under Belgian administration. In 1962, Ruanda became an independent republic and changed the spelling of its name from Ruanda to Rwanda. It is one of the most densely populated countries in the world.

ALSO READ: AFRICA, BURUNDI.

RWANDA

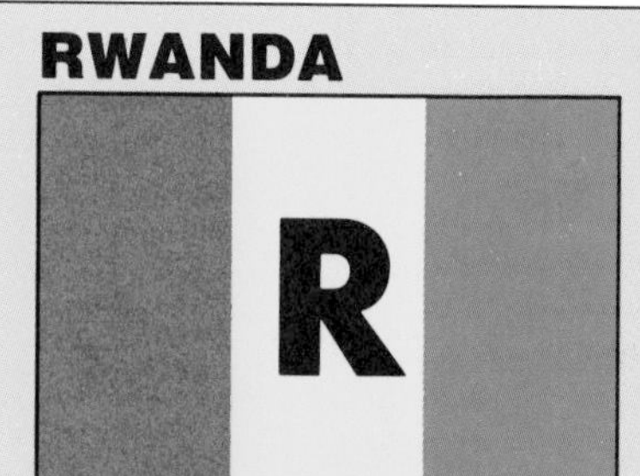

Capital City: Kigali (300,000 people).
Area: 10,169 square miles (26,338 sq. km).
Population: 7,276,000.
Government: One-party republic.
Natural Resources: Cassiterite, wolframite.
Export Products: Coffee, tea, tin.
Unit of Money: Rwanda franc.
Official Languages: Kinyarwanda, French.

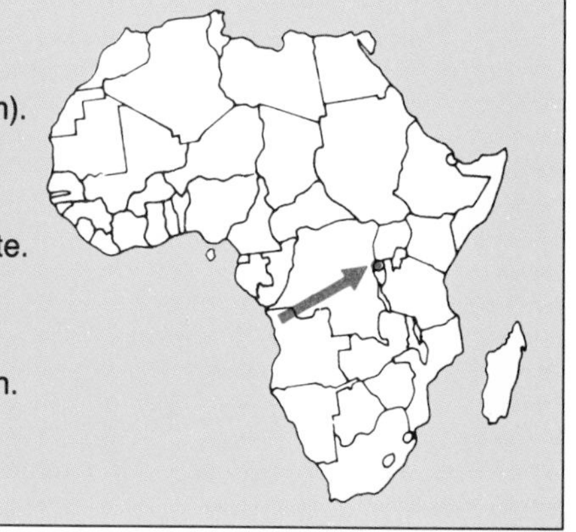

SAFETY "Safety First!" is a good motto for everyone to remember. Many of humanity's most daring feats—such as the moon landings—have been carefully regulated to ensure safety. Safety rules are designed simply to prevent accidents and injuries—not to stop people from having a good time.

Safety at Play Children who ride bicycles, tricycles, skateboards, wagons, or roller skates, can keep from getting hurt—or hurting someone else—if they learn how to use them safely. Don't cross driveways without looking both ways to be sure no car is backing out or approaching. If you coast down a hill, be sure you have enough room to stop safely. Don't try to cross a busy street by riding or skating to the other side. Get off your bike or skateboard and walk across. Take off roller skates and put them on after you are safely across. Put a light and a reflector on your bike or scooter if you ride at night. Don't show off on a bicycle by riding "no hands." An unexpected turn of the wheel could cause a bad spill.

Many children are badly hurt when sledding, skiing, or skating in wintertime. Coasting on sleds should be done only where there is no automobile traffic. Never "belly-flop" onto other sledders when they are coasting, or steer in front of other moving sleds. If you ride on a toboggan, always ride with an adult, and keep your arms and legs in close. Ask an adult or a police officer if the ice is safe before skating or sliding on a pond or

▼ *It is safest to cross a street at the crosswalk, especially where there are* WALK *and* DON'T WALK *lights or a police officer to guide you safely across.*

▲ *These canoeists are wearing life preservers as a safety precaution in case their craft capsizes on the rough river.*

lake. Always be sure the safety binds on your skis are carefully fastened. Carry ski poles at your side. At the top of a ski tow, get off quickly and move to one side.

Water-safety measures can prevent many serious and tragic accidents. Never go out in a boat by yourself unless you know how to swim! When you are in a boat, be sure you are wearing a life preserver. Be careful not to do anything that will upset a small boat or a canoe. It is a good idea for boys and girls to be "buddy swimmers." Always swim with a friend. You can learn how to swim in classes sponsored by the Red Cross, the YMCA, or the YWCA.

Safety at Home Carelessness with matches is one of the most common causes of home fires. Never play with matches or with electric appliances, such as irons and toasters. Don't tamper with electric wires or wall plugs. If your clothing catches fire, never run. Running makes the flames spread faster. Lie down and roll instead.

Never take medicines except when they are given to you by your parents or a doctor. Medicine that is good for one person's illness may be very dangerous for another person. Medicine bottles should always be carefully labeled. Insect killers, cleaning fluids, scouring powders, paints, varnishes, kerosene, and other common household products can be poisonous. Never try tasting them. Don't eat flakes of paint from peeling walls. This is a dangerous practice because the paint may contain lead, another poisonous substance. The home can be a dangerous place if you are not careful and sensible, particularly about electrical appliances.

▼ *Seatbelts in cars are a very important safety device. If your car stops suddenly, your seatbelt will hold you in your seat. Otherwise, you might be thrown through the windshield.*

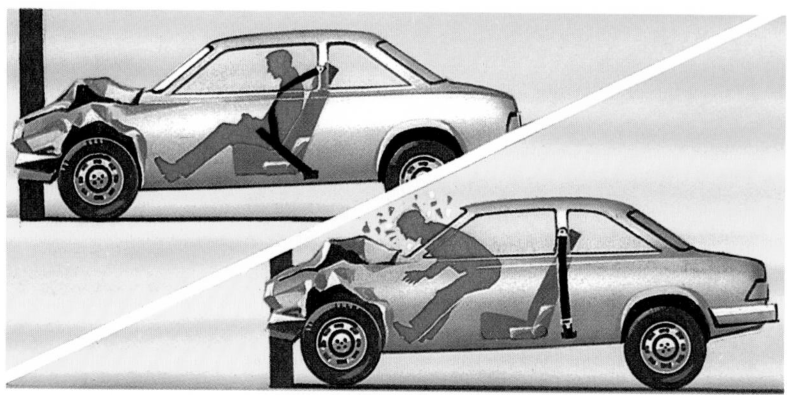

▲ *Two girls using the "buddy system" as a safety precaution when swimming in a class.*

ALSO READ: ARTIFICIAL RESPIRATION, FIRE PREVENTION, FIRST AID, LIFESAVING, POISON.

SAGA see MYTHOLOGY.

SAHARA DESERT The Sahara, in northern Africa, is the largest desert in the world. It stretches from the Atlantic Ocean to the Red Sea—a distance of more than 3,500 miles (5,630 km). The Sahara spreads over most of northern Africa including Egypt and large parts of Mauritania, Morocco, Algeria, Tunisia, Libya, Sudan, Chad, Niger, and Mali.

Flat, rocky plains cover most of the Sahara. Shallow valleys between the plains are filled with massive, shifting sand dunes. In some areas, barren mountain ranges rise out of the desert. Several underground rivers flow beneath the Sahara. At an *oasis*, where a spring or well brings this water to the surface, the land is green with date palms.

The Sahara receives very little rain—less than one inch (2.5 cm) in a year in some areas. On some days, the temperature climbs to 130° F (54° C).

But the nights are cold and sometimes icy in winter.

Farmers raise crops such as dates, wheat, and barley in the oases. But most of the people in the Sahara are wandering (*nomadic*) herders. They drive their herds of camels and goats from one watering place to another. The Saharan people are mainly Bedouin Arabs or Berbers (an ancient people of North Africa).

Until recent times, herders and traders, with *caravans* (trains) of camels, were the only travelers in the desert. Since the 1950's, rich deposits of petroleum and natural gas have been found in the northern Sahara. Minerals, such as copper and uranium, have also been found. Roads and pipelines have been built, and trucks now cross the desert.

ALSO READ: AFRICA, DESERT, NOMAD.

SAHEL In Africa south of the Sahara, there is a region of dry grassland called the Sahel. It extends from Senegal in the west to Sudan in the east. It includes parts of Senegal, Mauritania, Mali, Burkina Faso, Niger, northern Nigeria, Chad, and Sudan.

The Sahel has an average yearly rainfall of 4 to 8 inches (10–20 cm), most of which occurs in June, July, and August. But since 1968 there have been long droughts. When the rains fail, many plants die and the animals that graze on them also perish. The farmers and their families starve.

The farmers make things worse when they increase their herds in good years and overgraze the land. They also cut down trees for firewood. In these ways, they expose the soil. During droughts, winds remove the dry topsoil. This process, *soil erosion*, is causing the Sahara to spread south by 300 feet (91 m) a year in parts of the northern Sahel.

ALSO READ: EROSION, SAHARA DESERT.

SAILING Although sailing is generally considered a sport today, there was a time when sailing was the only way to travel across large stretches of water. Christopher Columbus and Leif Eriksson used sailboats when they made the first visits to the Americas. For years, sailing was the only way people could travel back and forth across the Atlantic. Once steamships were introduced, the widespread use of sailing vessels died out. However, sailboats are still used for carrying passengers and cargo in some parts of the world.

A sailboat's power source is the wind pushing against the sails. It is simple to sail a boat in the same direction the wind is blowing. It is easy, too, when the boat is at right angles to the wind, because the sails can be set at an angle so that the boat moves forward. But a sailboat cannot go directly upwind or into the wind. So, when sailors want to reach a point that is upwind, they must *tack* the boat. This means they must make a series of zigzag runs.

If the wind is coming from the *port* (left) side of the boat, the sailboat is on a *port tack*. If the wind is coming from the *starboard* (right) side of the boat, the sailboat is on a *starboard tack*. A sailboat is said to be *running free* when the wind is directly *astern* (blowing straight in from behind the boat). It is on a *close reach* when the wind is coming in from a forward angle. If the wind is blowing from the rear, but not directiy astern, the boat is being sailed on a *broad reach*. It is sailing on a *beam reach* when the wind blows in at a right angle.

Most large sailboats have *keels*, while smaller sailboats have *centerboards*. Both keels and centerboards are underwater supports. Their purpose is to prevent the boats from slipping sideways or turning over as they are driven by the wind.

A boat's ropes are usually called *sheets*, but the anchor rope is called a

▲ *The highest sand dunes ever measured are those of the Sahara Desert, in central Algeria. They stand up to 1,400 feet (425 m) high.*

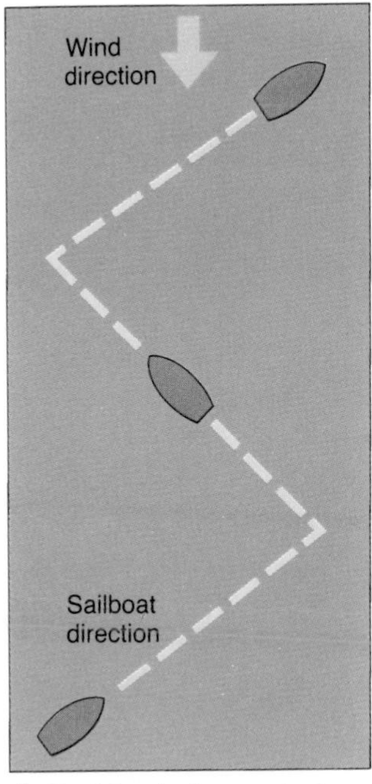

▲ *Tacking is the nautical term used to describe the technique of sailing a boat into the wind by making a series of zigzags, or tacks.*

▲ *An Egyptian* felucca *with a triangular (lateen) sail. Until the invention of the lateen sail, boats had square ones, which meant they could sail only when the wind was from behind or from the side. The lateen sail meant boats could sail into the wind.*

line. Small sailboats have only one or two sails, the *mainsail* and the *jib*. They are held up by a *mast*. Larger sailboats have more masts and additional sails. Sailboats are classified according to their size and *rigging*, or number and arrangement of their masts and sails. The different classes of sailboats include *cutters*, *sloops*, *catboats*, *yawls*, *ketches*, *schooners*, and *brigantines*.

Many sailors enjoy cruising in sailboats. They can go when they want and where they want, as long as the wind holds out. Sailboat racing is also popular, but it is not so free and easy as cruising. In sailboat races, a number of boats of the same size race one another around a *course*, which is marked by *buoys*. There are sailboat races for small one-person boats, as well as for larger sailboats with eight or ten sailors working as a team. The racing course is usually in the shape of a triangle, so that the boats must sail under a variety of conditions.

There is no special course on the long sailboat races, such as the big race from Newport, Rhode Island, to Bermuda. Another competition, called the America's Cup race, is an important international sailing event.

ALSO READ: BOATS AND BOATING, NAVIGATION, SHIPS AND SHIPPING.

◀ *Yacht racing is a popular sport. These bright sails are called spinnakers, used when running before the wind.*

SAILING SHIP see SHIPS AND SHIPPING.

SAINT A saint is a very good or holy person who is honored by a religious group after his or her death. The good deeds of certain people have earned them the right to be *venerated*—deeply respected by their church—after their death. Many people pray to saints, not to worship them, but to ask or thank them for help from heaven.

The best-known saints in the Western world are those of Christianity, especially those of the Catholic Church. In the early days of Christianity, all Christians were called saints. The term was later applied only to Christian martyrs (people who died for their faith) or Christian holy persons.

By the 1000's, the Orthodox and Roman Catholic churches had established a process called *canonization*. A person is officially named a saint of the Church once he or she is canonized. Only a few of millions of saints are ever canonized, Catholics believe. In the process, a person's life

▼ The Martyrdom of Saint Stephen, *painted by the Italian artist Annibale Carracci (1560–1609).*

is thoroughly investigated to see if the claims made about his or her holiness or ability to perform miracles are true. Once these things have been proved, the pope or the Orthodox patriarch declares the person to be a saint. A special day is celebrated in the saint's honor, and people may officially venerate him or her.

Protestant churches do not officially venerate saints. But they do respect most saints who were canonized before the Protestant Reformation. Muslims often venerate the very holy people of Islam, but there are no official Islamic saints.

ALSO READ: AQUINAS, THOMAS; BECKET,THOMAS À; CHRISTIANITY; EDWARD THE CONFESSOR; FRANCIS OF ASSISI; JOAN OF ARC; MORE, SIR THOMAS; NICHOLAS, SAINT; ORTHODOX CHURCH; PATRICK, SAINT; PAUL, SAINT; ROMAN CATHOLIC CHURCH.

SAINT KITTS-NEVIS see WEST INDIES.

SAINT LUCIA see WEST INDIES.

SAINT VINCENT see WEST INDIES.

SALAMANDER All salamanders are *amphibians*, which means that they live part of their lives in water and part on land. Most of them hatch from eggs in water. Baby salamanders (salamander *larvae*) look like tadpoles. They breathe underwater through feathery gills on the back of their heads. Adult salamanders lose their gills, develop lungs, and can breathe on land. They return to freshwater ponds and streams to lay eggs. Some species breathe through their skin and do not have either gills or lungs. Other salamanders look like large tadpoles. They spend all their lives in water and never lose their feathery gills. They are a special type of larvae called *neotenic larvae*. They can breed while in the larval form and may never turn into the adult, land-living form. However, if the conditions are favorable, they will become adult salamanders and breed as salamanders, not larvae. The Mexican *axolotl* is a neotenic larval form of salamander.

Salamanders are often called lizards, because the two animals look alike. They can both grow new tails or legs if the old ones are lost. The easiest and best way to tell the difference is by looking at the skin. The lizard is a reptile and has a dry, scaly skin. The salamander's skin is always soft, moist, and almost slimy. *Newts* are salamanders that look like lizards. Salamanders are cold-blooded. If they live where winters are very cold, they hibernate.

A big salamander that is sometimes mistaken for a fish is the mudpuppy, or waterdog. It measures from one to two feet (30–60 cm) in length and has gills.The hellbender, a salamander that can be more than two feet (60 cm) long, does not have gills. Giant salamanders, measuring four to five feet (120–150 cm) in length, are found in China and Japan and are caught for food.

Hundreds of years ago, people believed that salamanders were magic. It was thought that they could be in the middle of a fire and not be burned. A Roman naturalist named Pliny (A.D. 23–79) tried putting a salamander in a fire but found that it soon burned to a powder.

▲ *Saint Catherine of Siena was an Italian nun of the 1300's. She persuaded Pope Gregory XI to return to Rome and thereby end years of papal exile in Avignon, France. A poet and writer, she was named a Doctor of the Church in 1970 by Pope Paul VI.*

▼ *The fire salamander is recognized by its yellow markings. The spectacled salamander is bright red under the tail and legs.*

The most common salamander in the United States is the *red-spotted newt*. In its "red eft" stage, it is bright red in color and lives on land. When it returns to the water after a few years, it turns light green with red dots.

ALSO READ: AMPHIBIAN, METAMORPHOSIS.

▲ *Jonas Salk, who developed the first vaccine against polio.*

SALK, JONAS (born 1914) The U.S. doctor and research scientist, Jonas Salk, developed the first effective vaccine against polio (poliomyelitis), a virus disease that once crippled many people.

Salk was born in New York City and received a medical degree from New York University School of Medicine. At the School of Public Health at the University of Michigan, Salk helped develop vaccines for influenza, an infectious virus disease. Later, he moved to the University of Pittsburgh, where he taught and worked in bacteriology, preventive medicine, and experimental medicine. In 1963, Salk became director of the Salk Institute for Biological Studies in San Diego, California.

Salk discovered that polio viruses (which he grew in cultures of the kidney cells of monkeys) can be used as a vaccine when the viruses are killed with a special chemical. In 1955, the U.S. Public Health Service approved the use of the Salk vaccine, which has to be injected. Five years later, an effective oral vaccine, developed by Albert B. Sabin, came into use. The Salk and Sabin vaccines have almost eliminated polio in many parts of the world.

ALSO READ: CHILDHOOD DISEASES, IMMUNITY, VIRUS.

Between 1900 and 1904, Utah's Great Salt Lake almost disappeared because there was little rainfall. It became a desert of salt.

There will never be a shortage of salt. The world's oceans contain a staggering 45 trillion tons (50 trillion metric tons) of it.

SALT Salt is the most widely used flavoring in cooking. You need to eat a small amount of salt every day in order to be healthy. Usually, the amount of salt eaten in meat or used in cooking is enough. The salt becomes an important part of your blood. Also, salt aids digestion in your stomach. There are special areas on your tongue for tasting salt. However, eating too much salt has harmful effects, such as high blood pressure.

▲ *A traditional way to obtain salt is to flood coastal hollows (salt pans) and let the sun's heat evaporate the seawater.*

The salt you put on your food is a chemical compound called *sodium chloride*. It is made up of the chemical elements sodium and chlorine. But there are thousands of other salts made up of different elements. Most salts are poisonous.

Animals that eat only grass or leaves do not get enough salt in their food. Deer and other wild animals visit natural deposits of salt to lick it and supply their needs. Farmers buy large blocks of salt for cattle and other farm animals to use.

A huge amount of salt is dissolved in seawater. During the history of the Earth, whole seas have dried up. Large amounts of salt were left behind. This salt is called *rock salt* and is mined like any other mineral. Avery Island on the Louisiana coast and the state of Texas have large salt deposits. Salt is taken from the Dead Sea in Israel and the Great Salt Lake in Utah, where new salt deposits are constantly being added to the ancient ones. The big salt mines of Wieliczka, Poland, are like an underground city. Salt can also be obtained by allowing seawater to flow into large, shallow pits. Then the sun evaporates the water, leaving dry salt.

If salt is put on fish, meat, and other foods before they are stored or packed for shipping, they will be preserved for a long time. In the chemical industry, sodium chloride is a source of the elements sodium and chlorine. Sodium chloride is also used in making dyes, glass, pottery, and soap.

ALSO READ: ACIDS AND BASES, CHEMISTRY, ELEMENT.

SALVATION ARMY The Salvation Army is a Christian charitable organization. The men and women of the army devote their lives to helping people in need and spreading the Christian faith.

In the 1860's, an English Methodist minister named William Booth (1829–1912) and his wife, Catherine (1829–1890), began to work and preach among the poor people of east London. Their work was so successful that they founded an organization that, in 1878, became the Salvation Army. The organization gradually spread to other parts of the world, including India, Australia, Canada, and the United States. Ballington Booth (1859–1940) also set up a similar but separate organization in the United States, called the Volunteers of America.

Projects organized by the Salvation Army include medical care for the poor, inexpensive lodging for the homeless, and employment agencies to help people find jobs. The army runs programs to help prisoners and alcoholics and to encourage them to lead new lives. The army also runs fresh-air camps for children.

The Salvation Army holds many open-air religious meetings. Army members often play brass-band instruments at these meetings and take collections for the poor. People gather around to hear the music and listen to the army preachers.

The Salvation Army is supported entirely by gifts of money from people who admire its work. It is organized like a regular army. The members are known as officers or soldiers, and the chief officer is a general.

ALSO READ: EVANGELIST, MISSIONARY.

SAMOA see POLYNESIA, PACIFIC ISLANDS.

SANCTIONS If one country wishes to show disapproval of another (without going to war) it can impose sanctions. It may stop trade with that country of some or all goods. It may withdraw its ambassador and end airline flights. It may refuse to take part in sports competitions alongside that country. It may ask companies to close down their businesses there and stop loans of money and other forms of aid.

Sanctions are not always very effective. In the 1930's, for example, Italy invaded Abyssinia (Ethiopia). The League of Nations, the world body at that time, tried to make Italy end its invasion by imposing sanctions. But Italy took no notice.

More recently, South Africa has been condemned for its *apartheid* policy, which discriminates against blacks. Many countries have imposed economic sanctions against South Africa. The U.S. government has imposed economic sanctions against Libya because of that country's support for terrorism.

It remains a matter of argument whether economic sanctions are an effective way of achieving political changes in the world of international relations.

ALSO READ: UNITED NATIONS.

▲ *The Salvation Army has for many years been holding street meetings to spread Christianity. Here is a gathering that took place around the beginning of this century in New York City.*

▲ *William Booth, who founded the Salvation Army.*

▲ *Under the microscope, grains of beach sand and grains of desert sand look different. Grains of desert sand are more often rubbed against each other, and therefore are more rounded. Also, desert sand is made almost entirely of the mineral* quartz, *while river and sea sands often include softer minerals like* mica.

▼ *In deserts, dunes are created by the wind. In crescent-shaped dunes* (barchans), *sand grains are blown up the gentle windward slope. They then fall over the crest, down the steep leeward slope. Wind eddies keep this slope steep.*

SAND Sand is rock material in the form of grains. About one-fifth of the land area of the Earth is covered by sand. Geologists use the term "sand" for rock particles between .06 mm and 2 mm in diameter. Within these extremes the sand can range from very coarse to very fine. Most sand grains are formed when rocks are destroyed by weathering—the action of heat, cold, rain, and ice. Also, waves continually throwing pebbles against a rocky coast eventually break up the pebbles into sand grains. Most sandy beaches are formed this way. In fast-moving mountain streams, stones are pushed and tumbled along the rocky bottoms. This action eventually breaks down the stones into grain size, and sand accumulates in the lower parts of the streams.

Grains of hard minerals, usually *quartz*, form sand. Sand's color is determined by the color of the rocks that are broken up to make it. Usually, sand is yellow, brown, or red. Desert sands are often red because of iron compounds in them. Volcanic lava can create black sand. Grains of coral and shells form the sand on many island beaches.

Sand is used for making glass and for grinding and polishing. Sandpaper, for smoothing rough surfaces, was originally made of sand glued to heavy paper. Sand is used in making cement, mortar, plaster, and bricks that can stand very high temperatures.

ALSO READ: DESERT, ROCK, SILICON.

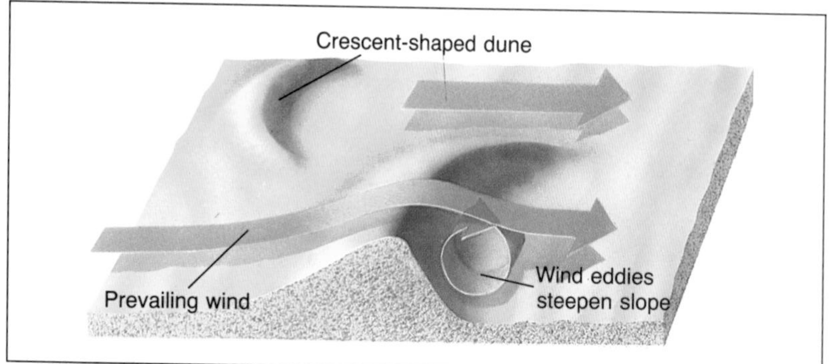

▲ *U.S. poet Carl Sandburg also collected and sang folk songs.*

SANDBURG, CARL (1878–1967) Carl Sandburg was a U.S. writer of both poetry and prose, and biographer of Abraham Lincoln.

Sandburg was born in Galesburg, Illinois. While in his early teens, he served in the Spanish-American War. He later attended Lombard College in his hometown and worked at railroad and farming jobs. Sandburg worked as an editorial writer for the *Chicago Daily News* for 15 years. He married Lillian Steichen in 1908, and they had three children. In 1914, the publication of his poem "Chicago" brought him his first public recognition. Sandburg's vigorous free verse was new in poetry. Of Chicago he wrote:

Hog Butcher for the World,
Tool Maker, Stacker of Wheat,
Player with railroads and the
  Nation's Freight Handler;
Stormy, husky, brawling,
  City of the Big Shoulders.

He wrote several books of poems that paint a realistic picture of U.S. life on farms and in the cities. Much of his poetry expresses a strong belief in our nation's future. Sandburg's *Complete Poems* won the Pulitzer Prize in 1951. Sandburg wrote an excellent biography of Abraham Lincoln, *The Prairie Years* (two volumes) and *The War Years* (four volumes). This work won the Pulitzer Prize in 1940. He wrote children's stories, too.

ALSO READ: POETRY.

SAN FRANCISCO is the second largest city in California. It lies on San Francisco Bay which is connected to the Pacific Ocean by a strait called the Golden Gate. The famous Golden Gate Bridge spans the entrance to this strait, giving the city its nickname of the "Golden Gate City."

About three-fifths of the people of San Francisco are white. Blacks form the second largest group. There are also large communities of people of Asian origin, and the colorful Chinatown district is one of the city's many tourist attractions. Another popular tourist site is Alcatraz, an island in the bay that had a famous prison from 1934 to 1963.

San Francisco is a major cultural city with a magnificent Performing Arts Center. It is also a major seaport and a great financial and industrial center. Its industries produce metal goods, processed food and clothes.

The city was founded by the Spanish, who built a fort and a mission called the Misión San Francisco de Asis (after St. Francis of Assisi) in 1776. U.S. forces captured the area during the Mexican War. The discovery of gold in California in 1848 caused the city to expand rapidly.

San Francisco occupies one of the world's most beautiful sites. But it stands on the San Andreas Fault, a huge crack in the Earth's crust. Movements of rocks along this fault cause earthquakes. In 1906, San Francisco was largely destroyed by fires that followed a severe earthquake. The city was rebuilt with structures designed to withstand earthquakes. Another major earthquake occurred in 1989.

ALSO READ: CALIFORNIA, EARTHQUAKE.

SANGER, MARGARET (1883–1966) Margaret Sanger was a leader of the movement that sought to make contraception (birth control) more readily available to women. She was born Margaret Higgins, in Corning, New York, on September 14, 1883. She was the sixth of 11 children.

She married twice. Her first marriage, to William Sanger, ended in divorce. Her second husband was Noah H. Slee. She spent some years nursing on the Lower East Side of New York City. There, she met many women whose lives were made difficult by poverty and poor housing, and whose problems were increased by constantly having new babies to care for. Margaret Sanger believed that, if women could plan their families through birth control, such social problems would be eased.

In 1916, she opened the first birth-control clinic in the United States, in Brooklyn. This got her into trouble with the law which at that time forbade such activities. She continued her campaign and gradually won public support.

In 1927, Margaret Sanger opened the first World Population Conference in Switzerland. She worked for birth control in Asia, particularly in India, and was the first president of the International Planned Parenthood Federation, founded in 1953.

SANITATION Sanitation includes all the efforts made by people to keep their community and their homes clean and healthful. The food people eat, the water they drink, and the places where they work and play must be kept clean to prevent the spread of sickness and disease.

Keeping water clean is a major sanitation problem. Sewage and industrial wastes are often dumped into rivers and lakes. *Sanitary engineers* (engineers who study sanitation problems) must find ways to filter the water and add germ-killing chemicals to make it safe.

Trash and garbage disposal is another sanitation problem. Almost ev-

▲ *One of San Francisco's famous cable cars, built to climb the many steep hills of this beautiful harbor city.*

▲ *Margaret Sanger, who pioneered the use of birth control in the United States.*

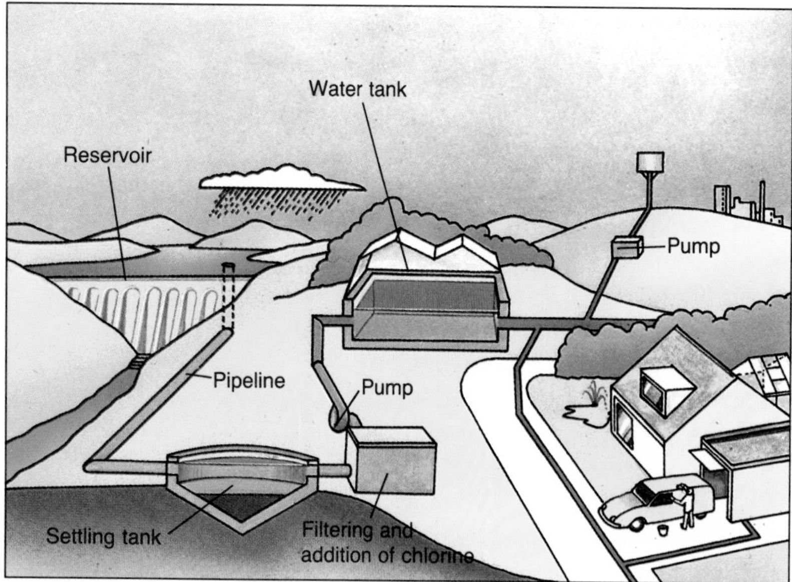

▲ *The water we take from reservoirs, lakes, rivers, and wells is not always fit to drink. Before it reaches our homes it has to be purified. Chemicals (like chlorine) are added to kill germs, and the dirt is removed from the water. The water also goes through filters to make it clean. In some places, chemicals called fluorides are added to drinking water to help keep our teeth healthy.*

ery community has a department of sanitation. The job of this department is to keep the streets and public places clean, and to collect trash and garbage from homes and business places and take it to be dumped. Waste and garbage that are not removed provide breeding areas for disease germs and for animals that spread the germs.

■ LEARN BY DOING

Many people today are trying to find uses for their garbage, rather than having it taken to the dump. Garbage can be *composted* and used as fertilizer for plants. You can compost garbage (*not* plastic or metals) easily by burying it in a hole two to three feet (30–60 cm) deep. Be sure to keep the garbage covered with a thick layer of dirt. Within a couple of months, your garbage will have merged with the organic matter in the soil. If you start your composting in the fall, you will have good fertilizer for spring planting. ■

State and local public health departments inspect restaurants and food-processing plants to ensure that food is produced, packaged, and served under clean, safe conditions. Public health officials also try to eliminate or have cleaned up any unsanitary conditions that exist in public and private places. Such conditions could be anything from a dirty drinking fountain to a rat-infested apartment building. The Department of Agriculture and Food and Drug Administration are agencies of the Federal Government that handle food sanitation problems.

There are various important ways in which you can help keep your city clean. You can be sure your own property is free of trash and unwanted dirt. Whether you are riding in a car or just walking, save your trash until you can find a trash can to put it in.

ALSO READ: AIR POLLUTION, DISEASE, ECOLOGY, FOOD, HEALTH, WATER POLLUTION.

SAN MARINO Europe's smallest republic, San Marino, is situated high in the Apennine Mountains of Italy. Italy surrounds this republic, which is only about the size of Manhattan Island. (See the map with the article on EUROPE.)

SAN MARINO

Capital City: San Marino (4,600 people).
Area: 24 square miles (61 sq. km).
Population: 23,000.
Government: Republic.
Natural Resources: Building stone.
Export Products: Building stone, wood machinery, chemicals, wine, postage stamps.
Unit of Money: Italian lira.
Official Language: Italian.

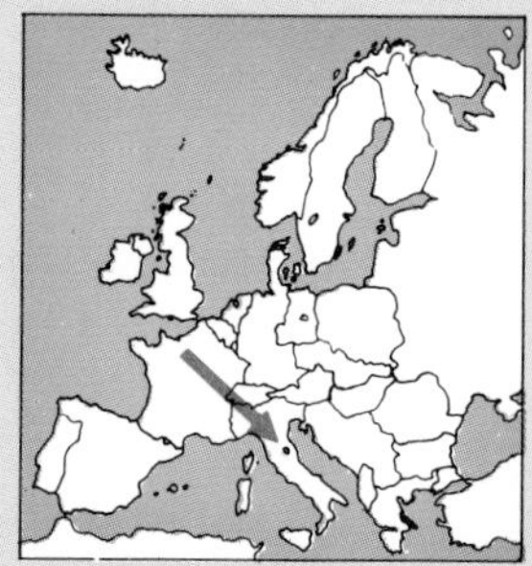

The tiny nation's capital, also named San Marino, is an ancient walled town. The three peaks of the mountain called Mount Titano rise above the town. Farmers grow wheat, corn, and grapes in the fertile valley at the foot of Mount Titano. Thousands of tourists come every month to enjoy the landscape and to buy wine, wool, and postage stamps.

Many of the people of San Marino are farmers and shopkeepers. The people claim that San Marino is the world's oldest existing republic. Their tradition of freedom began in A.D. 301, when a Christian stonecutter named Marinus was said to have fled to Mount Titano to escape persecution by pagan Romans. The people honor him as their patron saint.

ALSO READ: ITALY, REPUBLIC.

SANTA CLAUS see NICHOLAS, SAINT.

SANTA FE TRAIL This was one of the major trails that carried settlers and supplies into unsettled western lands. (See the map with the article on WESTWARD MOVEMENT.) The trail, about 780 miles (1,250 km) long, began in Independence, Missouri, and ended in Santa Fe, New Mexico.

William Becknell, a U.S. trader, blazed the Santa Fe Trail in 1821. After that, traders and settlers in wagon caravans traveled over it. The caravans usually left Missouri in the spring, crossed the Kansas plains to the Arkansas River, and then followed the river westward to Bent's Fort (near La Junta, Colorado). From there, they went south to Santa Fe. The entire trip took 40 to 60 days. About 5,000 wagons a year used the Santa Fe Trail in the late 1860's.

At Santa Fe, traders exchanged plows, farm tools, and clothing for silver, gold, furs, and mules. Regular passenger service by stagecoach began in 1848, but by 1800 the railroad had reached Santa Fe.

SÃO PAULO São Paulo is the city in Brazil, South America, where Brazil was declared to be a free and independent country separate from Portugal. In 1822, Dom Pedro, eldest son of the Portuguese King John VI, announced Brazil's independence in one of São Paulo's handsome parks, and declared himself Emperor Pedro I of Brazil.

São Paulo was founded by Jesuit missionaries in 1554. Today, it is the industrial center and largest city in Brazil. It is sometimes called the "Chicago of South America." It ranks as one of the world's fastest-growing cities in terms of population. More than 14 million people live in and around São Paulo. The city is the heart of the fertile southeastern highlands of Brazil, known for the best coffee in the world. The hills and good rainfall provide many places for dams and abundant hydroelectric power. As a result, São Paulo has become the leading industrial center in the Southern Hemisphere. The city's workers build machinery, make textiles, automobiles, shoes, clothing, and many other manufactured products used in Brazil and South America. São Paulo is near the Atlantic seaport city of Santos.

ALSO READ: BRAZIL, RIO DE JANEIRO.

▲ *Independence Square in São Paulo is packed with people on the sidewalks, some of whom spill over into the street. It is one of the most populous cities in the world.*

It has been calculated that by the year 2000 there will be 24 million people in São Paulo, making it the second biggest city in the world after Mexico City.

SÃO TOMÉ AND PRÍNCIPE The tiny volcanic islands of São Tomé and Príncipe lie in the Gulf of Guinea off the coast of west central Africa. Both islands consist of northeast and southwest lowlands with mountainous jungle in the interior. Together with two tiny islets, they form the Democratic Republic of São Tomé and Príncipe.

The islands were discovered in 1471 by the Portuguese, who brought con-

SÃO TOMÉ AND PRÍNCIPE

Capital City: São Tomé (40,000 people).
Area: 373 square miles (965 sq. km).
Population: 114,000.
Government: One-party republic.
Natural Resources: Timber.
Export Products: Cocoa, copra, coffee, bananas, palm oil.
Unit of Money: Dobra.
Official Language: Portuguese.

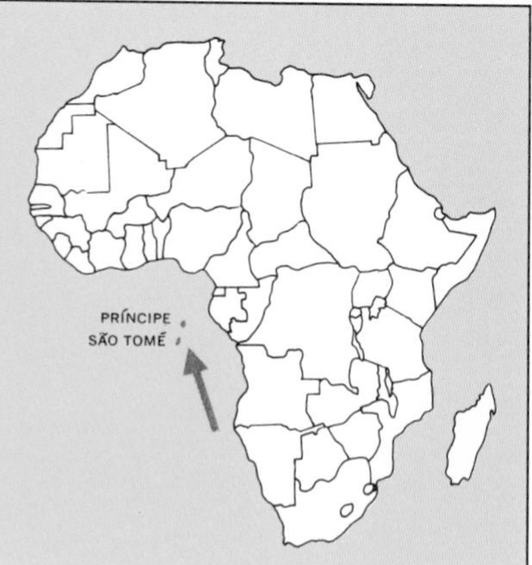

victs and exiled Jews to the islands. Slaves from the African mainland were used to run large sugar plantations. The slave trade became the principal economic activity until coffee and cocoa were introduced in the 1800's.

Most of the people are descendants of Africans and Portuguese settlers. Many laborers were imported from Angola and Mozambique to work on the plantations. When the islands became independent of Portugal in 1975, about 1,000 whites, who ran the plantations, and the Cape Verdeans, who were supervisors, left the country.

ALSO READ: AFRICA.

SARAWAK see BORNEO, MALAYSIA.

▼ *Street in Venice* by John Singer Sargent. This painting is now in the National Gallery of Art, in Washington, D.C. (Gift of the Avalon Foundation.)

SARGENT, JOHN SINGER (1856–1925) One of the greatest U.S. painters, John Singer Sargent was born in Florence, Italy. He was the son of a Philadelphia physician and his wife, who loved to travel in Europe. Young Sargent did not see the United States until he was 20.

He was just a small boy when his mother realized his extraordinary artistic talents and decided he should become a painter. His family moved to Paris when he was 16, so that John could study art. At 18, he entered the studio of a leading Paris painter, Carolus Duran. Sargent was an excellent student and very quickly mastered the techniques of painting. He went to Spain to study and paint for two years. The paintings he did after his Spanish visit are considered by many critics the best of his career. He was using dark, rich colors at this time. The little painting on wood shown here was done by Sargent at that time—in 1882. It is called *Street in Venice.* It is a simple street scene, but the color contrasts of light and dark shades are dramatic.

In 1884, Sargent did a portrait of a famous Paris beauty, Madame Gautreau. When it was exhibited, a furor began. Madame Gautreau did not like it. Neither did her friends or the Paris critics. Sargent, who had been the young favorite of Paris art circles, suddenly found himself an outcast. He moved to London and made many trips to the United States.

He painted many portraits of socially prominent people over the years. He switched to using the light colors of the Impressionists, although he did not adopt all their ways of painting. Many critics feel that his best paintings were done before he was 30.

ALSO READ: IMPRESSIONISM, PORTRAIT.

SASKATCHEWAN Saskatchewan is the middle of the three prairie provinces of Canada. It is a huge rectangle totaling a quarter of a million square miles (650,000 sq. km).

SASKATCHEWAN

Capital and largest city
Regina (173,400 people)

Area
251,866 square miles (652,330 sq. km)

Population
1,011,000

Entry into Confederation
September 1, 1905

Principal river
Saskatchewan River

Highest point
Cypress Hills 4,567 feet (1,392 m)

Famous people
Andrew McNaughton, Louis Riel

NORTHWEST TERRITORIES
ALBERTA
MANITOBA
UNITED STATES
Uranium City
Lake Athabasca
Wollaston Lake
Cree Lake
Reindeer Lake
Churchill Lake
Peter Pond L.
Churchill
La Ronge
Lac la Ronge
Doré L.
THUNDER HILLS
Montreal Lake
Meadow Lake
PRINCE ALBERT N.P.
Saskatchewan
North Saskatchewan
Lloyd Minister
Prince Albert
Nipawin
Melfor
North Battleford
Humboldt
Saskatoon
Big Quill Lake
Assiniboine
HIGH PLAINS
Kindersley
Last Mountain Lake
Wynyard
Kamsack
Rosetown
South Saskatchewan
Yorkton
Melville
Qu'Appelle
Swift Current
Moose Jaw
Regina
Maple Creek
Moose Mtn. 2 740 Ft. 835 M.
Old Wives L.
Assiniboia
Weyburn
Frenchman
Pinto Butte 3 340 Ft. 1 018 M.
Souris
Estevan
0 50 100
Miles

◀ *Regina, capital of Saskatchewan, lies in the heart of the province's vast, flat agricultural prairieland.*

PROVINCIAL FLOWER

Prairie lily

Isaac Newton was the first person to discuss the laws governing the flight of satellites. He did this in his book *Principia*, published in 1687. But it was not until 270 years later that the first space satellite was successfully rocketed into orbit.

▲ *On October 4, 1957,* Sputnik 1 *was the first artificial satellite to be launched into space.*

Its area is about the size of the neighboring states to the south, Montana and the Dakotas, combined. Alberta borders it on the west, and Manitoba on the east. The Northwest Territories are on the north.

The southern two-thirds of Saskatchewan, where most of the people live, is a great plain sloping gradually to the east and north. Much of this area is covered by fields of wheat, barley, rye, oats, and hay. The northern third of Saskatchewan is an undeveloped area. It is part of the Canadian Shield (or Laurentian Plateau) of rocky, forested country. Saskatchewan has a dry climate with long, cold winters.

People Most of Saskatchewan was settled only in the present century. In one generation, the population rose from a few thousand to more than a million. The province became known as a refuge for religious groups persecuted in Europe. The refugees were looking for a land that would give them new opportunities.

As a result, less than half of Saskatchewan's population is of English or French origin. Many are Germans, Ukrainians, Scandinavians, and Dutch. Some of these groups live by themselves in their own communities. They have their own schools, wear their own traditional clothing, and live as farmers. Canada wants to save the ethnic heritage of its peoples. Children in Saskatchewan schools must pass provincial examinations in English or in French. Once they have passed these examinations, they are free to study any subjects in whatever language they please.

Agriculture is Saskatchewan's most important business. Approximately 71,000 farms produce about two-thirds of Canada's wheat. Modern machinery and improved crops have permitted farmers to grow more grain than ever before. Beef, dairy cattle, and poultry are raised in large numbers. Mining is the fastest-growing industry in the province. Oil, potash, copper, and uranium are being extracted. The province also has deposits of coal and natural gas.

In the heart of Saskatchewan's farmland lies Regina, the capital and largest city. Its city streets are laid out on an almost perfect "grid" pattern. Chemical and meat-packing plants, flour and paper mills, and oil refineries are located in and around Regina. Saskatoon, the second largest city, is the home of the University of Saskatchewan. Moose Jaw, the third largest city, is an important dairy-product center. Camping and other recreation are enjoyed at Prince Albert National Park and in the provincial parks.

History Many Assiniboin, Cree, and Chipewyan Indians once lived here. The region was given by charter to the Hudson's Bay Company in 1670, and it soon became dotted with fur-trading posts. In 1870, the area was made part of the new nation of Canada. With the building of a transcontinental railway, settlers began arriving to farm the rich, flat lands.

Since Saskatchewan became a province in 1905, it has usually had a socialist or liberal government. Its legislature is unicameral (one-house). Many new ideas later used elsewhere, such as "Medicare" and "no-fault" automobile insurance, were first introduced in Saskatchewan.

ALSO READ: CANADA.

SATELLITE A satellite is a body that moves in an orbit about a larger body. Our moon is a satellite of Earth. Earth and the eight other planets are satellites of the sun. The moon and the planets are *natural* satellites—they are not artificial (man-made).

The Earth is not the only planet with a natural satellite—Saturn has at least 24 satellites (moons); Jupiter, at least 14; Uranus 15; Mars and Neptune, two each; and Pluto, one. Some of these moons are tiny—only a few miles across—but some are very large. Titan, a moon of the planet Saturn, is about 3,600 miles (5,800 km) across, which means it is larger than the planet Mercury. Two of Jupiter's moons, Ganymede and Callisto, are also larger than Mercury.

Artificial Satellites The Earth has many artificial satellites. The first was Sputnik I, launched by the Soviet Union on October 4, 1957. At the present time there are about 1,500 artificial satellites in orbit, as well as about 3,500 other orbiting bodies, consisting of pieces of rockets, empty fuel tanks, and other "space debris." Some will stay in orbit for centuries.

How long a satellite stays in orbit depends on its *perigee*—how close it comes to the Earth. If a satellite never gets closer than about 400 miles (640 km), it may stay in orbit almost indefinitely. The height of a satellite's perigee depends on how high its rocket carries it, and the angle at which the rocket pushes the satellite into orbit. The last push often follows the curve of the Earth's surface. A satellite must reach a speed of at least 18,000 miles (29,000 km) an hour in order to go into orbit. Most artificial satellites are used for research and communications.

The earliest artificial satellites were our first contact with space, and they made important discoveries. Two of the first three U.S. satellites, Explorers 1 and 3, launched in early 1958, led U.S. physicist James Van Allen to deduce the presence of doughnut-shaped belts of radiation circling the Earth. Oddities in the orbit of Vanguard 1, the second U.S. satellite, allowed U.S. physicist John O'Keefe to show that the Earth is *very* slightly pear-shaped.

Satellites can do jobs that scientists on Earth cannot do. They can take pictures of the Earth from space, and they can pick up radiation from space that is blocked by the Earth's atmosphere. Infrared radiation, ultraviolet radiation, and X rays are all better studied from outside the atmosphere. For example, IRAS (Infra Red Astronomical Satellite), launched by the United States in 1983, has found a ring of dust and gas circling the bright star Vega. It is thought that new planets are forming out of the dust and gas. Some years earlier UHURU (Explorer 42), an X-ray satellite, detected what is almost certainly a black hole—the first to be discovered.

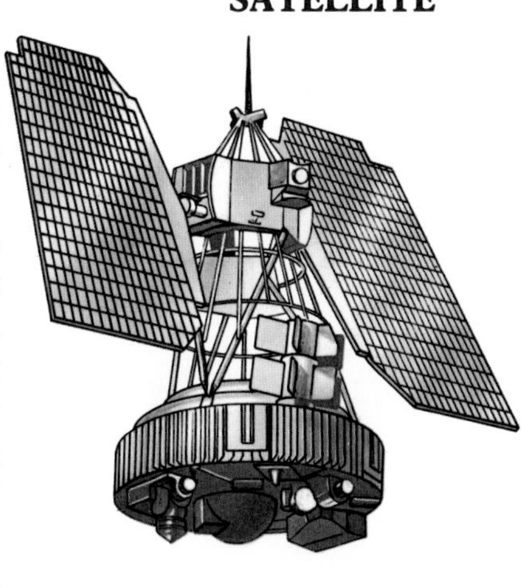

The Earth from Space Only about one-fifth of the Earth's surface is studied by ground-based weather stations. Meteorological satellites cover the gaps left by these stations. Tiros satellites have sent back television pictures of cloud patterns in the Earth's atmosphere. These and other satellites have provided information on surface winds and temperatures, ocean currents, and destructive storms, as well as details about the Earth's rotation and fault motions. Meteorological satellites are useful in forecasting weather and finding the cause of weather. Satellites have been used in biological research, too.

▲ *Orbiting above the atmosphere, satellites like this Nimbus satellite can photograph the Earth's cloud cover to tell us about the weather.*

▼ *Radio telescopes can be used to pick up signals from space satellites.*

COMMUNICATIONS. Communications satellites have had the greatest effect on our daily lives. They have made it possible for live radio and television broadcasts to be carried around the world.

A communications satellite is like a big mirror for radio and television signals. A television signal is sent from Japan high into space and hits the communications satellite. It bounces off the satellite and is directed toward the United States, where it is picked up by television stations and relayed to millions of viewers at home.

Communications satellites have been launched by governments and by private groups. The first communications satellite was Score, launched by the U.S. Army on December 12, 1958. The first commercial communi-

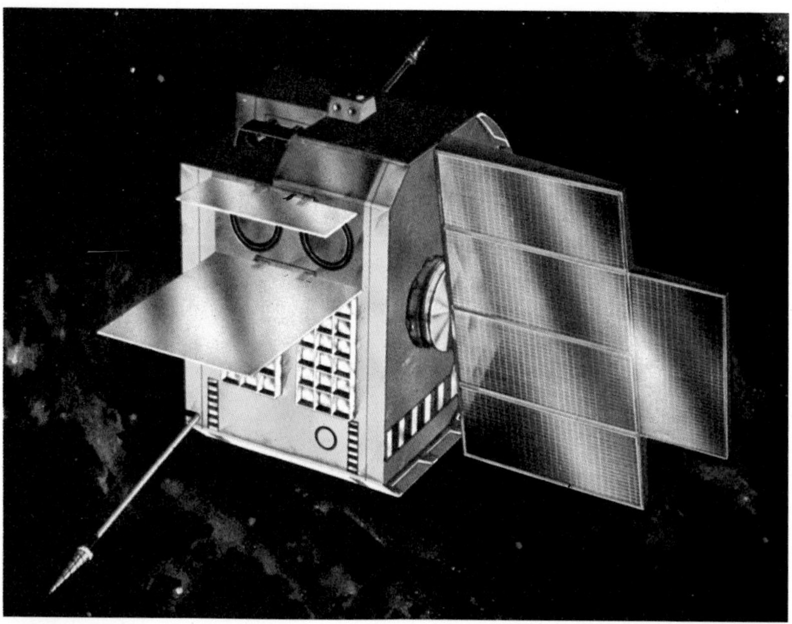

▲ *EXOSAT is a scientific satellite. It "sees" the stars not in visible light but in X rays. The X rays that stars and other bodies give out tell us a lot about what they are made of and how they work. Very few X rays can pass through the Earth's atmosphere, which is why satellites must be used for such work.*

cations satellite, Early Bird, or Intelsat I, was launched by the Communication Satellite Corporation, on April 6, 1965. Satellite television has had a major impact on broadcasting.

ALSO READ: ASTRONOMY, BLACK HOLE, COMET, COMMUNICATIONS SATELLITE, MOON, ORBIT, RADIO, SOLAR SYSTEM, SPACE RESEARCH, TELEVISION.

SATELLITE, NATURAL see MOON, SATELLITE, SOLAR SYSTEM.

SAUDI ARABIA is a large country that occupies much of the Arabian peninsula in southwest Asia. It is named for the Arab Saud family, which has ruled the country since it was founded in 1932.

Mountains border the Red Sea coastal plain in the west. East of the mountains are tablelands that slope down to the Persian Gulf lowlands. The southwestern Asir mountains have the most rainfall—about 15 inches (380 mm) a year. But most of the country is hot desert. The Rub' al Khali, or Empty Quarter, in the southeast is a barren, almost rainless sandy desert. Saudi Arabia has no lakes or permanent rivers.

Because of the climate, only 1 percent of the land is farmed. Dates and grains are the chief crops, while nomads (wandering tribespeople) raise sheep, goats, cattle, and camels. Saudi Arabia's real wealth lies underground in its huge reserves of oil. Saudi Arabia is the world's third largest oil producer after the Soviet Union and the United States. It is also the world's top oil exporter.

Arabic is the official language. Islam is the religion of the Saudis. The founder of Islam, Muhammad, was born in Mecca in Saudi Arabia in about A.D. 570. In 622, he went to Medina. He later led an army that conquered Mecca in 630. Today, Muslims regard both Mecca and Medina as holy cities. Muslims from all over the world make pilgrimages to them. Religion strongly influences daily life. Most people pray five times a day, and they do not eat between

SAUDI ARABIA

Capital City: Riyadh (1,300,000 people).
Area: 830,000 square miles (2,149,690 sq. km).
Population: 12,700,000.
Government: Monarchy.
Natural Resources: Oil and natural gas.
Export Products: Oil.
Unit of Money: Riyal.
Official Language: Arabic.

dawn and sunset during Ramadan, the Muslim month of fasting.

The Turks controlled Saudi Arabia from the early 16th century until World War I. In the 1920's, a local leader, Ibn Saud, worked to unite the people of Arabia and, in 1932, he founded the modern Kingdom of Saudi Arabia. The country is still ruled by a king, aided by a Council of Ministers. There are no elections and no parliament.

Until the 1950's, Saudi Arabia was a poor, backward country. There are still great differences between the rich Saudis in the cities and poor people in rural areas. But some of the income from oil sales has been used to create welfare services. Women once had no opportunities for jobs outside the home. But more and more girls are being educated, and women are now working in such occupations as nursing and teaching.

Water conservation and the production of fresh water from sea water are important priorities in this dry country.

ALSO READ: ARABIA, ISLAM, MUHAMMAD.

SAVINGS If you have a weekly allowance, you may already be familiar with the practice of saving. Let's say you want to buy a present for your mother, but it costs ten dollars. If your weekly allowance is two dollars, you must save all your allowance for five weeks in order to buy the present. Or you could save half your allowance for ten weeks. Similarly, most grown-ups put aside part of their wages for future use. Later on, they can use these savings to take a special trip or to buy things they need.

One of the best ways to save money is to open a *savings account* at a bank. When you do this, you are given a *bankbook* that shows how much money you have in your account. Each time you *deposit* (add) or *withdraw* (take out) money, the *balance* (amount you have left) is entered in the book. The bank also pays you a certain amount of money, called *interest*. The interest is a payment given to you for allowing the bank to use your money to make loans to people and transact other business.

Another way of saving is to buy U.S. government *bonds*. When you purchase a bond, you are investing your money in the welfare of the country. You can buy a bond for less than its *face* value. You allow the government to use the money for a certain number of years until the bond *matures* (comes due), at which time you can *redeem* (convert into cash) the full value of the bond.

ALSO READ: BANKS AND BANKING, MONEY, STOCKS AND BONDS.

▲ *Two small children in Saudi Arabia wear ankle-length clothes and colorful head scraves.*

SCALE A scale, or *balance*, is an instrument for weighing objects. Two arms are carefully balanced on a thin edge (*pivot*). Hanging from the arms are two pans. The scale is adjusted so that, when the pans are empty, the arms are perfectly level. The arms will also be level if weights put in the two pans are exactly equal. To use the scale, an object is placed in the left-hand pan. Known weights (*standards*) are put in the right-hand pan until the arms are level. Using a very sensitive scale (*analytical balance*), scientists can measure very small weights accurately.

Today, any weighing instrument is called a scale. Most use springs or electricity instead of standards.

ALSO READ: MEASUREMENT, WEIGHT.

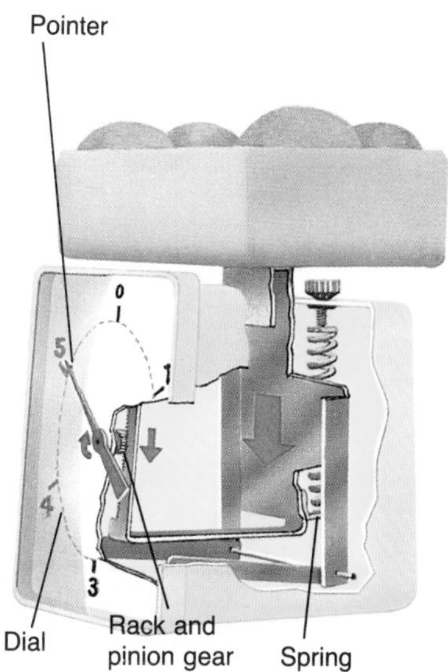

▲ *The kind of scale used in most kitchens is a* spring balance. *The weight put in the pan pushes down against a spring, and a gear system makes the pointer turn.*

SCANDINAVIA Three countries in northern Europe share the same way of life and a common history. Together they form Scandinavia. These countries are Denmark, Norway, and Sweden. Denmark lies on

▲ *The coastlines of the Scandinavian countries are cut up by countless* fiords. *These valleys were carved out by the glaciers during the most recent phase of the current ice age.*

the peninsula of Jutland, which is joined by Germany. Norway and Sweden share the Scandinavian peninsula. Finland is Sweden's eastern neighbor. (See the map with the article on EUROPE.) Iceland, which once belonged to Denmark, is often included as a part of Scandinavia. It is an island located about 550 miles (890 km) west of Norway in the North Atlantic Ocean.

No place in Scandinavia is far from the sea. Deep inlets, called *fiords*, cut into the coast, and thousands of lakes lie among thick forests. Northern Scandinavia is called the "Land of the Midnight Sun." Here, for several weeks during summer, the sun never sets.

ALSO READ: DENMARK, ICELAND, NORWAY, SCANDINAVIAN LANGUAGES, SWEDEN.

SCANDINAVIAN LANGUAGES

Scandia was the name given during the time of the Roman Empire to the lands of northern Europe. Today, the area is known as Scandinavia, consisting of the nations of Sweden, Norway, and Denmark. The people of these countries speak the Scandinavian languages, as do the people of Iceland, often counted as part of Scandinavia.

The Scandinavian languages were once a single language. This one language had developed out of an ancient language now called Germanic. As the people of the various northern European regions began to pronounce words differently and to add their own words, the single language developed into four languages—Danish, Icelandic, Norwegian, and Swedish. The Scandinavian languages were North Germanic, while Dutch and German were West Germanic. Icelandic is the most different language because its speakers lived for centuries in isolation on an island.

The Danes, Norwegians, and Swedes can understand each other without much difficulty. However, there are many different pronunciations of each language, and it is easy to tell where a person comes from the minute he or she speaks.

The language of Finland, which is also in northern Europe, is not a Scandinavian language. It belongs to a group of languages called Finno-Ugric.

English
Good morning, my name is Kathleen.

Swedish
God morgon, mitt namn är, Britt.

Danish
God morgen, mit navn er, Hans.

Norwegian
God morgen, mit navn er, Jens.

ALSO READ: LANGUAGES, SCANDINAVIA.

SCHOOL

If you were to reach the age of 14 or 15 without being able to read this page or write your name, you would be one of the millions of *illiterate* (unable to read and write) people in the world. Being literate helps you to be a more successful citizen in today's world. Being illiterate does not mean that a person is stupid. Some people have a little understood ailment called *dyslexia* that makes it hard for them to read. But many illiterate people cannot read because they have never had a chance to learn how to do so.

Learning can take place wherever you are and in many different ways. However, general information is probably most easily learned in school. All across the United States, school systems provide many kinds of education or learning for both young and older people. Some of these school systems are so small that they provide education for a village of only a few hundred people. Other school systems are so large that they are responsible for educating the people of huge cities. Whatever its size, a good school system tries to teach its students what they need to know to function most effectively in the world, and to develop whatever talents and abilities they already have.

Schools in the United States are either public or private. *Public schools* are financed mostly by local and state taxes. The Federal Government also

▲ *Singers from King's College School, Cambridge, Britain. Only boys with very good singing voices are accepted in this school. They are taught all the usual school subjects, too.*

contributes some financial support. Each state has complete authority over its own school systems, except for the federal rulings that all public schools must be integrated and must not promote any particular religion. In general, each city and county in a state has its own school system. *Private schools* are not usually supported by tax money. Church denominations, organizations, or groups of individuals support and control most private schools. Parents also help support the school by paying tuition fees (money charged for a child's attendance). Many of the nation's private schools are parochial—or parish-run under the sponsorship of the Catholic Church—but other religions often operate their own schools. Some military academies are private secondary schools for boys.

The levels of both public and private schools—from lowest to highest—are nursery schools, kindergartens, elementary schools, middle or junior high schools, senior high schools (sometimes just known as *high schools*), junior colleges, and colleges and universities.

Nursery Schools and Kindergartens Nursery schools are for three- and four-year-olds. Children learn mostly through play and informal instructions. They learn to get along with others their own age and begin to develop some basic skills—like tying shoelaces. Some preschool programs (educational experiences for children not old enough for regular school) are financed by public money. Most nursery schools, however, are privately supported.

Kindergarten is for children about five years old. A large number of school systems include kindergarten as part of their regular school programs, but many youngsters still go to private kindergartens.

Elementary and Secondary Schools Beyond kindergarten, those schools below the college level are known as elementary and secondary schools. Most often, elementary school includes grades 1–6 and secondary includes grades 7–12. Secondary schools are divided into grades in many ways. Grades 7, 8, and 9 may be junior high school, with 10, 11, and 12 as senior high school. Sometimes grades 7 and 8 are either included with elementary school or become part of a middle school (grade 5 or 6, 7, and 8), and their graduates go on to a four-year high school.

The aim of elementary education is to give students a firm background in reading, writing, and arithmetic. Other subjects, like science and social

▲ *Dartmouth College in Hanover, New Hampshire, was founded in 1769. The first classes were held before the log-cabin classrooms were finished, so they had to take place outdoors.*

▼ *A French classroom. The Ministry of Education in Paris decides what subjects must be taught in French schools, and how many hours must be spent each week on each subject by each pupil.*

▲ *Lessons need not always be in the classroom. In some countries they are often held outdoors.*

studies, are also taught.

In many elementary schools, students spend most of the school day in one classroom. When they go to junior and senior high, they move from class to class. Each subject is taught by a different teacher. In mathematics, instead of studying only arithmetic, they study algebra and geometry as well. In language arts, they study the structure of English, instead of just spelling and penmanship.

Senior high school is the last formal education or schooling some people will receive. For many, the subjects they take in high school are training courses for their life's work. High schools may prepare students for such vocations as auto mechanic, stenographer, keypunch operator, or carpenter. Good household management (nutrition, clothing, child care, and so on) and family and community life are taught in home economics courses.

Schools in Other Countries In Canada, the individual provinces control the school systems. The organization of most systems is similar to that of U.S. schools, but some predominantly French Catholic communities follow the French system. Children in these communities attend a preprimary school for three years and a primary school for seven years. Students may then attend either a two-year vocational training course or an eight-year course that prepares students for a university.

Britain and some other western European nations have a different school structure. Young people in Britain attend a primary school until they are about 11 years old. They then move to a middle school, and finally to an upper school. Their successes or failures in a series of examinations in different subjects, as well as their personal interests, determine the subjects they study in upper school. Some are prepared for college or university. Others study business or trade skills. Confusingly, "public" schools in Britain are those where parents pay tuition fees.

ALSO READ: COLLEGES AND UNIVERSITIES, EDUCATION, LEARNING, SPECIAL EDUCATION, TEACHING.

SCHUBERT, FRANZ (1797–1828)

The Austrian composer, Franz Peter Schubert, is best known for more than 600 German *lieder* (songs) that he wrote during his short lifetime. Schubert had a great gift for melody, for writing flowing lines of music filled with romantic feeling.

▲ *Franz Schubert, the great Austrian composer. Curiously, there was another composer called Franz Schubert who lived about the same time; he is now famous only because he was offended when people mixed him up with his brilliant contemporary!*

Schubert was born in Lichtenthal near Vienna. He had a beautiful singing voice as a boy. He studied singing at the Austrian emperor's choir school. He began to write songs when he was 14 years old. The words of many of his songs are poems by great German poets, such as Goethe and Schiller. Schubert's music beautifully portrays the mood of each poem. Most of his songs are included in *cycles*, or groups, such as *Winterreise* ("Winter Journey") and *Schwanengesang* ("Swan Song"). He also wrote many piano pieces and works for small groups of instruments, or chamber music. These include the piano fantasy "The Wanderer" and the *Quintet in A Major* ("The Trout").

Schubert's songs became very popular. But during his lifetime, people paid little attention to the symphonies, or large works for orchestra, that he wrote. He made little money from his music and spent most of his life in poverty.

ALSO READ: SINGING.

SCHUMANN, ROBERT (1810–1856)

Robert Alexander Schumann was a German composer. He wrote many of his most popular works for the piano. Schumann also edited a music magazine, which was widely read. His opinions were highly respected, and he encouraged several young composers of his day, including Chopin and Brahms.

Schumann was born in Zwickau, Germany. His mother persuaded him to study law, but Schumann was determined to become a great pianist. He took piano lessons and invented a mechanical device to strengthen his fingers. The device injured his hand, and he was forced to give up the piano.

Schumann turned to composing music. His early works include the happy piano pieces "Papillons" ("Butterflies") and "Kinderscenen" ("Scenes from Childhood"). Schumann's wife, Clara, was a famous pianist. She played many of his works in concerts. After their marriage, Schumann wrote several songs, including "Dichterliebe" ("Poet's Love"). Among his larger works for orchestra is the *Spring Symphony*.

ALSO READ: ROMANTIC PERIOD.

SCHWEITZER, ALBERT (1875–1965) Albert Schweitzer was a man who excelled in many fields. He is known throughout the world for his work as a doctor and missionary in Africa. He was also a brilliant musician, philosopher, and writer.

Schweitzer was born in the French region of Alsace (then occupied by Germany). He became a Protestant minister and served as head of a religious college in Strasbourg, Alsace. Schweitzer was a gifted organist and became a leading authority on Johann Sebastian Bach.

When he was 30 years old, Schweitzer decided to become a doctor. He studied medicine for six years and then traveled to Gabon in French Equatorial Africa. At Lambaréné, he built a hospital with many small houses, like a village. The people could live with their families in the village until they were well. Schweitzer often spoke of his "reverence for life." He felt that no person should kill another living creature. Even insects in his hospital were spared, and some people criticized Schweitzer for not keeping the hospital clean enough.

While he was in Africa, Schweitzer wrote several books about his philosophy of life and his religious faith. He was awarded the Nobel Peace Prize in 1952.

▲ *Robert Schumann, shown here with his wife Clara, who was also a composer.*

SCIENCE The Latin word for knowledge is *scientia*. The word "science," therefore, is used when we talk about studying in many fields of learning to gain knowledge about life, ourselves, the universe, how things work, how to solve problems, and so on. Science has been responsible for most of the things we use today and for showing us better ways of using other things.

History of Science Science developed very differently in the East and West. Since it is Western science that shapes our lives, here we shall trace the history of science in the West.

Science began with the stars. Babylonian astronomers observed (watched) the sky and kept careful records of the movements of the stars and planets. They used these records to construct a calendar. But observation is only the beginning of science. The next step is explanation. The Babylonians stopped with observation. They wanted to know *what* the stars were doing, not *why* they were doing it. For most early peoples, science was an arm of religion. Science observed, and religion explained.

▲ *Albert Schweitzer, French medical missionary, philosopher, and musician.*

The ancient Greeks moved away from a strictly religious way of looking at the world and closer to a scientific view. They studied the astronomy of Babylon and the medicine and geometry of Egypt, and they tried to

▲ *An alchemist. From around the 1st century* A.D. *through the Middle Ages, the alchemists tried to turn metals such as iron into gold. Of course, they could not succeed, but their experiments laid the foundations of the science of chemistry. But many alchemists believed their science was not just about making gold; they believed their experiments raised their souls to a higher spiritual level.*

find what caused things to happen. They tried to *explain* observations. The early Greeks also tried to explain more than they observed. They came up with remarkable theories, but they didn't always have the facts to back these theories.

After the Greeks, scientific thought slowed down in Europe for several hundred years. Science was kept alive by Arab scientists, mostly in mathematics, medicine, and astronomy. Then, in the 1200's and 1300's, Europeans rediscovered Greek science and Greek thought. In the next few hundred years, the Renaissance (rebirth) of knowledge spread throughout Europe. The discoveries of Galileo Galilei, Johannes Kepler, Isaac Newton, and other scientists changed the shape of science and changed people's view of the world. Galileo showed how bodies fall and found evidence that the sun is the center of the solar system. Newton proposed the law of gravitation, and Kepler showed how the planets move around the sun.

To some people, the universe was beginning to look like a big machine. They imagined that eventually they would be able to explain everything in mechanical terms.

But then scientists began to realize that perhaps there were limits to what they could learn. Albert Einstein's theories of *relativity* showed that distance and time were relative—they could be different for different observers. Werner Heisenberg proposed his *uncertainty principle*—that we can know *either* exactly where an atom or smaller particle is *or* the way in which it is moving, but never both at the same time. These and other ideas led to the realization that the universe is not just a machine, and that there are limits to what we can learn about it.

▶ *Isaac Newton was probably the greatest scientist of all time. Some of his most important work was on light. Here, he is using a prism to split up the sun's light into the band of colors called the* spectrum.

As science became more and more complicated, during the 1800's and 1900's, it became impossible for any one scientist to study more than a small part of it. Science became divided into the *physical sciences*—the study of matter, the *biological sciences*—the study of living things, and *mathematics*—the study of number and form. The physical sciences include *astronomy*—the study of space, *chemistry*—the study of the make-up of matter, *geology*—the study of the Earth, and *physics*—the study of energy, matter, and force. The biological sciences include *botany*—the study of plants, and *zoology*—the study of animals.

These fields of study can be broken down into still other fields. Zoology includes *vertebrate zoology*—the study of animals with backbones, and *invertebrate zoology*—the study of animals without backbones. Often two fields are joined together, as in *biochemistry*—the study of the chemistry of living things, and *biophysics*—the study of the physics of living things. The *social sciences*, including sociology, archeology, and anthropology, often use scientific methods to study society and behavior. Mathematics plays a part in almost all scientific study. It is not really a division of science but a tool of all the sciences.

Scientific fields can be divided in another way—into *pure* and *applied* science. Pure science observes and explains. Applied science uses the findings of pure science for practical purposes. Medicine is an applied science that uses the findings of biology, a pure science.

Scientific Method In the 1500's, Nicolaus Copernicus, a Polish astronomer, wrote that the Earth moved around the sun. Many people laughed at him. How could anyone imagine that the Earth was hurtling through space at thousands of miles an hour? Wouldn't a powerful wind blow all the time? They said that Copernicus was like an inexperienced sailor who imagines that the shore is sailing away from the ship.

But Copernicus was right. He had examined the movements of the planets, and he could find only one explanation to fit these movements—the Earth must be moving, too.

Copernicus used *inductive* reasoning—he started with a collection of facts and worked his way to a conclusion that would explain those facts. Inductive reasoning is the core of the *scientific method*, first formally proposed in the 1600's by Francis Bacon.

Scientists do not begin by trying to prove something but by trying to explain something. They begin by observing a phenomenon—something that happens. They collect as many facts as possible about the phenomenon. Then they try to come up with a *hypothesis*—an idea explaining the facts that they have. Experiments are designed to test the hypothesis. If enough experiments support the hypothesis, it becomes a theory. Other scientists use it and accept it as an explanation. If a theory can explain many different phenomena, and if it seems so obviously true that all scientists agree on it, it becomes a *general law*. Hypotheses are often disproved; theories are sometimes disproved; even general laws are occasionally disproved, but not often.

This is the way science is supposed to work, but things aren't always so neat. Many of the most important scientific breakthroughs have happened through luck and imagination. Charles Darwin's theory of evolution is an example. In the 1830's, Darwin sailed around South America on a ship called the *Beagle*. He went ashore on a group of islands called the Galápagos. The animals living on the Galápagos were interesting animals with curious ways.

Darwin made careful notes, although he was not sure what use or value his notes might have. When he got back to England, however, he happened to read a book that gave him a clue. Darwin studied and wrote for 20 years and produced his theory—that animals best suited to their surroundings are most likely to survive, and that variations (changes) in a species that make it better suited to its surroundings are also likely to survive.

Darwin was lucky in that he stumbled on the observations. But he was also imaginative enough to see what his observations might mean. Similar information had been available to other people, but they had not drawn the conclusions.

Scientists look beneath the surface. They hope that by doing this they will discover connections between things that are not obvious on the surface. They do not always take the easiest way of solving a problem, nor accept the most obvious explanation.

■ LEARN BY DOING

Try thinking like a scientist. Take a phenomenon and try to figure out how or why it happens. For example, you could try to figure out how waves move, how a magnet works, or why you have certain kinds of plants or animals in your part of the country. Make careful observations and record what you see. Make measurements if you can.

You might want to run some experiments. You can study waves in a shallow pan half full of water. Touch the water with your finger or with the edge of a ruler. Waves will move across the pan and reflect off the other end. Put a curved piece of metal in the pan and watch how the waves reflect when they hit the inside of the curve. Bend the curve until the waves

▲ *Scientists at work on a particle accelerator.*

▼ *Ernest Rutherford, famous for the work he did on atomic physics. In 1908, he won the Nobel Prize for Chemistry.*

▲ *A scientist using a device called a* thermocouple *to measure the temperature of the pile cap in a nuclear reactor.*

all reflect to the same point. Now see what happens when the waves reflect off the outside of the curve.

You can learn something about a magnet by seeing what objects it attracts and what objects it does not attract. How does distance affect the attraction? What happens when you put two magnets together? Will a magnet attract through glass or paper?

If you want to try your hand at zoological or botanical studies, you can count the animals and plants in a certain area and notice how weather and seasons affect them. If you had different weather, would you have different plants? If you had different plants, would you have different animals?

After you have collected your information and made your observations you can come up with a hypothesis—an explanation of what you have observed. You can check your explanation against books in the library or by asking a scientist or a teacher. ■

Becoming a Scientist If you are interested in solving problems and in finding out how things work and why the world is the way it is, you might like to become a scientist. In the past, there was no one way of becoming a scientist, but today almost all scientists go to college, where they study a broad range of subjects and begin to specialize in one field of science. Scientists who want to do more advanced work go on to graduate school, and in several years get a Master's degree or a Ph.D. (Doctor of Philosophy). Their work becomes even more specialized. A botanist may study one kind of plant. A physicist may study one kind of particle of matter.

Scientific work requires a great deal of patience and dedication. Scientists may spend their whole lives working on just one problem. They must keep a fresh and open-minded outlook. They should never become so attached to a pet theory or favorite idea that they are unwilling to give it up when the facts go against it.

On the other hand, a scientist should not give up an idea just because it is unpopular or seems to go against "common sense." Many of the greatest scientists have made important discoveries because they saw the world in a peculiar way. Often it was a long time before others came to agree with them.

The most important scientific breakthrough so far this century has probably been Albert Einstein's theory of relativity. This theory solved many problems that had been puzzling physicists for years. Einstein thought about these problems in a different way. Einstein thought not in words but in shapes, forces, and mathematics. He worked out his theory mathematically before ever translating it into words.

While pure science has changed the way we see the world, applied science has actually changed the face of the world. Airplanes, artificial hearts, skyscrapers, spaceflight, television, and frozen foods are all applications of science. Science has made our lives more comfortable and our machines more efficient, but it has also made our streets and skies more crowded and our wars more deadly. The uses to which science is put depend not just on scientists, but on the rest of us endeavoring to understand science.

▼ *The plasmatron equipment shown here has many uses in science. It can be used at high temperatures for metals research and for cutting and welding.*

For further information on:
Biological Sciences, *see* BIOCHEMISTRY, BIOLOGY, BOTANY, ECOLOGY, GENETICS, MEDICINE, NATURE STUDY, PALEONTOLOGY, PSYCHOLOGY, ZOOLOGY.
History of Science, *see* ARISTOTLE; BABYLONIA; COPERNICUS, NICOLAUS; DARWIN, CHARLES; EINSTEIN, ALBERT; EVOLUTION; FARADAY, MICHAEL; GALILEO GALILEI; GREECE, ANCIENT; KEPLER, JOHANNES; NEWTON, SIR ISAAC.
Mathematics, *see* ALGEBRA, ARITHMETIC, GEOMETRY, MATHEMATICS, SET.
Physical Sciences, *see* ASTRONOMY, CHEMISTRY, GEOLOGY, PHYSICS, QUANTUM THEORY, RELATIVITY.
Scientific Method, *see* BACON, FRANCIS; PHILOSOPHY; STATISTICS.
Social Sciences, *see* ANTHROPOLOGY, ARCHEOLOGY, ECONOMICS, PSYCHOLOGY, SOCIOLOGY.
For individual scientists see Index at name.

SCIENCE FICTION Have you seen the various *Star Trek* and *Star Wars* movies, or the movies *2001: A Space Odyssey*, *E.T.*, and *Back to the Future*? These movies tell science-fiction (S.F.) stories. If you watched them you would see space travel, robots, beings from other worlds, travel through time, telepathy ("mind-reading"), and many other S.F. themes.

Written S.F. is a form of *fantasy*. In a fantasy story, impossible things happen—like magic. In S.F., too, impossible things happen, but they are given scientific, or pretend-scientific, explanations, so readers believe such things really could happen.

People argue about which was the very first piece of S.F. Some say it was the *Odyssey*, written by Homer maybe 800 B.C. In the 2nd century A.D., another Greek, Lucian, wrote about people traveling to the moon. The great astronomer, Johannes Kepler, wrote about beings living on the moon. But the first real S.F. novel was *Frankenstein* (1818), by Mary Shelley. She told how a man made a living creature. Other important S.F. writers of the 1800's were Edgar Allan Poe and Jules Verne. Earlier this century, major writers like H.G. Wells, Aldous Huxley, and George Orwell wrote S.F.

The first magazine devoted to S.F. was *Amazing Stories*, founded in 1926 by Hugo Gernsback. Many other "pulp" S.F. magazines followed, but most S.F. today is published in general magazines or in books. Popular modern S.F. authors include Isaac Asimov and Arthur C. Clarke (who are both authorities on science subjects), Robert Heinlein, Larry Niven, John Brunner, Brian Aldiss, Ursula Le Guin, and Frank Herbert. Some of these have written S.F. especially for children, as have André Norton, Sylvia Louise Engdahl, and John Christopher.

Some people find S.F. rather tough going when they first start to read it—but it soon becomes easy. As Brian Aldiss once said, S.F. is no more written just for scientists than ghost stories are written just for ghosts!

ALSO READ: HOMER; HUXLEY FAMILY; KEPLER, JOHANNES; NOVEL; ORWELL, GEORGE; POE, EDGAR ALLAN; ROBOT; SHELLEY, PERCY AND MARY; VERNE, JULES; WELLS, H.G.

▲ *From being a highly successful science fiction television series starting in the 1960s,* Star Trek *became even more popular as a series of great special effects movies in the 1980s. Many of the U.S.S. Enterprise's designs were worked out with help from NASA (the National Aeronautics and Space Administration).*

The top four all-time most popular films, in terms of dollars earned, are all science-fiction films. They are *E.T. The Extra-Terrestrial* (1982) followed by the Star Wars film series: *Star Wars* (1977), *The Empire Strikes Back* (1980), and *Return of the Jedi* (1983).

▲ *A man in "traditional" Scots costume. In fact, this type of costume did not become popular among Scots until the 19th century.*

Scotland has always been famous for its engineers. The Forth railroad bridge in Scotland was the first large bridge in the world to be made entirely of steel. It took 3,000 men and 7 million rivets to complete it in 1890.

▼ *Eilean Donan Castle, in northwest Scotland.*

SCOTLAND The country of Scotland is part of the United Kingdom of Great Britain and Northern Ireland. It lies to the north of England, on the island of Great Britain. The Hebrides islands to the west and the Shetland and Orkney islands to the north are also part of Scotland. (See the map with the article on BRITISH ISLES.)

Scotland has a rugged coastline with many islands and deep inlets, or *firths*. The Scottish Highlands, in the north, is a region of mountains and deep valleys, or *glens*. Ben Nevis, 4,406 feet (1,343 m) above sea level, the highest peak in the British Isles, is located there. Sparkling lakes, or *lochs*, lie in many of the glens. The western part of the Highlands receives a large amount of rain.

South of the Highlands is a mostly flat region of rich farmland called the Lowlands. In this area are situated Scotland's major industries and its two most important cities, Edinburgh, the capital, and Glasgow, the largest city. A region of rolling hills, the Southern Uplands, lies between the Lowlands and the English border.

Scotland has been a part of the United Kingdom since 1707. The Scottish people have their own educational and legal systems and their own branch of the Christian church. A few Highlanders still speak their own language, Gaelic (also spoken in parts of Ireland). The Scots still have the tradition that all people with the same surname belong to a particular *clan*. Since the 1800's, each clan has had its own design of *tartan*, or checkered plaid, which is woven into cloth. The tartan cloth is made up into *kilts* (a type of pleated skirt), which many Scots still wear, especially on important occasions.

Scotland is not wealthy agriculturally, but it has become richer through the discovery of oil in the North Sea. The port of Glasgow, on the Clyde River, is the most important industrial center. Chemicals, iron and steel, and automobiles are all important industries. Scotch whisky (never spelled "whiskey"), woolens, and tweed textiles are exported all over the world. Tourists visit the Highlands to admire the beautiful scenery.

In the A.D. 400's, an Irish tribe called the Scots set up a kingdom on the west coast of what is now Scotland. By the 900's, the Scottish kings had conquered the whole country. The Scots fought many wars with the English, who often tried to gain control over Scotland. King James VI of Scotland, son of Mary, Queen of Scots, became King James I of England in 1603. He was the first of the Stuart monarchs of England, Scotland, and, usually, Ireland. In 1707, Scotland and England were united by the Act of Union. The Scots now send representatives to the British Parliament.

ALSO READ: BAGPIPE; BRUCE, ROBERT; ENGLISH HISTORY; JAMES, KINGS OF ENGLAND; MARY, QUEEN OF SCOTS; UNITED KINGDOM.

SCOTT, ROBERT (1868–1912) Robert Falcon Scott was a British explorer and naval commander. He led the second expedition ever to reach the South Pole. But all the members of the expedition froze to death on the return journey.

Scott first traveled to Antarctica in

1901. He spent the next four years exploring the region. He returned there in 1910 and began the expedition to the South Pole.

Scott and his companions pulled their sledges themselves instead of using dogs. After battling severe storms, they reached the South Pole on January 17, 1912. They found that the Norwegian explorer, Roald Amundsen, had arrived there a month earlier. Scott's expedition was hit by dreadful blizzards on the return journey. The explorers became weak from hunger and sickness. Petty Officer Edgar Evans died first. Then Captain Lawrence Oates became too sick to travel. He bravely went out into the storm to die, so that he would not slow down the others. But the remaining three men died shortly afterwards, only 11 miles (18 km) from their base camp. Scott's diary was later found. On his last day, he had written, "The end cannot be far. It seems a pity but I cannot write any more.—R. Scott."

ALSO READ: AMUNDSEN, ROALD; ANTARCTICA; EXPLORATION; SOUTH POLE.

SCOTT, SIR WALTER (1771–1832) Sir Walter Scott was one of the most popular of all story writers. He was born in Edinburgh, Scotland. As a boy, he was often sick and spent much time studying old legends. Scott attended the University of Edinburgh and then became a lawyer. He composed many successful books of poems, including *The Lay of the Last Minstrel* (1805).

In 1814, Scott published *Waverley*, a romantic story about Scottish history. This was the beginning of a long series of historical books, called the "Waverley" novels. *Rob Roy* (1817), *The Bride of Lammermoor* (1819), *Ivanhoe* (1819), and *The Talisman* (1825) are a few of these exciting tales. *Ivanhoe* is a novel about bitter enemies—the Normans and the Saxons. Robin Hood and Friar Tuck appear as two of the characters. Romantic knights in armor and lovely heroines, kings and queens, dwarfs and robbers are all part of Scott's colorful stories.

A much loved man, Scott got into trouble financially. From 1826, he tried to pay off the money he owed by writing more and more. Overwork destroyed his health and finally killed him. Scott's last years were spent at his home, Abbotsford, in southeastern Scotland.

ALSO READ: LITERATURE, NOVEL.

SCROLL see BOOK.

SCUBA DIVING The beauty of the underwater world is often explored by scuba divers. To do this, divers must wear *s*elf-*c*ontained *u*nderwater *b*reathing *a*pparatus, or "scuba" for short.

A scuba diver carries one or two tanks of compressed air strapped to his or her back on a frame. The diver breathes the air through a mouthpiece connected to a tube from the air tank. Wearing scuba gear, a diver can go deep and stay underwater for about an hour. However, if a diver does strenuous activity or dives very deep, the air supply will be used up more quickly. Scuba divers also wear a face mask, wet suit, weighted belt, flippers worn on the feet, and a flotation vest. The flotation vest may be inflated under water and bring the diver to the surface in an emergency.

In the 1930's, Jacques Cousteau, a French Naval officer, and Émile Gagnan pioneered the use of the *aqualung*, the first successful form of scuba. During World War II, frogmen carried out daring underwater missions. Divers began wearing rubber wet suits to keep them warm underwater, and underwater photography made great advances.

In the Caribbean, scuba divers

▲ *Captain Robert Scott, the British explorer who died trying to be the first to reach the South Pole.*

▲ *Sir Walter Scott, Scottish novelist and poet of the Romantic Period.*

▲ *A scuba diver raises the anchor of a sunken ship. Scuba divers have done much to increase our knowledge of ships of the past, and of the people who sailed in them.*

▲ *A Nigerian sculpture carved out of wood.*

have found the wrecks of Spanish treasure ships and have recovered gold and jewels from them. Archeologists have used scuba to explore the wrecks of ancient Greek and Roman ships in the Mediterranean Sea.

Skin diving is another underwater sport. But skin diving equipment is simple. A face mask, that enables the diver to see clearly, flippers that help the diver swim with less effort, and a breathing tube called a *snorkel* are all people need to explore shallow waters.

The diver holds one end of the snorkel in his or her mouth. The tube part of the snorkel is tucked under the face mask and extends above the surface of the water. The diver can breathe without taking his or her face out of the water. This way, a diver can swim face down and see schools of brightly colored fish swimming among coral reefs.

ALSO READ: COUSTEAU, JACQUES-YVES; SWIMMING.

SCULPTURE Sculpture is the member of the fine-arts family that you can touch, walk around, or set on a floor or table. While paintings are usually flat, sculptures are three-dimensional, with several surfaces. A sculpture changes appearance as you look at it from different angles and as the light that hits it changes. Paintings are usually made by applying paint to a flat surface, such as a canvas. Sculpture can be made out of almost anything—paper, wood, toothpicks, marble, bronze, clay, plastic, plaster, tin cans, cement, or rubber, to name just a few. Some modern sculptures have motorized parts that move. Others can be taken apart and put back together. Sculpture is exciting to look at and fun to make.

Sculptors are the artists who make sculptures. Sculptors carve, model, or construct their pieces. To *carve* something, the artist takes away material

▲ *A bas-relief (low-relief) Egyptian sculpture of Tutankhamen, who became the ruler of Egypt when he was only about 11 years old.*

from a solid block. Sculptures can be *constructed* by putting a number of parts together. Mobiles are constructed sculptures that hang from the ceiling and move with changing air currents. Alexander Calder (1898–1976) was a U.S. artist who made interesting mobiles. Some artists weld pieces of metal together with a hot gas flame to make constructed sculptures.

Sculptures are either in the *round* or in *relief*. Some ancient peoples such as the Egyptians and the Assyrians were especially good at making relief sculptures by carving into a flat surface to make a raised design. They usually made *low-relief* sculptures, where the figures stand out only a little from the background. Bernini, an Italian artist who worked in Rome in the 1600's, was an artist who carved sculptures in *high relief*. In high-relief sculptures, the figures stand out more from the background.

Some of the most beautiful sculptures ever made were done by the ancient Greeks. They loved to carve marble sculptures of the human figure in the round. Michelangelo, one of history's greatest artists, made sculptures in the round. Some of the best-known modern sculptures in the round were done by Henry Moore (1898–1986), a British artist. He cut holes into many of his figures so that you can look through them.

Some sculptures are cast into a metal such as bronze. These are usually sculptures that are large with long slender parts, such as arms.

Bronze casting is a complex process. A model of the sculpture to be cast is made by the artist in wax or clay. An *outer mold* is made by covering the model with wet plaster, or, in another method, with a special type of sand. Sections of the dry plaster or sand are then removed and reassembled. The inside of this hollow mold is exactly like the outside of the model. An *inner mold*, which is a slightly smaller version of the model, is fitted inside the outer mold. Hot, molten (liquid) bronze is then poured into the space between the two molds. In one method, the *cire-perdue* or lost-wax process, the bronze melts and replaces a layer of wax that is in the space. After the bronze has hardened, the molds are removed.

▼ Neapolitan Fisherboy, *a sculpture in white marble by Jean-Baptiste Carpeaux. (National Gallery of Art, Washington, D.C., Samuel H. Kress Collection.)*

▲ The Fountain of the Four Rivers, *in Rome, is one of the great sculptures of Gianlorenzo Bernini.*

In the early 1900's, some European artists began to study the art of less-developed civilizations. The art, especially the sculpture, of these people was simple, compact, and uncluttered. The artists particularly liked the African wood sculptures, such as the head shown on page 2178, which had plain shapes and few details. African sculptures have influenced Western sculpture ever since. Modern artists have gone one step beyond the African sculptors by making their pieces abstract (not realistic). For example, one of Barbara Hepworth's sculptures looks like a big apple that someone took a bite out of, but it was not meant to be a sculpture of an apple. She made it to express an idea or feeling. She used two colors and a variety of textures to add interest to her abstract.

■ LEARN BY DOING

Try carving a sculpture out of a solid block. A good material to start with is a large bar of soap. Soap can be cut with a blunt table knife and polished with the back of a spoon. To make unusual shapes, several pieces of soap can be stuck together by wetting the two surfaces to be joined and allowing them to dry. Textures can be added by carving into the basic shape

▼ Half Figure *by the British sculptor Henry Moore.*

▶ *A steel and aluminum sculpture in red, called* Early One Morning, *by Anthony Caro. These pieces are similar to those used for engineering or building purposes.*

The largest sculptures in the world are the mounted figures of General Robert E. Lee, Jefferson Davis, and General J. ("Stonewall") Jackson carved on the face of Stone Mountain, near Atlanta, Georgia. The sculptor Walter K. Hancock and others took more than eight years to complete the 90 foot (27 m) figures.

▼ *The gray heron stands motionless in or near water, then suddenly darts its head down to catch its prey.*

with fork prongs or toothpicks.

The easiest way to model a sculpture is to use self-hardening clay. Other objects, such as buttons, yarn, drinking straws, or toothpicks, can be pressed into the soft clay to add variety. Clay can be painted after it has dried. Special artificial clay is also fun to model with.

Make a constructed sculpture out of natural materials that you have collected. Gather shells, pieces of driftwood, rocks, or other materials and glue them together. Varnish or a little paint can be used to finish your sculpture. Some other things that you can use to make constructions are bottle caps, cardboard tubes, plastic straws and empty spools of thread. Can you think of any other materials that you could use? ■

For further information on:
History of Sculpture, *see* ABSTRACT ART, ART HISTORY, GREEK ART, ROMAN ART.
Methods of Sculpting, *see* CARVING, CLAY MODELING, PAPER SCULPTURE.
Sculptors, *see* CELLINI, BENVENUTO; EPSTEIN, SIR JACOB; MICHELANGELO BUONARROTI; RODIN, AUGUSTE.
Sculptured Mountains, *see* RUSHMORE, MOUNT; STONE MOUNTAIN.

SEABIRDS Some birds spend all their time far out on the ocean, except when they are nesting. Other birds spend most of their time on the ocean near the shore. These birds nest on land, too. All these birds are called seabirds. The places the birds choose as breeding grounds are sometimes called *rookeries*. Thousands of birds often nest on the same island or cliff.

Some kinds of birds soar over the ocean for hours. The *albatross* is one example. It is a large bird that lives in all the oceans except the North Atlantic. Albatrosses nest on islands in grassy or muddy areas. The *wandering albatross*, the largest type, has a wingspread of almost 12 feet (3.7 m), although its wings are only nine inches (23 cm) wide. As well as eating fish, albatrosses often follow ships and feed on the garbage that is thrown overboard. They soar behind the ship for hours, with hardly a movement of their wings. When garbage is tossed overboard the albatrosses alight on the water to feed. When they have finished feeding, they catch up to the ship.

The *fulmar* is related to the albatross. It is like the albatross, but smaller. Fulmars, too, spend much time over the ocean, except when breeding. They also eat fish and floating garbage. Fulmars nest in scooped-out areas on rocky cliffs.

Shearwaters are strong-winged seabirds that got their name from their habit of skimming close to the surface of the ocean. They are found on nearly all seas and oceans. They rarely fly far from land, but they come ashore only at nesting time. Some kinds of shearwaters nest in burrows, while others nest in caves or crannies in rocky areas. They are 12 to 20 inches (30–50 cm) long and have long, pointed wings and slender bills.

The *petrel*, related to the shearwater, is also a strong, tireless flier. The smaller *storm petrels*, or *Mother Carey's chickens*, are seen flying over very stormy seas. Their habit of patting the surface of the sea with their feet has given rise to sailors' tales of these birds walking on the sea. The petrels' breeding grounds are varied. Petrels, fulmars, shearwaters, and albatrosses are in a scientific group called tube-nosed swimmers. The nostrils of these birds are in short tubes on the bill.

The *frigate bird*, or *man-o'-war bird*, is a large soaring bird. It is black with white patches. The male has a bright red throat pouch. It is about 40 inches (1 m) long, and its narrow wings span seven feet (2.1 m). Frigate birds may be the best fliers of all birds, but they can hardly walk or swim. They build their nests in trees or on rocks. They pick some food from the surface of the ocean. They also snatch and eat chicks from unguarded nests of other birds. Frigate birds attack other birds that have caught fish and force them to give up their food.

The *auk* lives along coasts in the Northern Hemisphere. Although it is a poor flier, it is a very good swimmer and diver. It is very clumsy on land, where it rarely goes except to nest among rocks or on cliffs. The *little auk*, or *dovekie*, lives in the North Atlantic Ocean. It is about six or eight inches (15–20 cm) long. Eskimos eat dovekies and make their feathered skins into clothing. The *puffin* is a type of auk. Puffins live in the North Atlantic Ocean, as far north as the southern edges of the Arctic Ocean. Puffins are sometimes called *sea parrots* because of their large red bills, which are marked with yellow and blue. The back and wings are black, and the breast is whitish. A puffin can catch several fish and hold them all crosswise in its bill.

A *gannet* is a large seabird. Most gannets are white but a few are dark. They dive for fish from high in the air, often as high as 100 feet (30 m). Air sacs under the skin, in the breast region, cushion the bird as it hits the water. The air is then expelled from the sacs to enable the bird to stay

◀ *(1) Gannets do spectacular dives. (2) Terns are like small seagulls. (3) Oystercatchers are wading birds. (4) Shearwaters often fly close to the water—hence their name. (5) Puffins may build their nests in old rabbit burrows.*

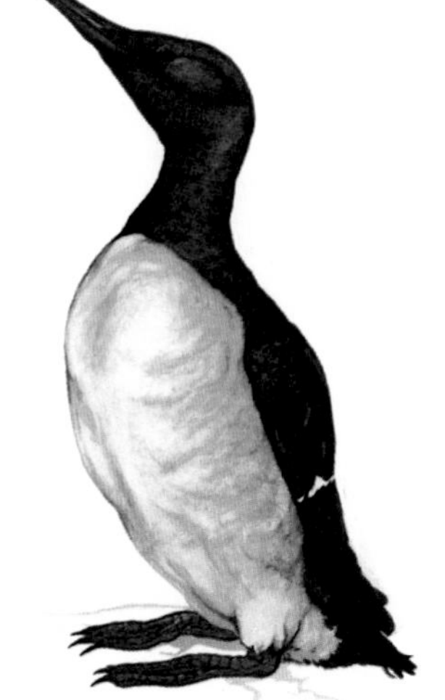

▲ *The guillemot is found around shorelines in the Northern Hemisphere.*

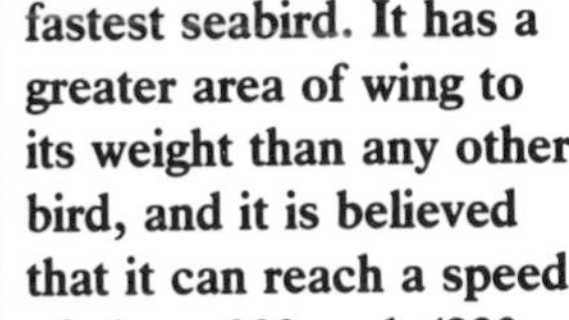

The frigate bird is the fastest seabird. It has a greater area of wing to its weight than any other bird, and it is believed that it can reach a speed of about 200 mph (320 km/hr).

▲ *Rugged cliffs make excellent nesting sites for gulls and other seabirds because few enemies can reach them.*

underwater for a long time. Gannets usually make nests of clumps of seaweed in rocky areas. The *booby* is closely related to the gannet. It is found in the oceans of the warmer parts of the world. It is an easy and powerful flier. Some types of boobies nest in trees, and others nest on the ground. Boobies feed on fish and squid, for which they dive into the water. This bird received its name because of its habit of alighting on ships and allowing itself to be captured easily. Sailors thought that this was stupid, so they called the bird a booby.

Gulls and *terns* are flying and swimming birds that live along the seacoast and in large lakes all over the world. *Pelicans* are swimming birds with a large pouch of skin under the lower jaw.

ALSO READ: BIRD, CRANE, DUCKS AND GEESE, GULLS AND TERNS, PELICAN.

SEACOAST A seacoast is the line along which land and sea meet. The sea is continually wearing away a seacoast in some places and building it up in others. The land itself slowly rises and sinks over periods of thousands of years. The seacoasts of the Earth are continually changing shape. The sea level rose after the melting of the ice at the end of the last ice age. Slowly rising seas flooded the land, causing the seacoasts to move inward, toward the centers of the continents. When the sea level falls, seawater runs off the land, moving the seacoasts outward.

The wearing away of land by the action of moving water is called *water erosion.* Ocean waves and currents cause erosion. Waves pound at the edges of continents. The waves carry rocks, pebbles, and sand, which are hurled at the rocky shores. This constant pounding wears away the shore. Shores composed of hard rock resist erosion, and the land rises up sharply from the sea in steep formations called *sea cliffs*. There are cliffs on the coasts of New England, Oregon, and Washington. When waves attack soft rock, they do not meet so much resistance, and a gently sloping area called a *wave-cut terrace* is formed. The terrace may be covered with sand by the waves. Waves pounding a sea cliff wear away the softer kinds of rock first, making sea caves. When a cave is cut all the way through a headland, it is called a *sea arch.*

In some places, sand makes up a *beach*. The landward side of a beach is the backshore. The part of the beach that is covered at high tide is the foreshore. Waves often create a nip, or low cliff, on the beach. The material eroded in forming the nip is deposited underwater, forming a sub-

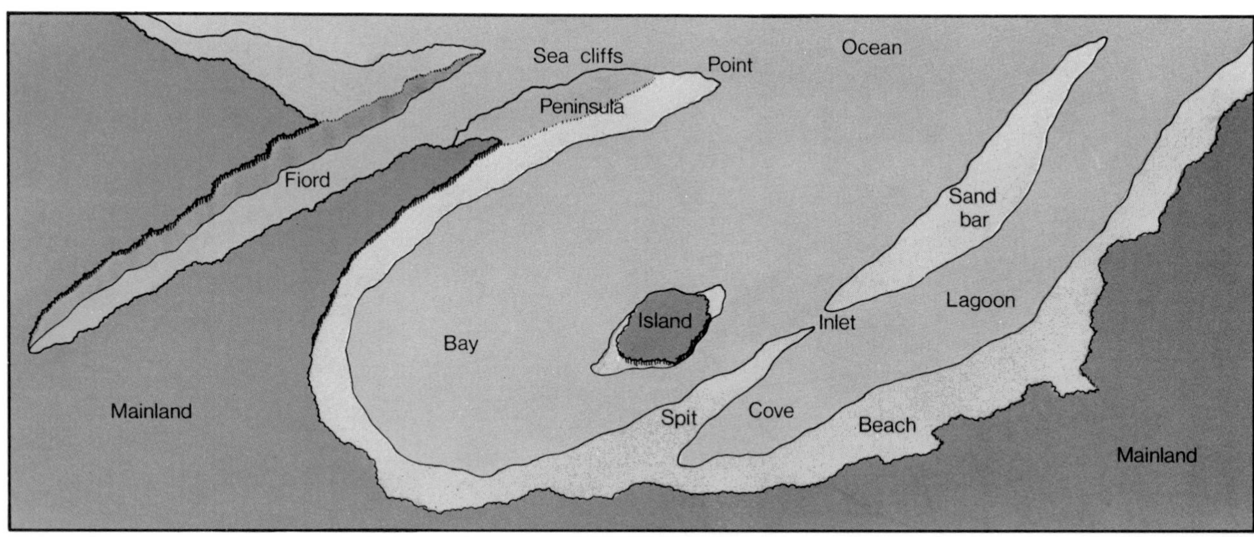

marine bar. The foreshore is covered with sand that slopes down to the sea.

Beaches are built up of pebbles, shingle (waterworn gravel), or sand. Sometimes currents move beach material along the shores and build *spits*, which are sandbars that project from the coast and are often curved. There are many spits along the Atlantic coast of the United States. Offshore sandbars, or *barrier bars*, may be underwater or exposed, when they are called *barrier beaches*. These long ridges of sand or shingle often occur on gently sloping coasts. *Lagoons* lie between them and the mainland. *Inlets* are breaks in the sandbar through which tidal water enters the lagoon. A long, narrow inlet between steep cliffs is a *fiord*. There are many fiords along the coasts of Alaska, Norway and New Zealand.

A *gulf* is a large area of water partly surrounded by land. The Gulf of Mexico is an example. A much smaller water area, similar to a gulf, is a *bay*. Bays and *coves* (small bays) are formed in less resistant rock than the surrounding headlands and are therefore eroded further inland by the waves. If the level of the sea rises and fills the mouth of a river, an *estuary* is formed. These estuaries are also called *inlets* or *rias*. Chesapeake Bay is an example of this kind of formation. *Points* and *capes* are pieces of land that stick out into the sea. Cape Cod is a very famous one. A *headland* is a point or cape that rises high above the ocean. A large area of land sticking out into the sea is called a *peninsula*.

ALSO READ: EROSION, OCEAN, TIDE.

▼ *People have changed many shorelines—most famously in the Netherlands—by building walls to keep the sea at bay.*

◀ *Chesil Beach in Britain. The beach has extended to cut off the river's exit, forming a brackish lagoon on the land-side of the beach.*

▲ *Atoll shorelines are ringed with white sandy beaches and gently lapping sparkling blue waters. Farther out, the coral reefs keep the rougher ocean waters at bay.*

SEAHORSE

SEAHORSE The seahorse is actually a fish with a long, tubelike snout, but with a head that looks like that of a tiny horse. Its body is covered with an "armor" of bony plates. It swims upright, head up and tail down. A seahorse cannot swim very fast. Its long tail does not even have fins. But the tail is *prehensile*, which means it can wrap around objects and hang on tightly. Seahorses spend much of their time clinging with their tails to underwater plants. They like shallow, quiet water and need the warmth of subtropical and tropical seas. Seahorses suck in tiny forms of ocean animal life, such as brine shrimp and other crustaceans. Seahorses snap up their food in tiny, toothless jaws and swallow it whole.

There are about 50 kinds of seahorses. One, the pygmy seahorse, is only an inch or two (2.5–5 cm) long,

The best place to see the horizon is on the seacoast. The horizon is the line where the Earth and the sky seem to meet. The distance to the horizon depends on how high you are above sea level. If you stand on the shore and your eyes are 5 feet (1.5 m) above sea level, you can see the horizon 3 miles (5 km) away. If your eyes are 20 feet (6 m) up, you can see for 6 miles. From the top of Mount Everest on a clear day you can see for a distance of nearly 250 miles (400 km).

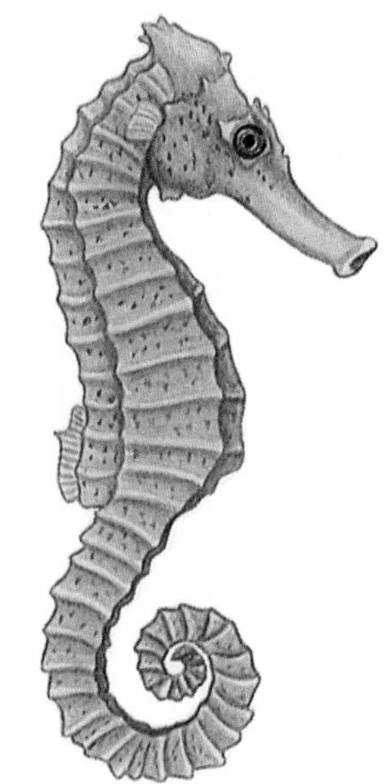

▲ *The seahorse gets its name for obvious reasons.*

or about as big as a paper clip. Common Atlantic Ocean seahorses are about four inches (10 cm) long. The biggest seahorses, found in parts of the Pacific Ocean, grow to be a foot (30 cm) in length. The mother seahorse puts her eggs inside a pouch in the male's body. The male carries the eggs until they hatch into living seahorses.

ALSO READ: AQUARIUM, FISH, OCEAN.

SEALS AND SEA LIONS Seals and sea lions make up two groups of fin-footed mammals that spend most of their time in water but come ashore to breed. The group called sea lions includes the fur seals as well as the true sea lions. These animals have small external ears, so they are often called eared seals. The other group of seals has internal ears—invisible to the casual observer—so they are often called earless seals.

Seals and sea lions are found in nearly all oceans, but most live in very cold water. They are protected from the cold by a thick layer of fatty tissue, called *blubber*, beneath the skin. The blubber also provides buoyancy (ability to float). Seals and sea lions are aided in swimming by webbed, paddlelike limbs called *flippers*. Many have claws on their flippers. Seals and sea lions are carnivorous animals that eat fish, shellfish, and seabirds. Some species will also eat other seals.

Seals and sea lions are large animals. The males are usually several feet—and several hundred pounds—larger than the females. The largest, the elephant seal, is about 18 feet (5.5 m) long and weighs several tons. The harbor seal—about six feet (1.8 m) long—is the smallest. Many types of seals are killed for their fur and for their flesh (for food and the oil in the blubber).

Seals and sea lions breed once a year on ice-covered or rocky shores and usually produce one or two young called *pups*. Adult males are called *bulls*, and adult females are called *cows*. Their breeding colonies, sometimes called *rookeries*, may be quite large, containing perhaps hundreds of thousands of animals. Pups are nursed for varying lengths of time and enter the water when they have developed enough blubber.

Eared fur seals are valuable to people because of their fur, which consists of two layers of thick hair. An insulating layer of short, fine hair is protected by a layer of longer, coarse guard hairs. The guard hairs, which grow from the blubber, are removed when the blubber is stripped away. So the seal fur used by people consists of the soft undercoat. Northern fur seals breed in the North Pacific Ocean, mostly on the Pribilof Islands. The bulls arrive in early spring. Each bull claims as much territory as he can. When the females arrive, the bulls try to collect as many mates as they can. The females give birth shortly afterward to pups conceived the previous summer. In late summer, after mating, the bulls leave for warmer waters, often near California.

▼ *(1) The elephant seal, the world's largest seal, is named for its great bulk and for the male's long, trunklike nose. Its homes include islands off California. (2) The smaller gray seal lives off coasts from North America east to the Baltic Sea. (3) The Californian sea lion is one of the eared seals. (4) The walrus lives only in cold waters.*

The cows and pups separate and leave about four months later, when the pups have been weaned.

True sea lions have longer limbs and necks than seals and can turn their heads all the way around. They can move more effectively on shore because they can move their hind limbs forward. This helps them to raise their bodies on the front limbs and slide along. Sea lions are also strong divers and can leap as much as five feet (1.5 m) out of the water. Performing seals are usually sea lions. Untrained sea lions often play catch with each other using a fish instead of a ball.

The group called earless seals includes both the smallest and biggest types—harbor seals and elephant seals. The largest subgroup, called northern seals, includes the harbor and hair seals. Harbor seals, because they prefer still water, live in bays and rivers along the Atlantic and Pacific coasts. They are friendly, tame animals. Hair seals live farther north along the Atlantic and Pacific coasts. Young hair seals have a fluffy, white coat of fur. For many years, these pups have been cruelly butchered for their white fur. These are the only earless seals killed for their fur because adult seals lack the soft undercoat. Ringed seals are unusual in two ways. They make holes in the Arctic ice where they live so they can swim under the ice and resurface as often as they please. The ringed seal is also the only species that digs a burrow (in the ice) for its young.

The elephant seal (or sea elephant) received its name because the male has a long—18 inches (46 cm)—trunk, or snout, similar to an elephant's. During the mating season, the male often fills his trunk with air (making it even larger) and then lets the air out, making a loud snorting noise. Elephant seals are also unusual in that they have very little hair and molt (shed their hair) once a year while they lie in the sun. These animals live primarily around the Antarctic Ocean, but some have been found along the Pacific coasts of South America and California.

▲ *The New Zealand fur seal is one of the species of eared seals. You can see how much like cats some seals are.*

ALSO READ: FUR, MAMMAL, WALRUS.

SEASON The four seasons of the year—spring, summer, fall (autumn), and winter—occur because of the way in which the Earth orbits the sun. The Earth is divided in half by an imaginary line called the equator. North of the equator is the Northern Hemisphere. South of it is the Southern Hemisphere. Another imaginary line, called the Earth's axis, runs through the center of the Earth from pole to pole. The Earth's axis is slightly tipped. The slant of the axis is always the same; the axis always points in the same direction throughout the year.

If you would like to "see" an imaginary axis (similar to the Earth's), spin a large coin, such as a quarter, on its edge. A line will *seem* to appear at the center of the spin. The imaginary line of the Earth's axis is much like the coin's, with the important exception that the Earth's axis leans to one side.

As the Earth orbits the sun, the slant of the axis exposes one hemisphere to more direct rays from the sun during half the year than during

The Weddell seal is believed to dive to depths greater than any other seal or sea lion. These animals have been known to reach depths of more than 1,600 feet (500 m) and stay underwater for an hour or more.

The longest migration of any mammal is by the Alaska seal, which does a round trip of 6,000 miles (9,600 km) from its breeding grounds on the Pribilof Islands in the Bering Sea to as far south as California.

▲ *The same scene in different seasons. This is near Lake Geneva, Wisconsin.*

▼ *Although not to scale, this diagram illustrates how the Earth's orbit around the sun produces the changing seasons in the northern and southern hemispheres.*

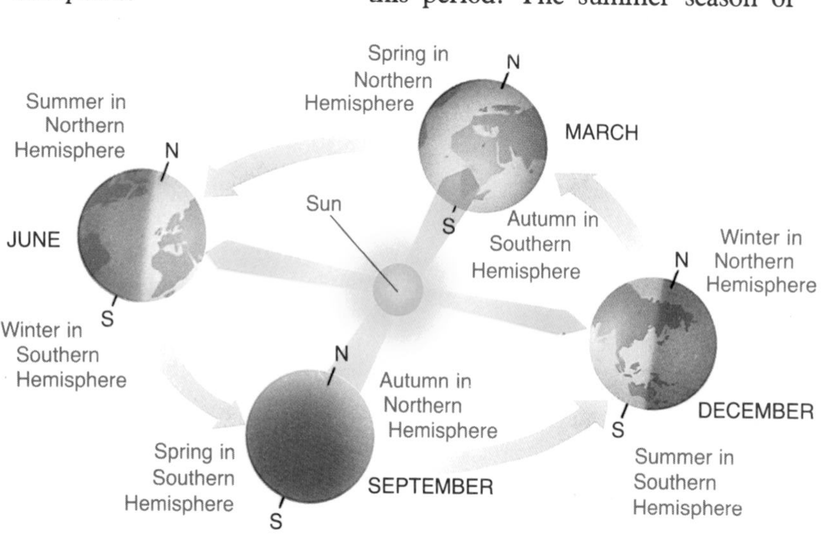

the other. The direct rays of the sun make that hemisphere warmer, so it is summertime there. As the Earth spins every 24 hours on its axis, that hemisphere also has more hours of daylight because it is tipped toward the sun. When it is summer in the Northern Hemisphere, it is winter in the Southern Hemisphere. The South Pole is then tilted away from the sun because of the tilt of the Earth's axis. The entire Southern Hemisphere receives rays from the sun at a slanting angle, so it experiences winter. As the Earth progresses in its orbit around the sun, the Southern Hemisphere comes into the position to receive direct rays, and the Northern Hemisphere receives the slanting rays. The seasons are then reversed.

Since the Earth's orbit of the sun is very gradual, the seasons change gradually. The months during which the weather gets warmer are called spring. The months during which the weather gets colder are called autumn.

The day of longest daylight (called the *summer solstice*) in the Northern Hemisphere is about June 21. That is the day of least daylight in the Southern Hemisphere. The North Pole is light all day and night around this time, because the tilt of the Earth's axis exposes the North Pole to sunlight for a full 24-hour period. The South Pole is completely dark during this period. The summer season of the Northern Hemisphere changes to autumn and finally to winter. The "shortest day of the year" or the day of least daylight (called the *winter solstice*) for the Northern Hemisphere is about December 21. In the Southern Hemisphere, the wintry climate has changed to spring and then to summer, so December 21 is the "longest day of the year." There are two days during the year when the lengths of day and night are about equal—the *vernal* (spring) *equinox* and the *autumnal equinox*.

One region of the Earth, however, has no change of seasons. That is the region close to the equator, where the sun's direct rays make it hot all year round. At the equator, day and night are always nearly equal.

ALSO READ: AUTUMN, CALENDAR, EQUATOR, NORTH POLE, ORBIT, SPRING, SUMMER, WINTER.

SEA WALNUT see COMB-JELLY.

SEAWEED see ALGAE.

SEEDS AND FRUIT Many of the plant foods we eat are seeds or fruits. Peas, beans, and lentils are useful seeds. Apples, pears, grapes, and cherries are popular fleshy fruits; wheat, barley, and other grains are important dry fruits. Some things we use as vegetables—tomatoes, squash, and peppers—are fruits. In a plant, seeds and fruits are a way of producing new plants.

A plant seed results from the fertilization of an egg cell by a sperm. The fertilized egg develops into an *embryo*. The embryo has the beginnings of the root, stem, and leaves of a fully grown plant. It also has a food supply called the *endosperm*. In many plants, the endosperm is largely used up in the growth of the one or two *cotyledons*, or seed leaves. In these plants the cotyledon carries most of the food. The embryo and its food supply are encased in a protective seed coat, or *testa*.

Some fruits and seeds have hooks or burrs that catch in the hair or skin of animals. The animals brush them off in distant places. Dandelion seeds have tiny parachutes, and the fruits of ashes and sycamores look like small wings. They can float on the wind for miles. Many seeds may also be carried by water.

When a seed falls on moist ground and the temperature is right, the seed will eventually sprout, or *germinate*. Warmer temperatures will often make the seed germinate more quickly, but too much heat will kill it. First, the root pokes its way through the testa and begins to grow downward. Then the first stem and the first leaves push through the soil into the air. In some plants, the cotyledons become the first leaves. In other plants, they stay underground and supply food.

■ LEARN BY DOING

You can watch a plant germinate step by step. Put some sand or sawdust at least an inch (2.5 cm) deep into a large flowerpot or box. Put about 12 beans into the box and cover them with a quarter-inch (about 0.5 cm) of sand or sawdust. Water the bean seeds and keep them moist—not soaking wet. Each day take out one seed and note how the roots grow and how the leaves begin to sprout. This is germination in action. ■

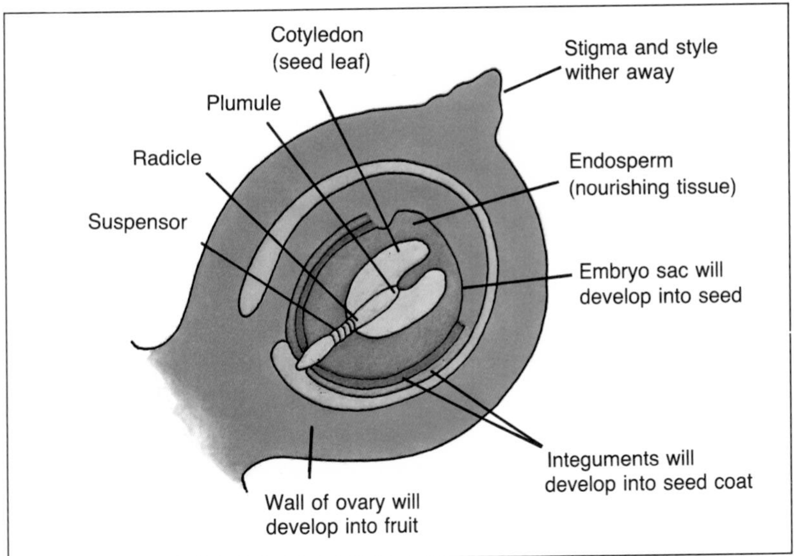

▲ *A simplified diagram of a seed forming in one of the carpels inside an ovary. You can see the miniature plant developing in the middle. It has a shoot* (plumule), *a root* (radicle), *and two seed leaves, called* cotyledons. *The cotyledons contain enough food to feed the plant until it can make its own food.*

Fruits Fruits grow only on flowering plants. A fruit is the ripened ovary of a plant, but sometimes it includes other parts of the flower, too. The fruit holds and protects the seeds and helps distribute them.

Look at an apple. On the side opposite the stem you will see the remains of the apple blossom. Split the apple in half, cutting from top to bottom. The seeds are almost in the center. The fleshy part that you eat not only protects the seeds but helps to distribute them. Animals eat the fruit and seeds. The seeds pass through their bodies undigested and are dropped in various places.

Fruits may be divided into two groups—*dry* fruits and *fleshy* fruits. Dry fruits include nuts and grains. Some dry fruits are only a seed with an outer coat formed from an ovary. Fleshy fruits include *pomes* (having a central seed-bearing *core*), such as ap-

▼ *Various types of seeds and fruits.*

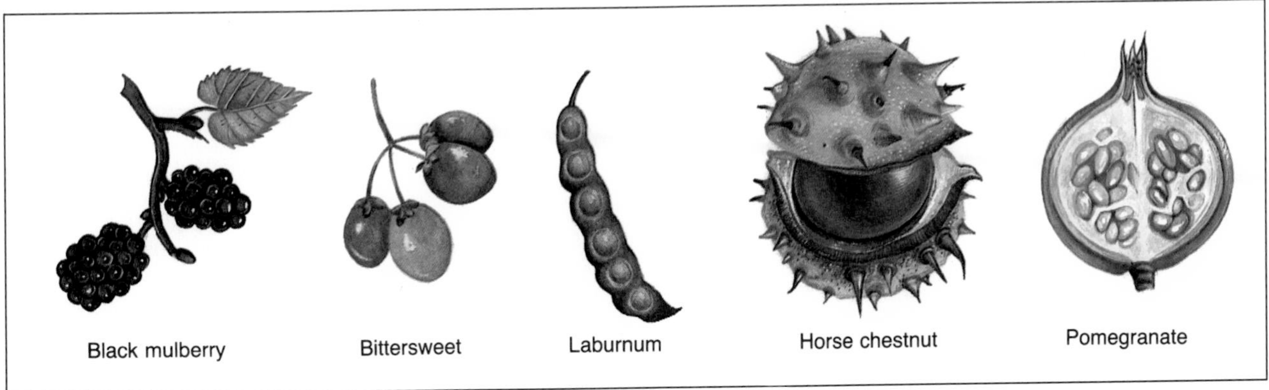

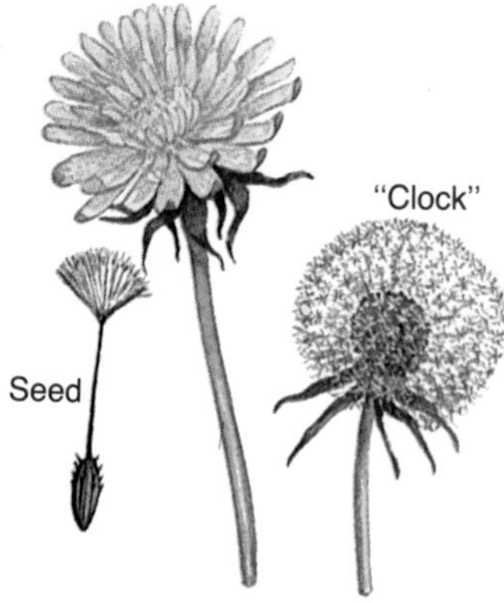

▲ *You have almost certainly seen the way the dandelion sends out its seeds!*

ples and pears; *drupes* (having a central *stone* or *pit* containing one seed), such as peaches and cherries; and *berries* (having seeds scattered in the flesh). Some fruits that are called "berries," such as raspberries and blackberries, are really many small drupes joined together.

People have been eating fruit since before history began. Fruit is mentioned in the first chapter of *Genesis*. All over the world all kinds of fruits are eaten raw, cooked, dried, canned, pickled, and preserved.

ALSO READ: FLOWER, FRUIT, PLANT, PLANT PRODUCTS, REPRODUCTION.

The world's biggest seed is a type of coconut that grows in the Seychelles in the Indian Ocean. Each single-seeded fruit can weigh as much as 40 pounds (18 kg).

SEISMOLOGY see EARTHQUAKE.

SELLING

SELLING Selling is the process of persuading people to buy something—either goods (manufactured or agricultural) or services. Just as people offer oranges or bicycles for sale, business people and technicians (such as plumbers and TV repairers) offer their services for sale. The business of selling forms a major part of any nation's economy, but especially that of the United States, with its emphasis on having more and newer things always available.

There are three major steps in getting goods from the manufacturer to the consumer. The manufacturer sells goods in large quantities to the *wholesaler*. The wholesaler sells smaller quantities to stores called *retailers*, which sell to individual customers. The wholesaler is sometimes called the "middleman," working between the manufacturer and the retailer. The manufacturer makes a profit in selling to the wholesaler. The wholesaler makes a profit by selling to the retailer. And the retailer makes a profit by selling to the consumer.

A producer, such as a farmer, might sell a corn crop to a company that will can or freeze the corn and sell it to grocery stores. The farmer is then like a manufacturer, the canning company and the wholesaler are middlemen, and the grocery store is the retailer. But the farmer might choose instead to sell the corn to individuals who stop at the farmer's roadside stand. In that case, the middlemen are eliminated and prices should be lower.

Selling is accomplished primarily through salespeople and through promotion, including advertising. Wholesale salespeople sell goods in large quantities, either to retail businesses or to other manufacturers who then use the goods in making other things. Retail salespeople usually work in stores, selling goods to customers. Door-to-door salespeople sometimes just show samples of their company's products, often cosmetic or housecleaning materials, and then take orders.

Wherever they work, salespeople try to persuade their customers that their products are the best to be had. Good salespersons must have several qualities to do this. They must know everything about the products—the advantages and disadvantages—and about competing products. They must also know what their customers are interested in and the things about their products the customers will find appealing.

Various official and voluntary orga-

▼ *Selling a second-hand automobile can be much harder than selling a brand new one. Although the model will be cheaper, the buyer is aware that more can go wrong with an older vehicle and so will be more wary of paying the asking price.*

nizations exist to promote *consumer protection*. They stop people from selling dangerous products, or products that are not as good as salespeople say they are. The U.S. Food and Drug Administration is one such official organization.

In the present century, distinctive packaging, brand names, and slogans have made consumers remember certain products. Marketing (selling) experts believe that the consumer is more likely to buy these products. Both goods and services are advertised on radio and television and in newspapers and magazines, all of which are largely supported by such advertising.

Whatever the product, the business of selling affects other kinds of businesses. Ships, airplanes, trains, and trucks carry goods to be made and sold. Factories make cartons, cans, and fancy packages to hold the goods that are later sold. Artists design labels, and printers print the labels. Clerks and other office workers must write letters and keep accounts. Practically all parts of the economic life of our country are affected by the sales of services and products.

ALSO READ: ADVERTISING, PUBLIC RELATIONS.

SEMICONDUCTOR

SEMICONDUCTOR Some materials, especially metals, are good *conductors* of electricity. Most other materials are *insulators*: they block an electric current. Semiconductors are materials that can change to allow different amounts of electric current to pass through them. These materials are very important in electronics. They are used to make electronic components in devices such as calculators, computers, television sets, and tape players.

Most semiconductors are made of crystals of silicon or germanium, with small amounts of other elements. These other elements change the way in which the semiconductor passes an electric current. The semiconductor can be made to pass low or high amounts of current, or to block a current. Through doing this, semiconductor components can produce and handle electric signals in electronic devices.

ALSO READ: ELECTRONICS, SILICON, TRANSISTOR.

▲ *In the making of semiconductors, the sausage-shaped block of silicon is sliced into wafers each holding 250 or more "chips."*

SEMINOLE INDIANS

SEMINOLE INDIANS This tribe's name means "runaway" in the Creek Indian language. The Seminoles were originally a racial mixture of several Indian tribes—including Creek—and of blacks from Africa.

At first, the Seminoles lived in Georgia and Alabama. But they moved to Florida in the 1700's. The Seminoles were prosperous farmers. They raised corn, beans, and squash and used runaway black slaves to work their fields. Adventurous Seminoles even sailed log canoes to Cuba and the Bahamas to trade.

The United States bought Florida from Spain in 1819. The U.S. government began to urge the Seminoles to move to what is now Oklahoma. Some Seminoles agreed to move. But other members of the tribe, led by a warrior named Osceola, began to fight to defend their land. They fought the U.S. Army from 1835 to 1842, until most of the Indians had been killed or forced to move. In 1837 Osceola was seized and imprisoned while having peace talks with U.S. officials. He died in 1838. A band of about 150 Seminoles managed to escape into the swampy Everglades in Florida. There they lived by hunting and fishing. They did not sign a peace treaty with the U.S. government until 1934.

About 1,500 Seminoles live on three reservations in Florida today. Some Seminoles earn a living by fishing, raising cattle, cutting lumber, or selling things to tourists. Others work in an electronics factory built on

▲ *Osceola, Chief of the Seminoles, stands before a group of Seminole dwellings. His father was an English trader, his mother a Cree Indian princess. Born about 1800, he died in 1838.*

▲ *A busy street scene in downtown Dakar, capital of Senegal.*

Seminole land. About 3,000 live on small farms in Oklahoma.

ALSO READ: FLORIDA; INDIANS, AMERICAN; INDIAN WARS.

SENATE see CONGRESS, UNITED STATES.

SENEGAL The Republic of Senegal lies on the westernmost portion of Africa, along the Atlantic coast. It is about the size of South Dakota. Guinea-Bissau and Guinea are to the south, and Mauritania and Mali to the north and east. Gambia is surrounded on three sides by Senegal.

The gleaming capital of Senegal is Dakar, one of the major ports of Africa. It is a true crossroads of the world, with an endless stream of ocean vessels from all countries sailing to and from its excellent harbor. The city is growing industrially. There is a modern airport, and the University of Dakar is renowned as an excellent center of learning. The people of Senegal wear both European and traditional African clothing.

Senegal is the world's top exporter of pet birds.

Peanuts are the country's chief crop and export. Millet, sorghum, cotton, and rice are other crops. Fishing is an important business. Phosphates, to be used in fertilizers, are the main mineral resource. Chemicals and cement are major industries.

Senegal was the first French colony in Africa. The Senegalese had representation in the French parliament as early as 1848. Full independence for Senegal came on June 20, 1960.

A number of states were founded here in medieval times by peoples who lived in the area, among them the Tukulor and the Wolof empires. The first European contact came in 1444 when the Portuguese reached Cape Verde. They later established trading stations along the Senegalese coast. In the 1600's, the French established settlements in Saint Louis. The British arrived in the 1750's and controlled some of the French parts until the French took over again in 1815.

Senegal's first president, Léopold Sédar Senghor, was one of the foremost intellectuals of Africa. A member of the Serer tribe, he was educated in France where he gained fame as a poet and teacher. Senghor resigned in 1981, and Abdou Diof became president. In 1982, Senegal and Gambia joined together in a confederation, called Senegambia.

ALSO READ: AFRICA, GAMBIA.

SENSE ORGAN Your senses are the way you learn about the world around you and about the state of your own body. The five *external* senses are sight, hearing, touch (including sensations of heat and cold), smell, and taste: these senses respond to outside stimuli. You have also *internal* senses: balance, hunger, thirst, muscle tension, and proprioception

SENEGAL

Capital City: Dakar (1,300,000 people).

Area: 75,750 square miles (196,192 sq. km).

Population: 7,700,000.

Government: Republic.

Natural Resources: Phosphates.

Export Products: Peanuts, fish, phosphates.

Unit of Money: Franc of the African Financial Community.

Official Language: French.

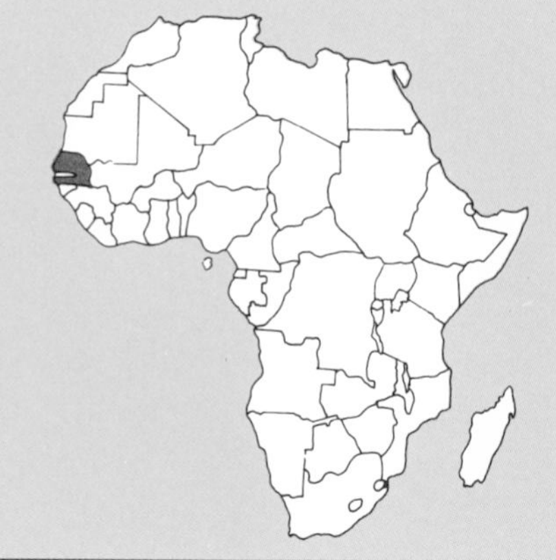

(the sense of how your bodily parts, such as limbs, are positioned at any particular moment).

For each external sense there is a sense organ that receives certain stimuli. The sense organ turns the stimulus into a nerve impulse, which it sends to the brain. Eyes, the organs of *sight*, receive light stimuli. Ears, the organs of *hearing*, receive sound; the inner ears contain also the mechanism responsible for *balance*, an internal sense. *Touch* and knowledge of *heat and cold* depend on nerve endings in the skin and in the linings (mucous membranes) of the mouth, nose, and so on. No one knows how the olfactory organ in the upper part of the nose enables you to *smell* things. *Taste*, a sense closely allied to smell, depends on sense organs, called taste buds, in your tongue.

Internal senses are usually more generalized. For example, many things tell you when you are hungry.

ALSO READ: BRAIN, EAR, EYE, NERVOUS SYSTEM, NOSE, SKIN, SMELL, TASTE, TOUCH.

SEPTEMBER The month of September has 30 days. It is the ninth month of our year. The word September comes from *septem*, the Latin word for seven. Long ago, people used a different calendar, and September was the seventh month in the year. In 153 B.C., the Romans changed the months of the calendar around. They made September the ninth month, but they did not change its name.

In the northern part of the world, September is an in-between time. Summer ends and autumn begins on the autumnal equinox, which falls between September 21 and 23. But sometimes the weather in September can surprise us by being as fine as any during the summer. In the southern part of the world, springtime begins in September.

DATES OF SPECIAL EVENTS IN SEPTEMBER

1 • Canadian provinces of Alberta and Saskatchewan were formed (1905).
• Germany invaded Poland, touching off World War II in Europe (1939).
2 • Great Fire of London began (1666). It lasted nearly a week and destroyed much of the city.
• United States Department of the Treasury was formed (1789).
• Japan surrendered to the United States on V-J Day, formally ending World War II (1945).
3 • Treaty of Paris was signed by Britain, ending the American Revolution (1783).
• Labor Day was first observed as a legal public holiday (1894).*
5 • First Continental Congress assembled in Philadelphia (1774).
• Jesse James, U.S. outlaw, was born (1847).
6 • President William McKinley was shot by Leon Czolgosz. The President died eight days later (1901).
7 • Brazil proclaimed its independence from Portugal (1822).
8 • St. Augustine, Florida, was founded, the earliest lasting European settlement in territory that was later added to the United States (1565).
• Senator Huey Long of Louisiana was assassinated (1935).
9 • California admitted to the Union (1850).
10 • Oliver Hazard Perry won a great naval victory over the British on Lake Erie (1813).
12 • Henry Hudson explored the river later named for him (1609).
• First rocket to the moon was launched by the Soviet Union (1959).
14 • "The Star-Spangled Banner" was composed by Francis Scott Key during a British attack on Fort McHenry (1814).
15 • President William Howard Taft was born (1857).
• Tanks first used in warfare by the British in World War I (1916).
16 • The *Mayflower* sailed from England (1620).
• First U.S. military draft in peacetime began (1940).
17 • United States Constitution was signed (1787).
• Citizenship Day honors native-born U.S. citizens and foreign-born immigrants who have become U.S. citizens.
18 • Quebec surrendered to the British (1759).
• Chile proclaimed its independence from Spain (1810).
• *The New York Times*, an important newspaper, printed its first edition (1851).
19 • Battle of Saratoga began. The British were defeated (1777).
• President James Garfield died from an assassin's bullet (1881).
20 • Robert Emmet, Irish patriot, was executed by the British on grounds of treason (1803).
22 • Nathan Hale, U.S. patriot, was executed by the British for spying during the American Revolution (1776).
• President Abraham Lincoln proclaimed the preliminary Emancipation Proclamation (1862).
23 • The *Bonhomme Richard*, commanded by John Paul Jones, defeated the *Serapis*, a British ship, during the American Revolution (1779).
25 • Christopher Columbus set sail on his second voyage to the Americas (1493).
• Pacific Ocean discovered by Vasco Núñez de Balboa (1513).
28 • William the Conqueror landed in England, beginning the Norman conquest of that country (1066).
29 • Michaelmas, a Christian holiday honoring Saint Michael the archangel. In Europe, people sometimes celebrate with a hearty meal of roast goose. An old English proverb says,
"If you eat goose on Michaelmas Day, you will never want money all the year round."
30 • Blockade of Berlin by USSR ended after successful counter-blockade airlifts by U.S. and British planes (1948).

* It is now celebrated on the first Monday of the month.

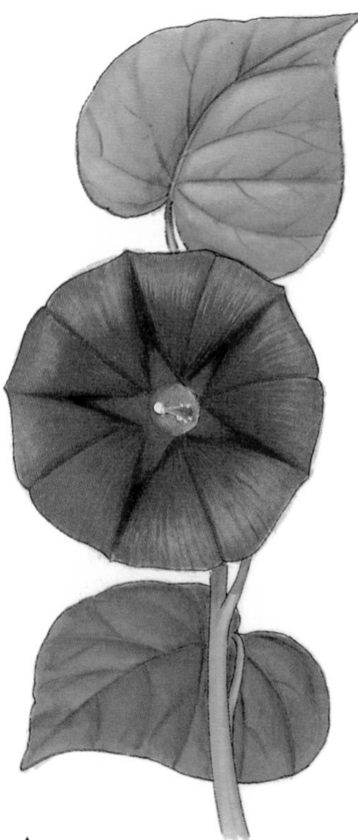

▲ *Morning glory, September's flower, is a flowering vine widely grown in North America. At night its blossom closes up.*

▲ *Sequoya holding a copy of the alphabet he invented. The alphabet had symbols for the 85 sounds that make up the Cherokee language.*

The first full month of school is September. Flower gardens are still in bloom, especially with the soft white and purple of asters. The aster, or morning glory, is September's special flower. September is harvest time. Its birthstone is the sapphire.

Labor Day is September's major holiday in the United States. Several Jewish holidays, including the Jewish New Year, Rosh Hashanah, and the Day of Atonement (Yom Kippur), usually come in September.

ALSO READ: CALENDAR, HOLIDAY.

SEQUOYA (about 1770–1843) Sequoya, or Sequoyah, was a Cherokee Indian who invented an alphabet that enabled his people to read and write their own language.

Sequoya was born in Loudon County, Tennessee, the son of an Indian mother and a white father. His father's name was believed to be Gist, and Sequoya was also called George Gist, or Guess. Sequoya was at first a hunter, but he was crippled in a hunting accident. He then became a silversmith and trader. Sequoya had no education, but he knew that reading and writing were important. He began to work in the evenings on an alphabet for the Cherokee language. In 1823, after 12 years of work, his alphabet was ready. Sequoya's alphabet consisted of symbols for 85 sounds that make up the Cherokee language.

Within a few months, several thousand Cherokees learned to read and write using the new alphabet. They could write to friends and relatives. They could also write poetry. Soon a Cherokee newspaper called the *Phoenix* was being published. Its columns carried news in both English and Cherokee. Using their new alphabet, the Cherokees adopted a written constitution and organized a legislature.

Sequoya became a teacher. He moved to Arkansas and later to Oklahoma where he continued to teach the Cherokee alphabet. The huge sequoia trees that grow in California are named in his honor.

ALSO READ: INDIANS, AMERICAN.

SET The idea of a set has been borrowed from everyday life. For example, we speak of all the raisins in a box, all the pages in a book, or all the cars in a parking lot. When we use the phrase, "all the cars in the parking lot," we mean that those cars, all together, form a set, or collection, of cars, distinct from the set of all the cars that are *not* in that parking lot.

This is what the mathematicians mean by the word "set." For example, if they said, "The set of whole numbers from 4 to 8," they would mean exactly the numbers 4, 5, 6, 7, and 8. A short way of saying "the set of" is to use brackets like this: { }. Written this way, the set would be: {4, 5, 6, 7, 8}.

The members of a set are called *elements*. In the examples above, cars are the elements of one of the sets, and numbers are the elements of the other. Almost anything can be an element of a set. In mathematics, one could have a set with points as elements (a set of points) or a set with triangles as elements (a set of triangles) or even a set with sets as elements (a set of sets).

A set can contain any number of elements. A *finite* set contains a limited number of elements. An *infinite* set contains a limitless number of elements (for example, the set of all whole numbers). An *empty* set contains no elements. *Equivalent* sets contain exactly the same elements. *Overlapping* sets contain some of the same elements.

Usually, a set has a rule so that we can tell if something is in the set, or not. In the first example, the rule is "cars in the parking lot." The set excludes cars that are not in the parking lot, and people or things that are in the lot but are not cars. What was the rule for {4, 5, 6, 7, 8}? Why isn't 2 in the set? Can you give a rule for {2, 4, 6, 8, 10}?

ALSO READ: ALGEBRA, ARITHMETIC, MATHEMATICS, NUMBER.

SEVEN WONDERS OF THE WORLD The ancient Greeks and Romans often made lists of the greatest man-made works. The works most often mentioned are known as the Seven Wonders of the World.

Of these seven ancient wonders, only the *Pyramids of Egypt* survive today. They were built around 2500 B.C. as tombs for the Egyptian pharaohs (kings). The pyramids were made of huge blocks of stone and sloped upwards to a point at the top.

The Hanging Gardens of Babylon are thought to have been built by King Nebuchadnezzar II. Scholars believe he designed them in the 500's B.C. to please his best-loved wife. The gardens were planted on terraces laid over arches and seemed to hang in the air.

The Temple of Artemis at Ephesus was built by Greek settlers in Asia Minor (now Turkey). Artemis was the Greek goddess of the moon and the hunt. The temple was carved from white marble. It had over 100 columns, each 40 feet (12.2 m) high. The temple took 120 years to build and was completed around 430 B.C. It was destroyed in 356 B.C.

The Statue of Zeus at Olympia, Greece, was made around 430 B.C. Zeus was leader of the Greek gods. The majestic statue was made of gold and ivory, and stood 40 feet (12.2 m) high. It was carved by the Greek sculptor, Phidias. The statue disappeared long ago, but pictures of it can still be seen on ancient coins.

The Mausoleum at Halicarnassus was an enormous tomb. Mausolus was king of an ancient land called

SEVEN WONDERS KNOWN IN THE MIDDLE AGES

1. The Colosseum in Rome, a huge amphitheater built during the Roman Empire.
2. The Catacombs of Alexandria, a series of underground chambers and tunnels where early Christians escaped persecution.
3. The Great Wall of China, a huge, fortified structure built to keep out invaders. It took more than 1,000 years to complete.
4. The ruins of Stonehenge in England, a series of huge stone slabs built in prehistoric times.
5. The Leaning Tower of Pisa, a leaning bell tower completed in the 1300's in the city of Pisa, Italy.
6. The Porcelain Tower of Nanking in China. It was built in the 1400's but was destroyed in 1853.
7. The Mosque of Saint Sophia at Constantinople (now Istanbul) in Turkey. It was completed in A.D. 548 as a Christian church. It later became a Muslim mosque, and is now a museum.

SEVEN NATURAL WONDERS OF THE WORLD

1 Mount Everest on the Nepalese-Tibetan border.
2 Victoria Falls on the Zimbabwean-Zambian border.
3 Grand Canyon of the Colorado River in Arizona.
4 Great Barrier Reef of Australia, the largest coral reef in the world.
5 Mauna Loa, the world's largest active volcano, in Hawaii.
6 Rainbow Natural Bridge in Utah, the largest in the world.
7 Yellowstone National Park, the world's largest geyser area.

Today's sewing machines use more than 2,000 different techniques for different operations. Some of the processes have been automated so that several different sewing operations are performed at the same time.

Caria (now part of Turkey). After his death in 353 B.C., his widow ordered the magnificent tomb to be built. A pyramid supported by columns was built above the tomb chamber. On the very top was a statue of a chariot with four horses. The word "mausoleum" is used today to mean any large tomb.

The Colossus of Rhodes was an enormous bronze statue. It loomed over 100 feet (30.5 m) high at the entrance to the harbor of Rhodes, a Greek island. It was built in the early 200's B.C. but collapsed during an earthquake in 224 B.C. Ships were said to have sailed between the legs of the statue.

The Pharos, or *Lighthouse, at Alexandria*, Egypt, was built about 270 B.C. It was more than 400 feet (122 m) high and was made of marble. A fire in the lighthouse guided ships into Alexandria's harbor. It was destroyed by an earthquake in 1375.

ALSO READ: PYRAMID.

SEWAGE see SANITATION.

SEWING People have been sewing clothes ever since they first learned to fasten two animal skins together. Today, sewing is both an art and a craft. Beautiful, complex designs in embroidery and tapestry are shown in galleries, along with paintings and sculpture. Useful sewing can clothe, decorate, shelter, and protect. People sew things of leather and plastic, as well as fabric. Upholstered furniture, many book bindings, baseballs, and, of course, clothing are sewn.

Most sewing today is done by factory machines. Commercial sewing machines can perform many different tasks, such as sewing on buttons and making invisible hems. Many modern home sewing machines can do these things too. You can make buttonholes, long and short stitches, and trimmings just by changing a small part. Your machine may also be able to make embroidered decorations.

Anyone can learn to use a sewing machine. Most schools teach sewing in home economics classes. Stores that sell sewing machines give lessons for a small fee. But a beginner can just as easily learn from a friend who sews.

Hand Stitching Every person should know how to sew by hand before trying to make a garment by machine. Even the simplest skirt or vest requires some hand sewing. The most common hand stitches are the basting stitch, running stitch, backstitch, and hemming stitch.

The *basting stitch* is used to make a temporary seam, often to make fitting the garment easier. Basting simply consists of long stitches.

The *running stitch* is used for making gathers and tucks. To make this stitch, take several tiny stitches on the needle at once and pull through.

The *backstitch* is the strongest hand stitch. It is used for making permanent seams by hand—perhaps for mending when you do not want to use a machine. To make the backstitch, take one small stitch forward and then one backward, part of the length of the first stitch.

The *hemming stitch* is used, of course, for making hems—stitching the material that has been turned up at the bottom of a garment. Hemming consists of tiny, slanted stitches about one-half inch (about 1 cm) apart. Each stitch pierces a few threads of the inner side of the body of the garment and a few threads of the fold or the seam binding stitched over the fold.

Buying a Pattern and Fabric Before you begin sewing, you must buy a pattern and fabric for the garment you want to make. Fabric stores and the dry-goods sections of department stores sell patterns, fabrics, threads, zippers, seam tape, and whatever else you may need for sewing. There are patterns for all kinds of clothing in the latest fashions. Most pattern companies sell easy patterns with only a few pieces for beginners. You can look through the catalogs and find a becoming style. Simple styles are best to begin with.

You will have a wide variety of fabrics to choose from. Cotton, wool, and silk are available at department stores. The textile industry now produces synthetic (man-made) fabrics that are attractive, wrinkle-free, and washable. The variety of fabrics often puzzles the beginner, but a salesperson can help find the appropriate fabric for a certain pattern. Beginners usually find it easier to sew with fabrics that combine cotton with a synthetic fiber.

Pattern makers solve problems about how much fabric to buy by listing the yardage needed for the width of the fabric. Most fabric comes in a width of 36, 45, 54, or 60 inches. Once you know the width of the fabric you are buying, you can find the yardage (length) of fabric needed by looking at the pattern envelope. The envelope also lists other things needed, such as buttons, thread, zipper, and seam binding. These things can be color-matched.

CUTTING. It is tempting to start cutting new fabric immediately. But the beginner is wiser to read the pattern's guide sheet first. The yardage estimates were based on the manufacturer's cutting diagrams, which vary with the width of fabric. Unless the pieces are cut as the manufacturer suggests, you may not have enough material for all the pattern pieces. Circle the cutting diagram for your size and fabric width. This will help you find the proper diagram quickly while you are pinning the pieces. Those pattern pieces that are shaded (darker) in the diagram must be placed face down on the fabric. Be sure the arrows printed on the paper pattern run *with the grain*. That means they should follow the woven threads down the length of the fabric.

Cut all notches as they are shown on the pattern. They will guide the joining of major pattern pieces. Mark all darts, slashes, centers, and dots on the fabric. These show where special steps will be necessary. You may mark with tailor's chalk or with a tracing wheel and carbon paper. These are sold at fabric stores and dime stores.

SEWING. When all pieces are marked, the pattern's illustrated, step-by-step instructions become your guide. If you are a beginner, you may have trouble if you fail to follow this guide.

You should press each seam and dart as soon as you have sewn it. This is easy to do if the ironing board is near the sewing machine. A dress made with this iron-as-you-go method looks more attractive and fits better.

▲ *Detail of a beautiful embroidery supposed to have been sewed by Mary, Queen of Scots. It shows the thistle and the rose.*

▼ *Inside a vast textile factory in Israel, where the workers are busy sewing clothes.*

▲ *An early version of one of the sewing machines invented by Isaac Singer.*

▲ *One of the first sewing machines, developed by Elias Howe. It was because of a dream that he realized sewing machines could be much more efficient if the hole were near the point of the needle, not the other end.*

Fitting and Finishing Experienced sewers can fit clothes on themselves, but beginners should get help. Fitting should be done when the body of the garment is joined, but before facings and sleeves are added. Changes made at this time should require little ripping or resewing.

Even with modern sewing machines, most clothing construction ends with hand finishing. Facings at necklines must be *tacked*, or fastened with small stitches, in shoulder seams or at back zippers. Hooks and eyes and snaps usually must be added by hand. Most people prefer doing buttons and hems by hand.

Once you have mastered the principles of sewing, you will want to try more complicated garments. You also can buy precut outfits to sew. By using these, you can learn more about sewing seams before you go on to learn how to cut and fit pattern pieces.

ALSO READ: NEEDLEWORK, PIN, SEWING MACHINE.

SEWING MACHINE Sewing machines are designed to stitch together pieces of fabric, leather, or other materials. They are very popular home appliances, and they are widely used in many kinds of industries.

Early machines sewed chain stitches, a series of stitches made with one thread. Some commercial models still make this stitch. Most modern machines use two threads to make the lockstitch. In this type of stitching, the top thread goes through the fabric and catches on a hook below. The hook twists the top and bobbin (lower) threads together. This lockstitch holds tightly and makes a strong seam. Commercial and home sewing machines make this stitch. Slant-needle models and "zigzag" machines do several other kinds of stitching as well.

The earliest sewing machines were used in industry. Crude machines for sewing heavy materials were patented by a British inventor, Thomas Saint, in 1790 and by a French tailor, Barthélemy Thimmonnier, in 1830. In the United States, two inventors, Walter Hunt in 1832 and Elias Howe in 1846, built lockstitch machines. Howe made the breakthrough of putting the eye (the opening for the thread) at the pointed end of the needle, a feature now used in all sewing machines. In 1850, Allen B. Wilson found a way to feed fabric automatically through the machine. The earliest models were powered by hand-turned wheels located on the side of the machine. In 1851, Isaac Singer invented the treadle machine, which was foot-powered by a wide, pedal-like device (the treadle) beneath the machine. Singer also invented the presser foot, a flat piece of metal that holds the fabric in place under the needle. Soon Singer's machines were to be found in nearly every U.S. home.

By 1900, nearly all the principles used in present-day sewing machines had been invented. As electricity came into everyday use, other people built small motors for sewing machines. Today, most sewing machines run on electric power. In these, the treadle has been replaced with a foot-operated switch or a knee-operated lever. Many machines can be programmed to do fancy stitches automatically.

Special kinds of commercial sewing machines are used in manufacturing. These machines sew clothing, tents, awnings, leather goods and furs.

ALSO READ: ELECTRIC APPLIANCE, INVENTION, SEWING.

SEX see REPRODUCTION.

SEYCHELLES The island nation of the Seychelles, correctly known as the Republic of Seychelles, lies about

SEYCHELLES

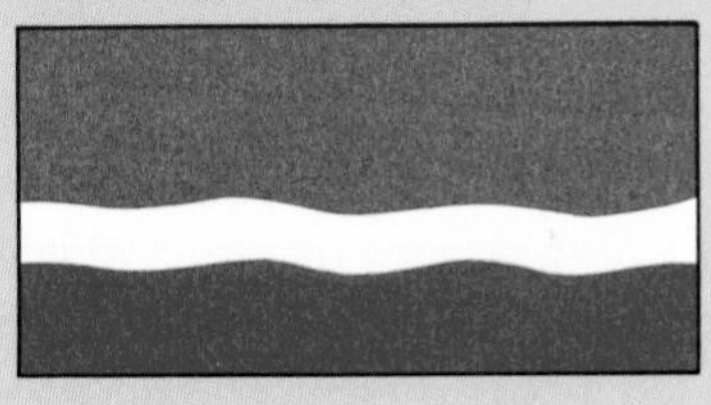

Capital City: Victoria (23,000 people).
Area: 108 square miles (280 sq. km).
Population: 68,000.
Government: One-party republic.
Natural Resources: No commercial mineral reserves.
Export Products: Copra, fish, cinnamon.
Unit of Money: Rupee.
Official Languages: Creole, English, French.

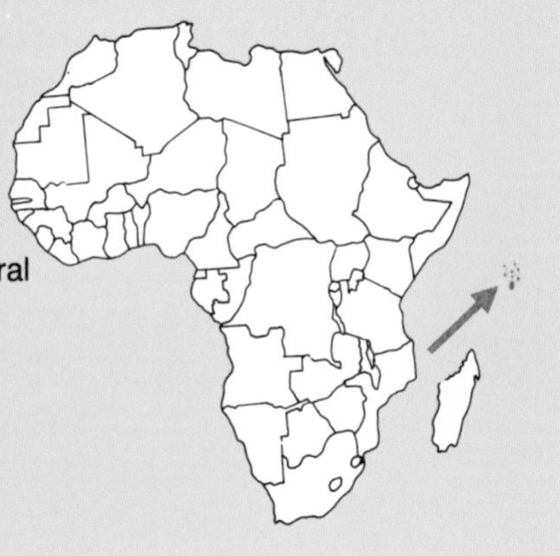

1,000 miles (1,600 km) off the east coast of Africa in the Indian Ocean. It is made up of 87 scattered islands. Victoria, the capital, lies on Mahé, the largest island. Other important islands are La Digue, Praslin, and Silhouette.

The islands were colonized by the French in 1768 but seized by the British in 1794. The Treaty of Paris in 1814 ceded them to Britain, which ruled them for 162 years. In 1976, the Seychelles were granted independence.

The country has volcanic mountains, sweeping sandy beaches, and coconut-palm plantations. Tourism is a major business. Many Europeans and others are attracted by the beautiful scenery and warm climate. Most of the inhabitants of the Seychelles are of mixed African and European ancestry. They speak Creole (a French dialect) and English. Copra (dried coconut meat), cinnamon, and vanilla are important products. Fishing helps support the large population of the Seychelles.

ALSO READ: AFRICA.

SHAKESPEARE, WILLIAM

(1564–1616) Scholars and writers have called William Shakespeare the greatest dramatist of all time. People all over the world have read his plays in their own languages or seen them performed. Two famous annual festivals at Stratford, England and Stratford, Canada feature his plays.

Shakespeare's Life William Shakespeare was born in the English town of Stratford-upon-Avon, and baptized there a few days later, on April 26, 1564. His father, John Shakespeare, was a tradesman. William was probably educated at Stratford grammar school. In 1582, at age 18, Shakespeare married Anne Hathaway, who was eight years older. They had three children, Susanna and the twins Hamnet and Judith. Little more is known about Shakespeare's life until he was about 28 years old. He was then in London, working as an actor and writing plays. Actors in Shakespeare's time usually worked together in a group, or *company*. The company often owned a theater, where they produced most of their plays. Sometimes, one of the actors would write new plays for his company to perform. Shakespeare worked for most of his life with a company called the Lord Chamberlain's Men (later the King's Men).

In 1599, Shakespeare and his company started their own theater, the Globe, just outside London. There were no actresses at that time. Men played all the women's parts. By 1598, Shakespeare had become a very popular actor, and the plays he wrote were extremely successful. Shakespeare spent his last years in Stratford, where he is buried. In the parish church, his death is recorded as being on April 23, 1616.

It has been estimated that Shakespeare made about $12 from writing each of his 37 plays. It is unfortunate that the world's greatest playwright didn't leave us one word about himself.

Scholars have calculated that William Shakespeare had a vocabulary of about 32,000 words.

▲ *The English playwright and actor, William Shakespeare.*

▲ *The house where Shakespeare was born is a popular tourist attraction in Stratford-upon-Avon, in England.*

▲ *A monument in Stratford-upon-Avon honors its most famous resident, William Shakespeare.*

William Shakespeare's *Hamlet* is his longest play, with nearly 30,000 words. The play also has Shakespeare's longest speaking part—by Hamlet himself.

Shakespeare's England In the busy city of London, Shakespeare was at the very center of events in England. He lived during one of the most exciting times in English history. Explorers were returning from far-off lands with fascinating stories. Writers were creating brilliant works of literature. Shakespeare knew many of the famous people of his time. His company acted more than once at the palace of the magnificent and powerful English queen, Elizabeth I, and later for her successor, James I. Shakespeare put all the sights, characters, and activities that surrounded him into his plays—Elizabethan England seems to come alive in them.

The Works of Shakespeare Shakespeare wrote 36 plays and collaborated with John Fletcher (1579–1625) on two others. His plays are usually divided into three basic types—histories, tragedies (sad plays), and comedies. Many of the people in Shakespeare's plays are completely human and believable. The characters in his historical plays may actually be quite different from the men and women they represent, but they are realistic, believable characters, and their motives and actions are understandable to readers and audiences. When people think of figures such as King Henry V, King Richard III, or Julius Caesar, it is usually Shakespeare's characters that they remember.

Shakespeare's tragedies—more than any of his other plays—show his deep understanding of human nature. The brilliant and moody prince in *Hamlet* is such a complicated character that no one completely understands him—but this only makes him more real. Some of Shakespeare's tragedies are about great and noble people who are destroyed by one weakness or flaw in their character. The Scottish nobleman in *Macbeth* is doomed by his own ambition. The old king in *King Lear* is destroyed by his love of flattery. Shakespeare's tragic play, *Romeo and Juliet*, tells how innocent people are destroyed by the pride and intolerance of others.

Some of Shakespeare's comedies are lively and romantic. *A Midsummer Night's Dream* takes us into a magical world of fairies—an enchanted world in which a fairy queen can fall in love with a comical craftsman with a donkey's head. Other comedies make fun of people's faults and stupidities. For example, in *Twelfth Night*, the conceited steward Malvolio is brought low by his own vanity.

Shakespeare Today Shakespeare's plays are still popular because his characters have human passions and weaknesses that are common to all of us. We can all find something of ourselves in his plays. Many of the events in his plays are the same tragic and comic situations that people are still living through today.

Another reason for Shakespeare's reputation is the language of his plays. His characters speak words that seem as sincere and beautiful to us as they must have seemed to Elizabethan audiences. The sonnets (14-line poems) that Shakespeare wrote contain some of the most beautiful poetry in the English language. Shakespeare's poetry, in both his plays and his sonnets, is so powerful that many people today—centuries after it was written—consider it the best in the English language. As Shakespeare wrote in one of the sonnets,

Not marble, nor the gilded monuments
Of princes, shall outlive this powerful rhyme.

ALSO READ: ACTORS AND ACTING, DRAMA, ELIZABETH I, ENGLISH HISTORY, ENGLISH LANGUAGE, THEATER.

SHANGHAI Shanghai is the major seaport of China and the largest city in that country. About 11 million people live in Shanghai. The city lies a short distance from the China Sea near the mouth of the Yangtze River in central China. Its location makes it both an ocean and a river port.

Shanghai was founded 800 years ago, but really began to grow in the 1840's. China had been opposed to foreign trade, but in 1842 the United States and European powers insisted that Shanghai and other ports be opened to foreign settlement and commerce. Much of the modern business area along the waterfront was built under British and U.S. direction in an area for foreign residents called the "International Settlement."

Shanghai was occupied by the Japanese during World War II. When the Chinese regained the city, they ended foreign control. Communist Chinese captured Shanghai in 1949 and drove out almost all the remaining foreign residents.

Shanghai is a center for education, art, and culture in China. The city is a fascinating mixture of modern Western-style office buildings and old-fashioned huts and homes, of large, busy factories and tiny, makeshift family workshops. Once mainly textiles were made here, but now Shanghai has steel mills, chemical plants, and other heavy industry. Raw materials for the factories come mostly from inland China.

ALSO READ: CHINA, YANGTZE RIVER.

SHARKS AND RAYS Sharks and rays are related. Both of these fish are *carnivores* (meat-eaters). They feed on fish and other sea animals, both large and small. Some are found in cold waters, but the largest number live in tropical seas.

Sharks and rays look and live much as their ancient ancestors did 140 million years ago. Over the years, although other fish developed bony skeletons, sharks and rays did not. Instead, they kept the tough *cartilage* skeleton that all fish once had. (The flexible part of your nose is of cartilage rather than bone.) As time passed, other fish developed *swim bladders*, which are sacs of air inside the body to help keep the fish afloat. Sharks and rays do not have swim bladders. If a shark stops swimming, it sinks. The skin of sharks and rays is rough like a file and has toothlike scales different from those of bony fish.

Many sharks are savage hunters and powerful and swift killers. Their sharp, pointed teeth can tear through skin and bone. In a second, a medium-sized shark can rip a bucket-sized hunk of flesh out of a big fish. However, certain kinds of sharks, including the enormous whale sharks and basking sharks, eat only tiny fish and plankton.

Sharks have sharp senses. They

▲ *A gray shark glides through the shallows on its long, outstretched pectoral fins.*

▼ *Not all sharks are huge or ferocious like the great white shark featured in the movie* Jaws *(1975). The humble dogfish is at most about 3 feet (90 cm) long, and harmless, as is the vast whale shark, up to about 60 feet (18.3 m) long.*

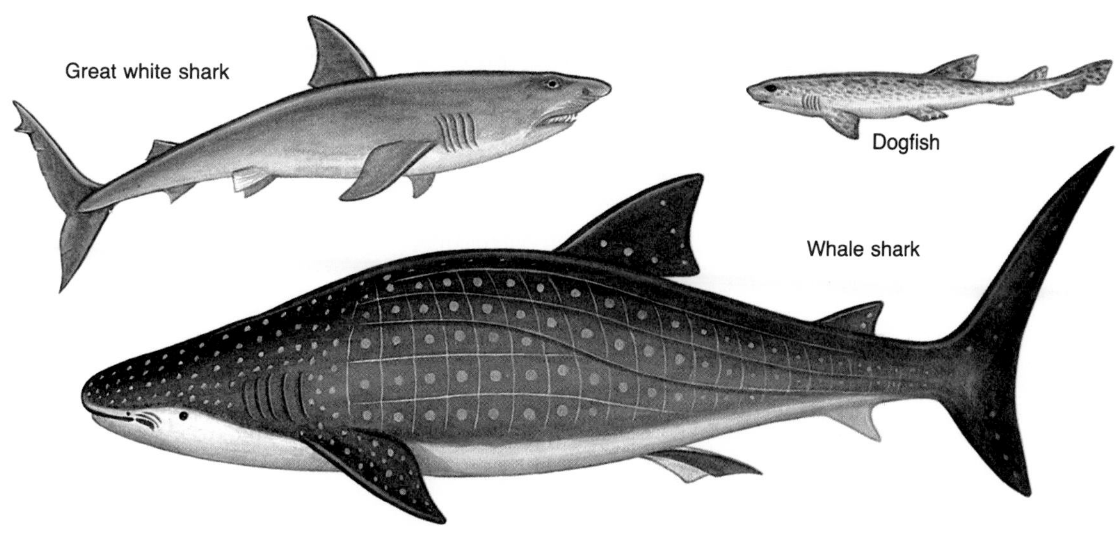

▲ *Rays are fishes closely related to the sharks.*

▲ *George Bernard Shaw, Irish-born dramatist and drama critic.*

can follow a smell across miles of ocean. They see well, even in dim light, although they cannot see colors. Like many fish, sharks also learn about their surroundings through a *lateral line*. The lateral line is made of special canals that run along the side of the body, under the skin, from head to tail. The lateral line senses pressure waves and vibrations in the water. For instance, a swimming fish makes tiny waves that are picked up by the shark's lateral line. The shark knows the fish is there, even if it cannot see, hear, or smell it.

There are about 250 different kinds, or species, of sharks in the world. The *Greenland shark* is found in glacier-cold waters of the north. The *whale shark* is the largest fish in the world. An average whale shark is 30 feet (9 m) long, but big ones may grow to be about 60 feet (18.5 m) long—the length of four average automobiles placed end to end. One of the smallest sharks is the three-foot-long (90-cm-long) *dogfish*. Some sharks live in deep water far out at sea. Others, like the *sand sharks*, usually live close to land. Most sharks give birth to live young, but some hatch from eggs.

How dangerous are sharks? Many underwater divers have worked in the midst of sharks without being attacked. However, many people have been attacked, wounded, and killed by sharks. Nobody ever knows what a shark will do; their behavior is unpredictable. The *great white shark*, or *man-eater*, is sometimes called the most dangerous shark. It may grow to be 35 feet (10.7 m) long. Even small sand sharks have attacked swimmers off beaches. Sharks circle their prey for a while before moving in to attack.

Rays look somewhat like flattened sharks. Their *pectoral fins*, or side fins, are especially large and shaped like pointed flaps, or wings. Most rays live in the ocean, usually close to the bottom or half-hidden in sand or mud. *Stingrays* have a long tail armed with spines. The whipping tail can give a painful sting. Some rays live in fresh water. Giant rays of the open ocean, such as the *manta ray*, can grow to be 22 feet (6.7 m) across and weigh over 3,000 pounds (1.36 metric tons). They look like huge bats flapping through the water. But they are harmless to human beings. They eat small kinds of animal life in the ocean. *Skates* are small rays that live in cooler parts of the ocean, usually clinging to the muddy bottom. They have no stinging spines.

ALSO READ: FISH, MARINE LIFE.

SHAW, GEORGE BERNARD

(1856–1950) The Irish writer George Bernard Shaw was the author of more than 50 plays.

Shaw was born in Dublin, Ireland, but he spent most of his life in London. Shaw was very concerned about the poverty and misery that he saw among most English working people. He helped to start a socialist club called the Fabian Society, organized by people who wanted to reform British society and government. Shaw criticized the British way of life in many of his plays. He had a biting sense of humor. His characters often make us see a particular subject in a way we had never thought of before.

Some of Shaw's most familiar plays are *Man and Superman* (1903), *Caesar and Cleopatra* (1901), *Saint Joan* (1924), *Major Barbara* (1905), *Androcles and the Lion* (1913), and *Pygmalion* (1913). In *Pygmalion*, a professor of speech turns an uneducated flower girl into a lady by teaching her to speak perfect English. It is a delightful story that makes fun of society's false values. The musical *My Fair Lady* (1956) was based loosely on *Pygmalion*. Shaw also wrote criticisms of plays, music, and art for various newspapers.

ALSO READ: DRAMA, LITERATURE.

▲ *Australian sheep account for nearly a third of all the wool produced in the world.*

SHEEP Sheep are among the oldest domesticated (tamed) animals. People have raised these four-footed mammals for food and clothing for thousands of years. Sheep have supplied meat, milk, and cheese. Both the skins of sheep and their fleeces (wool) are used for clothing. Sheep are members of the Bovidae family, which also includes cattle, goats, and antelopes. The seven species of sheep are in the *Ovis* genus.

Sheep range in height from about 2½ to 4 feet (76–122 cm), from their hoofs to their shoulders. They weigh from 100 to 350 pounds (45–160 kg). Sheep fleeces can be white, gray, brown, or black. Sheep like to live together in flocks. Domesticated sheep are timid animals and will usually try to run away from any real or imagined danger, although the *rams* (males) can attack people. Both male and female wild sheep have horns for protection, but not all domesticated sheep have horns. In some breeds of domesticated sheep, only the rams have horns. Female sheep, called *ewes*, usually bear one or two babies, or *lambs*, in the springtime.

▼ *Sheepshearing in New Zealand. In New Zealand there are 20 times more sheep than there are people.*

Sheep eat all day long. Their favorite foods are grasses, leaves, and small plants. Like their relatives, the goats, and like cows, sheep are *cud-chewers*. A sheep swallows its food and stores it in a division of its stomach called the *rumen*. The food is partially digested in the rumen and then passed back into the mouth. The sheep then finishes chewing this food, called *cud*, and swallows it.

Domesticated sheep are raised throughout the world. There are about 200 breeds of domestic sheep, all probably descended from a type of wild sheep called the Asian red sheep. Wild sheep live in hilly and mountainous areas in Europe, Asia, and North America. Wild sheep have longer faces and tails than domesticated sheep. Their fleece is generally coarser than that of domesticated sheep. Domesticated sheep are raised primarily for their wool or for their meat (called *mutton* or *lamb*). Sheep raised for their meat are called mutton sheep. A variety of British breeds produce very good-quality meat. Among these are the Dorset, Hampshire, Suffolk, Southdown, and Shropshire breeds. Some of these also produce fine wool.

A Spanish breed, the Merino sheep, is perhaps the best wool-producing sheep. Its thick fleece grows to be long and shaggy and makes a fine grade of wool. A French

▼ *The mouflon is a type of wild sheep that is found in southern Europe, in Sicily, and Corsica.*

▲ *Bighorn sheep are found in the Rocky Mountains. They are agile climbers, as are the Rocky Mountain goats that live in this region.*

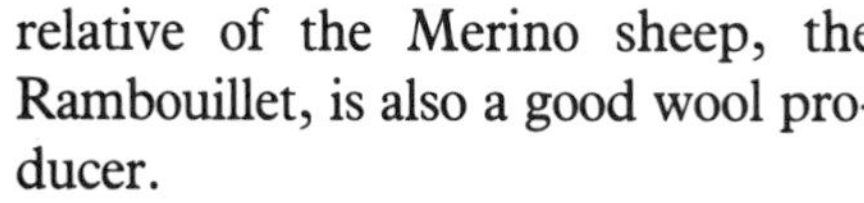

relative of the Merino sheep, the Rambouillet, is also a good wool producer.

The wild bighorn sheep of North America may be related to the wild sheep of Asia. The California bighorn is in danger of becoming extinct (dying out). Many are being killed by hunters, and the animals lack grazing land.

ALSO READ: ANIMAL, CATTLE, GOAT, HOOFED ANIMALS, HORNS AND ANTLERS, MAMMAL.

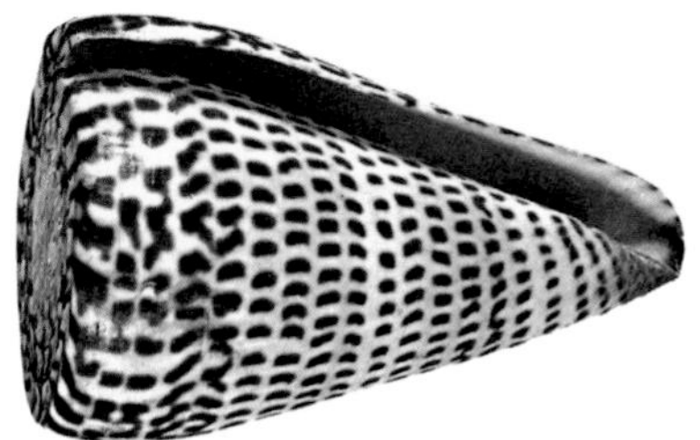

▲ *The marbled cone is the shell of a type of snail. It is very popular with collectors.*

▲ *The tiger cowrie, whose shell this is, lives in the Indian Ocean and in some parts of the Pacific Ocean.*

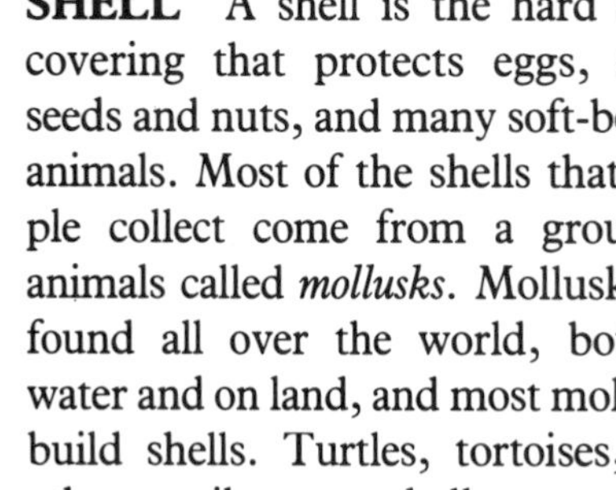

SHELL A shell is the hard outer covering that protects eggs, some seeds and nuts, and many soft-bodied animals. Most of the shells that people collect come from a group of animals called *mollusks*. Mollusks are found all over the world, both in water and on land, and most mollusks build shells. Turtles, tortoises, and other reptiles grow shells, too.

Among the thousands of kinds of mollusks are clams, oysters, snails, conchs, abalones, and chitons. People who collect mollusk shells are really saving the old "homes" of these animals. Each kind of mollusk builds a shell that is different from all the others. However, all mollusks make their shells in just about the same way. The material for the shell comes from a part of the mollusk's body called the *mantle*. The mantle is soft and usually surrounds the mollusk like an envelope. The mantle produces material (mostly calcium carbonate) that hardens into shell, covering the mantle and the body within it. The mantle usually keeps on making shell as long as the mollusk lives.

▼ *A selection of shells that are actually fossils, millions of years old. The shells' shapes and ridges have been preserved, so they look just like modern shells.*

▲ *For thousands of years people have used shells for personal decoration, often stringing them into necklaces and bracelets.*

The shell is formed in two layers. The outer layer is thicker, since it must protect the animal from external danger. Often, color is added to the outer layer, so many shells are beautiful and have interesting patterns. This layer is usually brightly colored, often striped or in several shades. The inner layer, next to the mantle, is composed of many thin, flat crystals. The colors in this layer change as you look at them from different angles. The inner layer is often called *mother-of-pearl* because of its similarity to the pearl produced inside the shell of some mollusks.

Mollusks produce several kinds of shells. *Univalves*, such as garden snails, have shells made in one piece. As the shell grows, it may form a coil. Univalves from the sea include conchs, whelks, and limpets. *Bivalves* have two shells joined together by a hinge. Clams, oysters, scallops, and mussels are familiar bivalves. *Tooth shells* make curved, tubelike shells that often look like tusks. *Chitons* have shells made of interlocking plates.

Many shells are pretty and decorative. Some are carved to make jewelry and other ornamental items. Old cameos (gems) were carved from helmet shells. Freshwater mussels provide mother-of-pearl. Many early peoples used shells for money. North American Indians made shell-money, or wampum, from clam shells.

ALSO READ: CRUSTACEAN, EGG, MOLLUSK, PEARL, SEEDS AND FRUIT, TURTLE.

SHELLEY, PERCY AND MARY

Percy Bysshe Shelley (1792–1822) was one of the great poets of the English language. Shelley's second wife, Mary (1796–1851), wrote several novels including the famous science-fiction story, *Frankenstein* (1818), the tale of a doctor who created a monster.

Shelley was born in Warnham, England. He was expelled from Oxford University in 1811 for writing a pamphlet against religion. He married Harriet Westbrook that same year but left her in 1814. In 1816, after Harriet had drowned herself, Shelley married Mary Godwin. Mary was the daughter of the philosopher William Godwin and the radical writer Mary Wollstonecraft, who had died giving birth to her. Two years later, Shelley and Mary went to live in Italy. Mary wrote *Frankenstein* after the Shelleys and a few friends, notably the poet Lord Byron, had challenged one another to write a horror story.

Shelley's poems tell of his innermost emotions and beliefs. He believed that a person should struggle to be free from worldly tyrants and from the laws of religion. He tells of such a struggle in his long dramatic poem "Prometheus Unbound." His poem "Hellas" was inspired by the Greek war of independence from the Turks. The poem "Ozymandias" tells how all tyrants die and are forgotten. Shelley wrote "Adonais" to the memory of John Keats, another famous English poet. "Ode to the West Wind" is one of Shelley's best-known poems and tells a great deal about his own life.

Shelley was drowned when his schooner sank off the coast of Italy during a storm. His body was washed ashore. Byron had it burned in the manner of the ancient Greeks.

ALSO READ: POETRY.

SHELTER

SHELTER A shelter is an enclosed or safe place that gives protection from enemies and from bad weather. Most animals in the world use some type of shelter. Human beings are unusual in that they also use their shelters for privacy—to be alone with their family groups or by themselves.

Different climates and different building materials have always caused great variations in types of shelters. Other differences are caused by the way people obtain their food, the types of tools they use, and the way their societies are organized.

Some of the earliest bones and tools of Stone Age people have been found in natural caves and rock shelters. The cave dwellers lit fires at the entrances of the caves to cook food and to frighten away animals. Most of the caves were occupied for only a short time because these people moved from place to place following and hunting herds of wild animals.

The Stone Age hunters who lived on the flat, treeless plains of central Asia learned to build their own shel-

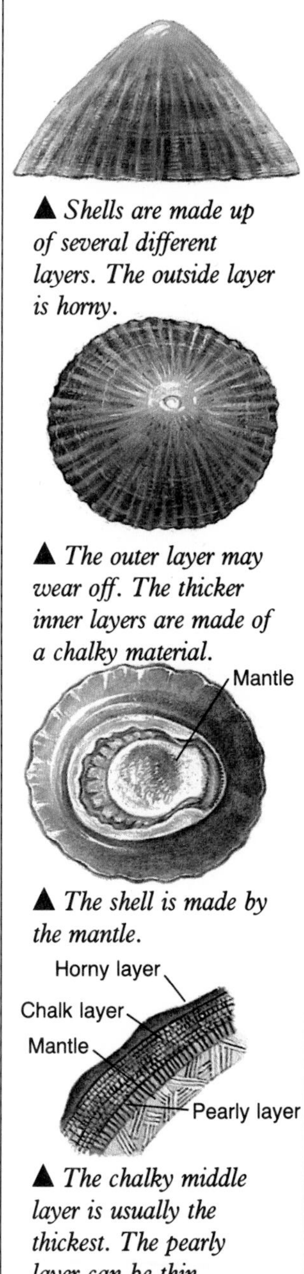

▲ *Shells are made up of several different layers. The outside layer is horny.*

▲ *The outer layer may wear off. The thicker inner layers are made of a chalky material.*

▲ *The shell is made by the mantle.*

▲ *The chalky middle layer is usually the thickest. The pearly layer can be thin.*

▲ *Percy Bysshe Shelley, English poet.*

▲ *In North America hunters built their wigwams from birch poles covered with birch bark.*

▲ *The type of lakeside settlement lived in by the Scots when the Romans occupied much of Britain.*

ters. They often used the huge tusks and bones of the mammoths (a type of elephant) that they hunted. The bones were stuck into the ground in a circle, and skins were stretched over them to make the earliest type of tent. Nomadic hunters would have been able to carry this type of shelter with them as they moved.

People began to build permanent shelters after they learned how to domesticate (tame) animals and cultivate (grow) plants for food. The farmers had to stay in one place all year to tend their crops and animals. They began to build groups of houses around a well or spring. In this way, the first "civilized" towns and cities grew up. Permanent fortifications, such as walls and ditches, were built around the settlements to defend them from human enemies as well as wild animals.

Farmers in the hot countries of the Middle East built their houses with bricks made out of dried mud. They were built so close together that they formed a solid wall around the edges of the city. People climbed into their houses through the flat roofs, which also served as cool sleeping quarters.

In the colder, rainy regions of central and northern Europe, farmers built houses of logs with clay pressed between the logs. The roofs were *pitched*, or sloping, so that the rain and snow would run off easily. The houses were often arranged in a large circle, and the settlements were defended by earthen banks and ditches. Most of the houses could hold several families. They were similar to the long houses of the Iroquois Indians of North America.

▼ *Shelters made of dried-mud brick, common in the Middle East. The flat roofs provide cool sleeping areas.*

▲ *Shelters in tropical areas are often made of reeds, palm leaves, or bamboo stalks. The roofs are usually thatched.*

Modern houses in cities today are similar throughout much of the world. But if you travel out into the countryside, different types of houses can still be seen. In places where there is little rain, such as Arabia and parts of Mexico, you will see houses built of mud brick (adobe). In Norway, farmers still build log houses. Eskimos sometimes build houses, called igloos, out of ice. People of the Pacific Islands use palm leaves and bamboo as building materials. Even city dwellers return to the simplest type of shelter—the tent—on camping expeditions.

Nuclear Shelters Many governments and individuals have built underground shelters in which people could hide should nuclear war break out. They hope that people could survive the explosions and then remain safe until the poisonous radiation died down. But no such shelter could survive a direct hit or near miss by a nuclear bomb, and it is believed that the outside world would be uninhabitable for decades or centuries after a nuclear war.

ALSO READ: ANTHROPOLOGY; ARCHEOLOGY; ARCHITECTURE; CAVE DWELLER; CIVILIZATION; CLIFF DWELLERS; FORTIFICATIONS; HOUSE; HUMAN BEING; INDIANS, AMERICAN; IROQUOIS INDIANS; LAKE DWELLERS; NOMAD; STONE AGE; TENT.

SHERMAN, WILLIAM T. (1820–1891) William Tecumseh Sherman was one of the great Union (Northern) commanders in the U.S. Civil War. His whirlwind "March to the Sea" across the state of Georgia greatly helped to win the war for the North.

Sherman was born in Lancaster, Ohio. His middle name, Tecumseh, came from a famous Indian chief. Sherman attended the U.S. Military Academy at West Point. He became an officer in the U.S. Army and fought in the Mexican War. After the Civil War broke out in 1861, Sherman joined the Union Army. He fought bravely at the first battle of Bull Run. He was then made a commander of the Union forces in Kentucky. Sherman was wounded at the Battle of Shiloh, where he fought under General Grant.

In 1864, Sherman was made commander of the division of Union armies of the Mississippi. In September, he captured Atlanta, Georgia. Much of the city was destroyed by fire during the fighting. Sherman then led his army of 62,000 soldiers on the famous 250-mile (400 km) march from Atlanta to Savannah on the coast. Sherman's forces destroyed crops and food supplies in their path, saving little except what they needed themselves. From Savannah, Sherman marched north through the Carolinas. He defeated Confederate forces under General Joseph E. Johnston at Raleigh in April 1865. That same month, the Confederates surrendered. Sherman served as supreme commander of the U.S. Army from 1869 to 1883. Sherman is reported to have said later, "War is hell."

ALSO READ: CIVIL WAR; GRANT, ULYSSES SIMPSON.

SHINTO Shinto is the religion native to Japan. The word "Shinto" means "the way of the gods." Unlike other major religions, Shinto does not teach the existence of one supreme force or being or a universal law. Its main idea is that there is an eternal truth, *kami*, to be found expressed in all forms of life. Trees, mountains, lakes, and rivers, as well as all other forms of nature, are seen as expressions of *kami*.

All over Japan there are holy places, or shrines, dedicated to different *kami*. Here, people may make offerings of food, or play music, dance, and sing. To purify the body, a Shinto believer may fast (go without food) or walk many miles.

Shinto is a very ancient belief. It has been influenced by other religions, including Buddhism, Chinese Confucianism, and Christianity. One form of Shinto, Imperial Shinto, is centered on the emperor of Japan who is believed to be a direct descendant of the sun goddess.

ALSO READ: JAPAN.

SHIPS AND SHIPPING A ship is a large vessel on which people travel and goods are transported across large bodies of water, such as lakes, seas, and oceans, or along major rivers and seaways. In the past, all ships were made of wood. Today, ships are constructed of steel. Passenger ships are often called *liners*. Cargo ships are

▲ *A Mongol camp on the vast Gobi desert looks much like it did hundreds of years ago. The felt tents used by the Mongols for their shelter are called* yurts.

▲ *William Tecumseh Sherman, Union Army general in the Civil War.*

▲ *A Phoenician galley. The ship was powered partly by the sails, partly by oarsmen.*

▲ *A Roman trading ship.*

Robert Fulton, who built the first steam-powered boat in 1807, began his career as a jeweler's apprentice. He became a talented painter of small pictures called miniatures, and then went to London to study art. He became interested in mechanical inventions from the friends he made there.

known as *freighters* (for dry goods) and *tankers* (for liquids, such as oil). *Warships* include aircraft carriers, destroyers, submarines, and other naval vessels. Some warships are freighters and carry troops or military supplies.

History of Ships The earliest people known to have constructed true ships (rather than boats, barges, rafts, and canoes) were the Phoenicians. Since ships at that time were made of wood, they eventually disintegrated. Art works or written descriptions from ancient times are usually the only means of finding out about these early ships.

Phoenician vessels were propelled by oarsmen placed in rows along each side of the ship. Greek warships were powered by oarsmen who were assisted by one or two sails. They were called *biremes* if they had two ranks of oarsmen on each side, *triremes* if they had three ranks of oarsmen on each side.

The ancient Romans copied the design of the Greek trireme and added a *forecastle* (raised structure) on the bow (front end) of the ship. The forecastle was used during wartime to help sailors climb onto an enemy ship and attack its crew.

In ancient times, warships were shaped differently from *merchant ships* (ships that carry cargo). Merchant ships were built wide and deep to hold as much cargo as possible. Warships were built shallow and narrow so that they could move swiftly from place to place. Merchant ships were usually rigged for sailing, whereas warships depended also on oarsmen for power. A warship powered only by sails was in danger of becoming stranded on a windless sea during battle, without any way of maneuvering or escaping from enemy attack.

The Vikings of Scandinavia were excellent shipbuilders. They developed fleets of very light, fast ships powered by combinations of sails and oars. Most Viking ships were warships (*snekkjas*), but the Norse people also made a wider, deeper ship (the *skuta*) that was used on exploratory voyages. Ships used on long voyages had to be larger in order to hold enough provisions for many days or weeks at sea.

During the Middle Ages, especially in Spain and Italy, people built great war galleys that held double rows of giant oars. The oars were balanced on *outriggers* (bars set out from the ship's body and extending the length of each side). Each oar needed two or three people to pull it. These outrigged galleys were the main kind of warship until the cannon was invented. Once cannon fire blasted the oars, a ship was helpless because it did not have sails strong enough to pull it out of danger. Warships of the Renaissance were patterned after merchant ships, which were equipped with all kinds of sails. Use of sails enabled ships to carry more provisions in place of the oarsmen. More provisions meant longer voyages, and by the 1500's the era of exploration by sea had begun.

SAILING SHIPS. Several different types of sailing ships (ships powered only by sails) were developed between the 1500's and 1800's. Sailing ships were grouped according to the type and arrangement of *rigging* they carried. The rigging of a ship included the masts, sails, spars, and lines (ropes) used to power and steer the

▼ *Various types of boats and ships used from the distant past to the present day.*

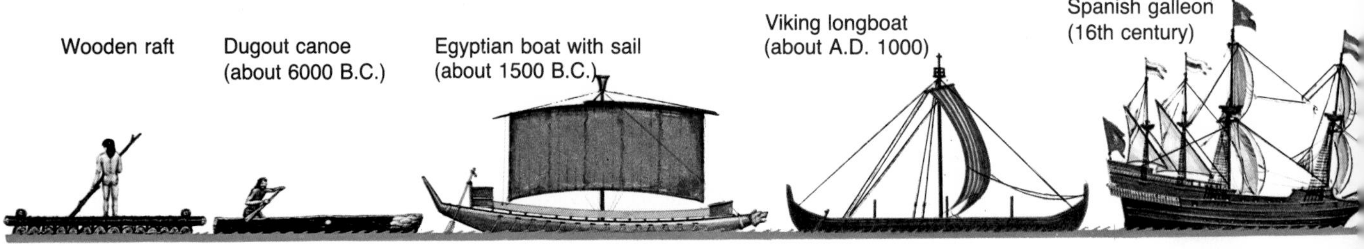

ship. The *masts* were tall poles placed along the center line of a ship. *Spars* were rods placed at various heights on each mast in such a way as to support an unfurled (open) sail.

Sails were of two types. *Fore-and-aft* (or *lateen*) sails were triangular in shape. When unfurled, they flew parallel to the length of the ship. Small vessels, such as sloops and schooners, were rigged mainly with fore-and-aft sails. *Square* sails were four-sided in shape. When unfurled, they flew crosswise—parallel to the width of the ship. Larger vessels, such as clippers, frigates, and naval ships of the line, were mainly square-rigged. Sails were raised, lowered, unfurled, and furled with ropes. When sails were in use, the lines (ropes) were tied to different parts of the ship.

The *caravel* was a fairly small vessel, made mostly in Portugal and Spain. It was rigged with three or four masts carrying fore-and-aft sails. Only the foremast (front mast) carried a square sail. Columbus sailed in a rigged vessel similar to this on his voyages to the New World. The *galleon* was a larger type of caravel.

By 1750, shipbuilders in the North American colonies were making fast-sailing *sloops* and *schooners* rigged with fore-and-aft sails. The sloop had a single mast. The schooner had two or more masts, the mainmast (in the center of the ship) being taller than the others. Both of these vessels were merchant ships.

The long, slender *clipper* ships, developed during the 1800's, were the speediest type of merchant sailing ship. They were fast, sturdy, and able to hold more cargo and passengers than earlier ships. U.S. clippers were

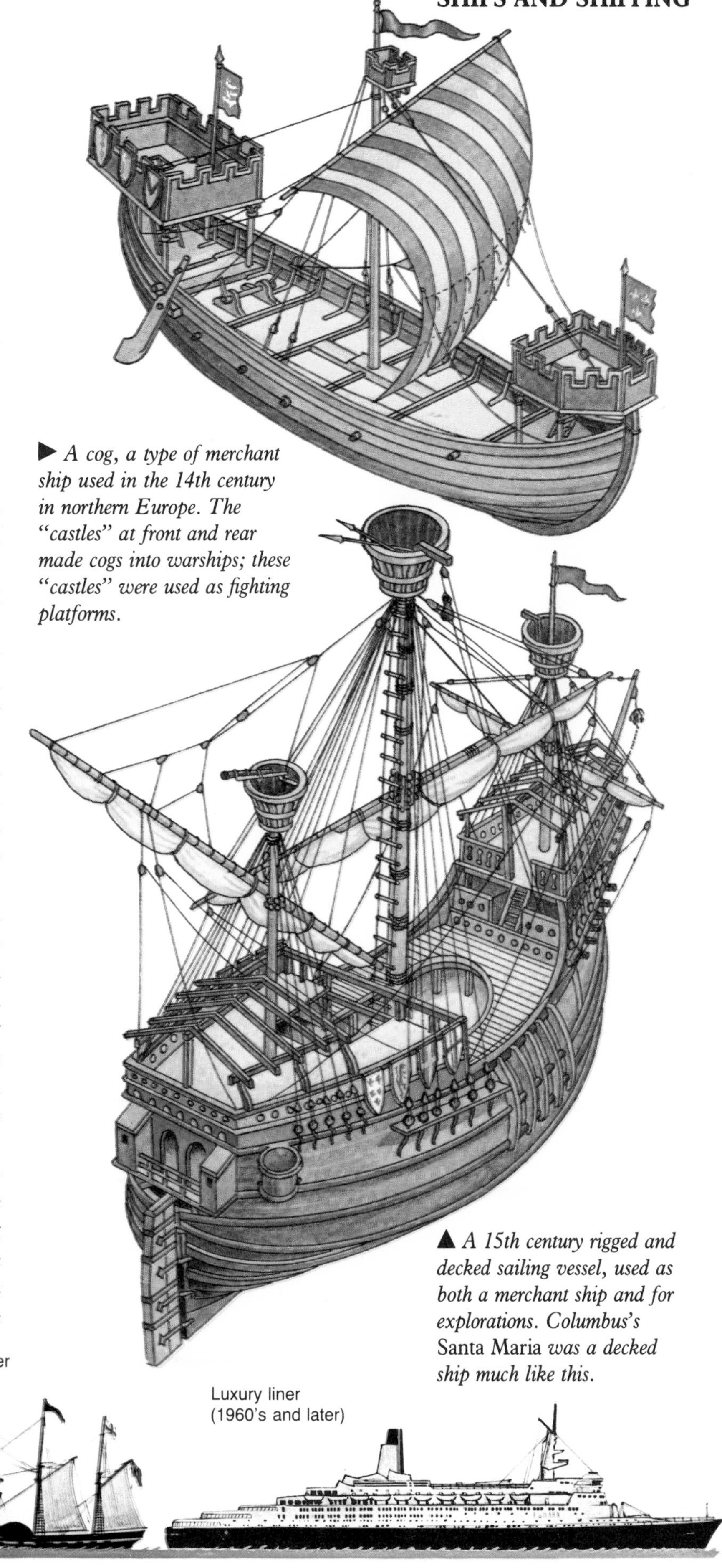

▶ *A cog, a type of merchant ship used in the 14th century in northern Europe. The "castles" at front and rear made cogs into warships; these "castles" were used as fighting platforms.*

▲ *A 15th century rigged and decked sailing vessel, used as both a merchant ship and for explorations. Columbus's* Santa Maria *was a decked ship much like this.*

▲ *This is how a seaman looked 300 years ago. There was no uniform. Most of the food and drink on ships was stored in barrels like the one here.*

used during the 1800's in the Pacific trade with China and in extensive trade with Europe. During the California gold rush of 1849, clippers were used to transport passengers quickly from the eastern United States around the tip of South America to the California coast. This was the beginning of extensive passenger trade from coast to coast. It lasted until fast overland transportation became available.

ENGINE-POWERED SHIPS. The U.S. inventor, Robert Fulton, built the first steam-powered paddle-wheel boat in 1807. Within a few years, paddle-wheel boats were being used to carry passengers and cargo along coastal areas and inland waterways in the United States and Europe. Early steam engines were not very practical because they used huge quantities of coal for fuel. For this reason, steam-powered oceangoing vessels were not used until about the 1860's to 1880's, when more efficient steam engines were developed. At about the same time, steel ships began to replace

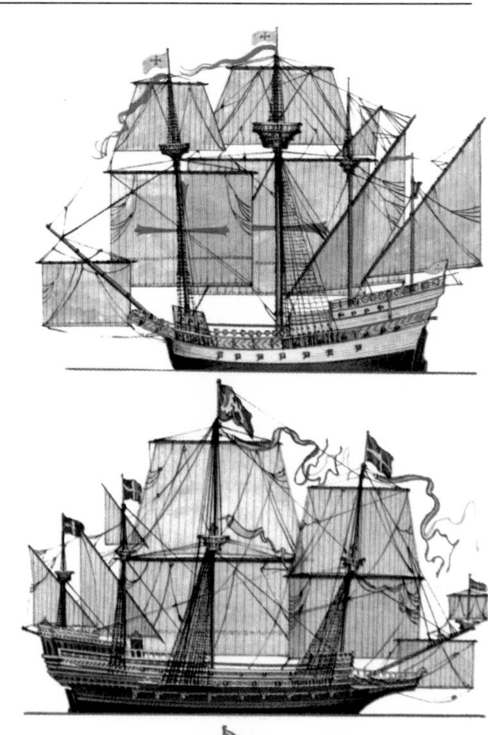

▲ *A Spanish galleon from about 1550 (top); a Dutch man-of-war from about 1613 (middle); and an English "First Rate" dated about 1780 (bottom).*

▶ *Inside a galleon: (1) forecastle; (2) gun deck; (3) orlop deck; (4) bitt; (5) anchor cable; (6) store ballast; (7) cookhouse brick fire; (8) water pump; (9) cannonball store; (10) capstan; (11) sail locker; (12) storeroom; (13) rudder attached to (14) the tiller and (15) whipstaff; (16) captain's cabin.*

SHIPS AND SHIPPING—SOME KEY DATES

about 2515 B.C. The oldest surviving boat is built. It was buried near the Great Pyramid of Cheops, in Egypt.
480 B.C. The Greeks defeat the Persians in a great sea battle near the island of Salamis. Thousands of Persians die because they cannot swim.
about 238 B.C. Pytheas sails from the Mediterranean to discover Britain.
about A.D. 986 Eric the Red sails from Norway to establish a colony on Greenland.
about 1000 Leif Eriksson becomes the first European to sail across the Atlantic to the Americas. He arrives in what he called Vinland—probably Nova Scotia.
1492 Christopher Columbus reaches the Americas. His expedition consists of the three ships *Santa Maria, Pinto, Niña.*
1500 About this time the first large "ship-killing" guns are used on warships. Gunports are added to the ship's sides, so that the big guns can be carried lower down in the hull, where they are less likely to make the ship top-heavy.
1570–1580 Race-built galleons are constructed for speed.
1571 The battle of Lepanto, the last great battle between oared warships. Don John of Austria, commanding a fleet of 200 galleys and galleasses from Spain, Genoa, and Naples, destroys the Turkish navy in the Gulf of Corinth.
1577–1580 Francis Drake sails around the world in his galleon *Golden Hind.*
1588 The Spanish Armada—a great fleet of sailing vessels—sails against England, but is defeated in the English Channel because the English use the swifter-moving race-built galleons.
1620 Cornelius Van Drebbel, a Dutchman, demonstrates the earliest known submarine.
1776 David Bushnell invents his submarine, the *Turtle.*
1805 The battle of Trafalgar. The British navy, under Admiral Horatio Nelson, defeats a combined French and Spanish fleet off southern Spain.
1827 The *Curaçao* is the first steamship to cross the Atlantic.
1912 The *Titanic,* widely hailed as unsinkable, sinks on its maiden (first) voyage, with the loss of many lives.
1915 The *Lusitania,* a British liner, is sunk by a German submarine. Because many U.S. citizens die, the United States enters World War I.
1938 The *Queen Mary* wins the "Blue Riband" for the fastest crossing of the Atlantic.
1952 The *United States* wrests the "Blue Riband" from the *Queen Mary.*
1954 The first nuclear-powered warship, the U.S. submarine *Nautilus,* is built.
1959 First full-scale hovercraft, invented by Christopher Cockerell, is used at sea—it crosses the English Channel.
1961 Launch of the world's largest-ever ocean liner, the *France* (renamed the *Norway* in 1979). It is 1,035 feet 7½ inches (315.66 m) long.
1969 Launch of the *Queen Elizabeth II,* the famous luxury liner.

▲ *Robert Fulton's ship,* North River Steamboat of Clermont. *The insets show views of the engine built by the British company Boulton & Watt. This ship was the world's first steamboat to run at a profit.*

▲ *Isambard Kingdom Brunel, the 19th-century engineer, created three famous early steamships, including the* Great Western.

wooden ships, first in naval and later in merchant fleets. With the development of improved steam engines and the steam turbine, ships were able to run on less fuel. The space taken up by fuel storage could then be used for cargo or passenger space. The development in the early 1900's of the *internal combustion* engine and the diesel engine made long-distance sea travel even more practical because these engines required even less fuel. By the late 1950's, engines run by nuclear power had been developed for ships.

Shipbuilding The basic shape of a ship has changed very little since ancient times. The way ships were built also did not change much until steel ships came into use and very large vessels began to be built. Ships are built in *shipyards*—wide, open areas next to bodies of water. Within a yard are workshops and factories where a ship's parts are manufactured.

Wooden and steel ships are built in almost the same way. First, the *keel*—a long piece of steel or timber that serves as the spine of the hull—is laid between wooden tracks called *ways*. The ways support the hull while it is being built. *Ribs*, which frame the sides of the hull, are fixed to the keel. Other members running the length of the hull connect the ribs. Partitions called *bulkheads* are built within the hull. Some of these add to its structural strength and some are watertight, dividing the hull into compartments that will help keep the ship afloat if the sea gets into one part. The *shell* of the hull, its outer watertight covering, is made of steel plates or wooden planks. So are the *decks*, which serve as floors. All parts of the hull work together to strengthen it against the huge strains that it undergoes in a heavy sea. Even the shell and the decks are important in resisting the forces that push and pull on, and attempt to twist, the hull. Ships have to be a little flexible—they might crack if they were not—but strong, girderlike construction is still needed.

In sailing ships, masts are fastened to the keel. The masts extend upright through the decks and high above the

▲ Sirius, *the first ship to cross the Atlantic under sustained steam power.*

▶ *The motor ship* Selandia *(1911) had an exhaust pipe instead of a funnel.*

ship. Wooden planking is *caulked* (made watertight) by filling in open spaces with binding materials, such as tar and resins. Spars, sails, and lines are then rigged to the masts, and all wood is varnished and painted to help protect it from the seawater.

Sections of a steel ship are often built in factories and then transported to a shipyard for assembling. Each section of a modern ship may weigh several tons. A steel ship is made watertight by welding the metal plates together.

The launching of a ship is a very special event. The ship is released and allowed to slide down the ways into the water. As it begins to move, the ship is "christened": a bottle of champagne is broken against its bow, and the ship is given a name.

Shipping All the cargo-carrying ships of a nation are that nation's *merchant fleet* or *merchant marine*. The U.S. Merchant Marine is under the control of the U.S. Maritime Administration and the Federal Maritime Board (both branches of the Department of Commerce). These agencies decide how much merchant ships can charge and what kinds of services they can provide. They provide government money for the building of new merchant ships, and they keep a fleet of government-owned merchant ships for use in time of war. U.S. merchant ships as well as U.S. ports and shorelines are protected by the U.S. Coast Guard.

Men and women of the Merchant Marine are the officers and crews of the U.S. merchant ships. They sail the ships, collect the transport fares, and see that the fleet is kept in good repair. Large fleets of merchant ships owned by big companies usually have regularly scheduled routes. Ships

▶ *A giant supertanker being built in a dry dock. Soon the cranes and scaffolding will be removed, and the ship will be floated out for her trials.*

▲ *It is always a big event when a new ship is launched.*

called *tramps* do not have regular routes. They sail to wherever their particular loads of cargo must go.

In recent years, ships have gotten bigger while the crews to man them have grown smaller in number. The biggest of all, the supertankers, are used particularly for transporting oil. Yet less than forty men are needed to work them. They are awkward things, requiring radar and computers to work out their movements far ahead and to adjust course and speed in time. They are too large for most docks. They are loaded and off-loaded by pipeline while anchored off-shore.

While mail and light cargo have been taken over by airlines, ships have become bigger to take more cargo because it becomes cheaper per ton to carry. Many new ships have been built for special cargoes. There are refrigerated ships to carry perishable foodstuffs and gases frozen into liquids. There are container ships that link with road and rail depots for onward transport by land, or link with barge-carriers which travel the inland waterways.

ALSO READ: AIRCRAFT CARRIER; AIR CUSHION VEHICLE; BOATS AND BOATING; CANAL; COAST GUARD; DIESEL ENGINE; ENGINE; FULTON, ROBERT; HARBORS AND PORTS; KNOT; LIGHTHOUSE; MERCHANT MARINE; MONITOR AND MERRIMACK; NAVIGATION; NAVY; NUCLEAR ENERGY; OCEAN; PANAMA CANAL; PIRATES AND PRIVATEERS; SAILING; SEACOAST; SIGNAL; SUBMARINE; SUEZ CANAL; TRADE; TRANSPORTATION; TRAVEL.

▲ *A large oil tanker also called a supertanker. Supertankers transport oil around the world, but when they sink, their oil spillage devastates the sea and its wildlife.*

SHOES Take a close look at one of your shoes and try counting all the separate pieces. You can see that shoes are not simple to make. A shoe manufacturer must buy the right materials and then cut and fit them to

▼ *The world's major shipping lanes.*

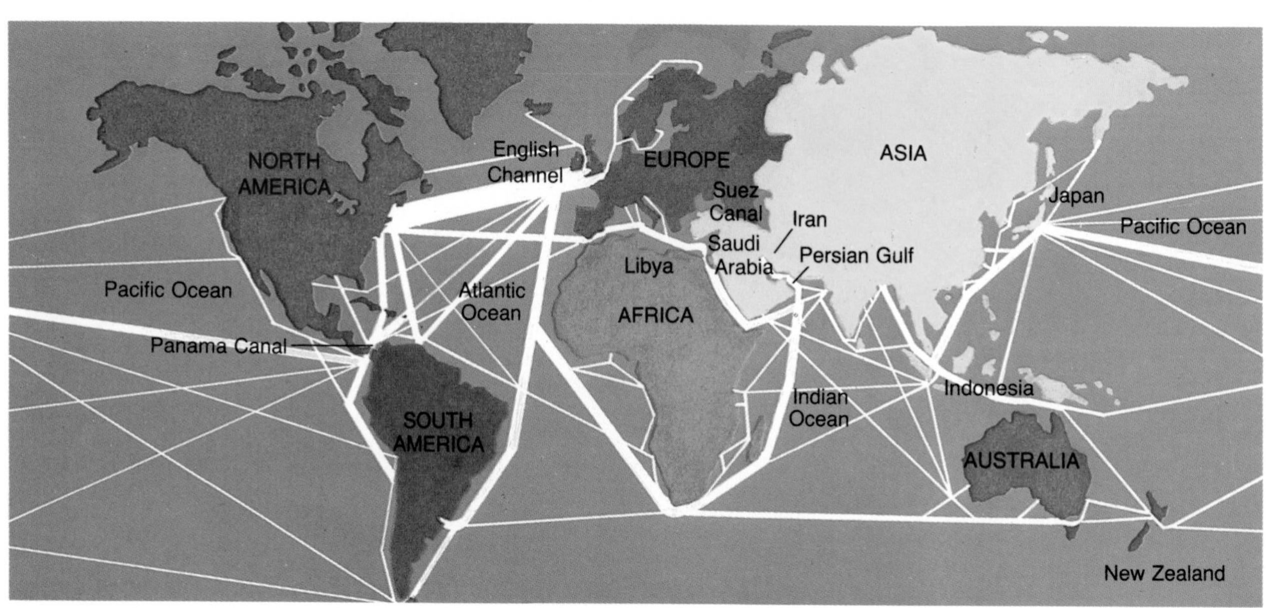

follow the lines of a person's foot. Pieces of sturdy leather (cowhide, pigskin, or other hide), bolts of fabric (such as canvas for tennis shoes), or large sheets of plastic imitation leather are cut in different sizes to fit various sizes of feet. Shoe linings of soft material are also cut to fit the inside of the shoe. The cut materials are then stitched together and the linings sewn or glued into place. The completed top part of the shoe is called a *shoe upper*. After stitching, designs, lace holes, and button or buckle holes are punched into the shoe upper.

In the stock-fitting room, the lower parts of the shoe are made and fastened together. The *outsole* (bottommost part of the shoe) is cut from sheets of leather, rubber, or cork. Some soles are made of plastic materials. The *insole* is a layer of leather material that attaches directly to the shoe upper. The outsole is attached to the bottom of the insole by sewing, gluing, or nailing. This process is called *bottoming*. *Counters* and *box toes* (pieces of stiff material that give strength and shape to the heel and toe of a shoe) are also made in the stock-fitting room.

The upper and lower parts of the shoe are then assembled on a last, a wood or metal form that is shaped like a foot and gives shape to the shoe. The counters and box toes are inserted between the leather and the lining, and the sole is sewn to the shoe upper. The heel is attached to the back sole with cement or nails, and the soles are scoured and waxed. Lastly, the entire shoe is cleaned and polished. Laces, bows, buttons, buckles, and other ornaments are attached, and the shoe is packed for shipping to stores.

Some of the earliest shoes were worn by people of the ancient Middle East. They wore sandals made of hide or braided reeds that were held to the foot by cords. In colder areas, moccasins were made by stitching leather bags for the feet and tying them around the ankles with cords. In very cold weather, feet and legs were covered with wrappings of hide that were held in place by crisscrossed leather cords. The first boots were made by attaching leg wrappings to a sandal sole.

In ancient and medieval times, shoes were a mark of rank. The fancier and more elegant shoes were worn by people of high rank. Important Greeks, Romans, Egyptians, and Chinese wore shoes with complicated decoration, often encrusted with jewels and gold. Highly decorated shoes were very popular among the nobility during the Middle Ages, when pointed-toed shoes also became fashionable. One shoe, called the *Crakow*, had such long, pointed toes that the wearer had to hold each toe up with a chain in order to walk.

The common people of medieval Europe wore *buskins*—soft fabric shoes with soft soles. Russian peasants wore *bast* shoes made from birch bark. Hard soles did not come into extensive use until the 1400's. In the 1500's, *jackboots* became popular. These were thigh-high boots with a high heel and a wide cuff at the top. They were so heavy and fitted so tightly that people had to be helped to put them on and take them off. At various times throughout history, high heels

▲ *Shoes through the ages: (1) Egyptian sandal, 2000* B.C.*; (2) wooden clog to keep feet dry, Middle Ages; (3) Italian Crakow, 1400's; (4) Venetian pedestal shoe and clog, 1500's; (5) English lady's brocade shoe, 1660; (6) English lady's shoe, 1700's; (7) English whiteboot with flat-sided galosh, 1632; (8) man's shoe, 1736; (9) woman's closed laced boot with patent cap, 1905; (10) button balmoral with black patent galosh; (11) man's shoe, 1963; (12) stiletto heel, 1958.*

America's earliest known cobbler was Thomas Beard, who came to the Massachusetts Bay colony of Salem in 1629.

▲ *A shoemaker sews pieces of leather which eventually will make up a complete shoe.*

▲ *Target shooting requires tremendous accuracy. It is a fun sport as well as an Olympic sport.*

have been in style for both men and women. One type of high-heeled shoe worn in the United States is the *cowboy boot*—the lengthened heel giving good foot support in a stirrup.

Before the 1800's, most shoes were made by local shoe craftworkers called *cobblers*. Cobblers were skillful leather workers, but they paid little attention to how a shoe fitted. Most shoes were made to fit either foot. Since shoes did not exactly follow the lines of the foot, new footwear had to be "broken in" by the wearer. This was often a painful process, and many foot deformities were traced to the wearing of poorly fitted shoes. Most cobblers worked at home or in little shops; some went from house to house, making and selling their shoes.

In parts of Europe, people have for centuries been wearing wooden shoes (called *klompen* or *sabots*) to keep the feet dry when working in moist fields. The Chinese and Japanese have worn a raised, wooden-soled shoe for walking in muddy areas. They are still part of the Japanese woman's traditional costume.

ALSO READ: CLOTHING, FASHION, HANDS AND FEET, INDUSTRIAL REVOLUTION, LEATHER.

SHOOTING Have you ever set up a target and tried to hit it using a slingshot, a bow and arrow, or an air rifle? If so, you have enjoyed the sport of shooting.

Two main types of shooting are performed in competitions like the Olympic Games. In *archery*, contestants use a bow and arrow. In *marksmanship*, the shooters use pistols or rifles, and either the shooter or the target, or both, may be moving. Many hours of practice are required before someone can become a good *sharpshooter* (marksman or markswoman).

Whether they use a bow and arrow or a gun, beginners should have an experienced shooter with them for advice and supervision. Beginners should certainly know how to handle a gun safely before they ever fire it.

Beginners should start with a *short-range* target—one that is fairly close to the shooter. The area behind the target should be a steep bank or hillside to stop stray bullets. Target shooting for handguns is done standing up. Rifle shooting can be done standing, kneeling on one knee, sitting, or lying on the stomach. Shooters able to get tight groups—closely bunched bullet holes in the target—are considered good marksmen or markswomen.

In *clay pigeon shooting*, or *trap shooting*, saucer-shaped targets are fired into the air, and the shooter must try to hit as many as possible. In *skeet shooting*, measures are taken to make the flight of the targets similar to that of game birds.

ALSO READ: ARCHERY, GUNS AND RIFLES.

SHORTHAND Shorthand is a type of writing in which symbols (signs) are used instead of letters of the alphabet. Some symbols are used in place of whole words. A person can write much faster in shorthand than in longhand or ordinary writing. Shorthand is most often used to copy down the words of a person speaking at normal speed. A person who is employed to take down shorthand in this way is often called a *stenographer*. Secretaries use shorthand to take down letters. Clerks and newspaper reporters use shorthand to record speeches, interviews, and press conferences. Students find shorthand useful for taking notes in class. Many court reporters use a Stenotype machine, which prints alphabet letters in a shorthand system, to record hearings and trials in courts.

Many different methods of shorthand have been invented. The first known method was invented about 63 B.C. by a Roman named Marcus Tullius Tiro. The most common methods used today have symbols or letters that represent the different sounds used in speech. Two of these methods are Gregg Shorthand and Pitman Shorthand.

Pitman Shorthand was invented in the 1830's by an Englishman named Sir Isaac Pitman. In this method, lines and curves are used to represent consonant sounds. Similar consonant sounds, such as F and V, have similar symbols. But the soft F is written with a light stoke, and the hard V is written with a heavy stroke. Most vowel sounds are shown by dots and dashes written close to the consonant symbols.

Gregg Shorthand is most commonly used in the United States. It was invented in the 1880's by John Robert Gregg. In this method, consonant sounds are shown by lines and curves, as in the Pitman method. Similar-sounding consonants, such as F and V, are shown by symbols of different length. Vowel sounds are represented by hooks and circles. These are joined to the consonant symbols. In both the Gregg and Pitman methods, some common words and phrases (groups of words) are represented by a single symbol. This helps greatly increase the speed of note taking.

Another method of shorthand popular today is SPEEDWRITING®. In this method, letters of the alphabet are used to show sounds or common words. SPEEDWRITING® is easy to learn, but it is not usually as fast as the other methods of shorthand.

■ LEARN BY DOING

You can invent your own shorthand system, just as Gregg and Pitman did. Write down the 26 letters of the alphabet. Choose a symbol for each and write it beneath the appropriate letter. Make sure that the symbols you invent can be written more quickly than letters in longhand. (If not, your shorthand won't be very short!) Perhaps you can make up your own abbreviations for words you use often in school. Then write something in the shorthand you've invented. See how many sentences you can make up in your new system. ■

if u c rd th msg
u c bkm a sec
& gt a gd jb

▲ *A sample of* SPEEDWRITING®, *a type of shorthand that uses Roman letters. This reads: "If you can read this message, you can become a secretary and get a good job."*

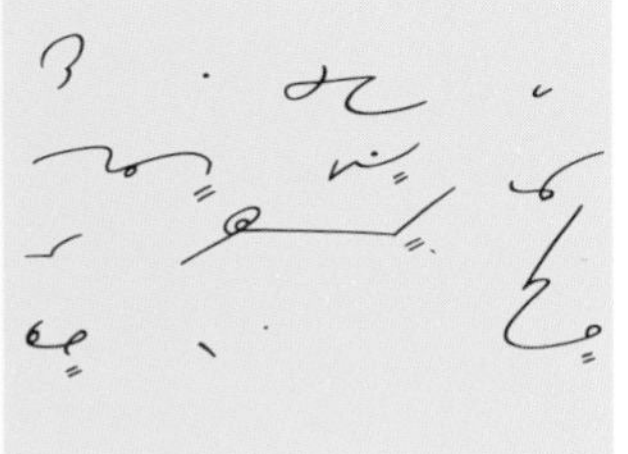

▲ *This sample of Gregg Shorthand says: "This is a sample of Gregg Shorthand written in the Diamond Jubilee Series." (Used with permission of Gregg Division, McGraw-Hill Book Company, copyright owner and proprietor of Gregg Shorthand.)*

SHORT STORY

SHORT STORY You have probably listened to short stories from the time you were able to talk. When you started to read, many of the things you read were stories. Nearly everyone has read fairy tales such as "Cinderella." These are short stories, too. A story is a short, fictional work of prose. Short stories may vary in length, but they can usually be read in less than an hour or two.

The short story is similar to other fiction in that it not only tells a story but also usually makes a statement (its theme) about human character or experience. But, because of its shortness, the short story is much more compact in scope and form than the novel. The plot is usually very much simpler. Most short stories contain just a few characters, and only one or two are fully developed. The setting is usually also more compact—short stories usually take place in one or two places during a short period of time. But some short stories have many characters or take place over a long time! So many types of short stories exist that it is impossible to define everything that a short story is and does.

People have been telling stories as long as they have been communicating with each other—long before they developed a system of writing. Many of the myths and legends of ancient people were short stories. Many inci-

The first Latin shorthand was invented by Marcus Tullius Tiro in 63 B.C. His system lasted for over a thousand years.

▲ *A scene from a short story by Mark Twain, called "Tom Sawyer Abroad."*

dents in the Bible stand out as excellent short tales. *The Arabian Nights* is a collection of some of the most ancient stories. During the Middle Ages, several types of stories were popular. Chaucer's *Canterbury Tales* was a collection of all kinds of short tales.

In the 1800's, several authors (especially the U.S. writer, Edgar Allan Poe, and the Russian writers, Nikolai Gogol and Anton Chekhov) gave short fiction a more definite form and purpose—made it the type of literature called the short story. In the past century, the short story has won increasing respect and popularity. Writers have developed a variety of styles and kinds of short stories. There are so many types of short stories to choose from—including adventure stories, horror stories, science-fiction stories, and realistic stories—that everyone can find some to his or her liking.

ALSO READ: CHAUCER, GEOFFREY; CHEKHOV, ANTON; LITERATURE; NOVEL; POE, EDGAR ALLAN; SCIENCE FICTION.

▲ *Washakie was a Shoshone Indian Chief who was born about 1804, and who died in 1900.*

SHOSHONE INDIANS The Shoshone (also spelled Shoshoni) were a group of Indian tribes who lived in the western plains of Wyoming, Utah, Nevada, and Idaho. Life in this semidesert region was difficult. The Shoshone lived by hunting small animals and gathering nuts, fruits, and seeds. Most Shoshone lived together in small family groups. An older person in the group was the leader. Each group was known to the others by the type of food that was plentiful in its particular region. The "Sheep Eaters" and "Seed Eaters" were two such groups. The Shoshone worshiped the spirits of animals. Their chief god was the spirit of the coyote, a wolflike animal that lived in the region.

In the 1700's, the Shoshone received guns and ammunition from the Spanish. Some of them then became hunters like their neighbors, the nomadic Comanche tribe.

Perhaps the most famous member of the Shoshone tribe was Sacagawea, the woman who accompanied Meriwether Lewis and William Clark on their expedition across the West. The Shoshone were friendly with white settlers, and they helped U.S. forces in their battles against the Plains Indians.

Today, more than 10,000 Shoshone Indians live on or near reservations in the western United States. Most work as ranchers, farmers, and laborers.

ALSO READ: COMANCHE INDIANS; COYOTE; INDIANS, AMERICAN; INDIAN WARS.

SHOW JUMPING see EQUESTRIAN SPORTS.

SHREW see MOLES AND SHREWS.

SHRUB A shrub is a woody plant with more than one stem. It is taller and sturdier than most nonwoody plants, and shorter than most trees. Trees usually have a thick central trunk, while shrubs branch into thin stems just above the ground. Shrubs may be evergreen or deciduous. Evergreen shrubs bear leaves all year. Deciduous shrubs lose their leaves in the fall. Some shrubs have colorful fruit, and many have flowers.

Shrubs can grow wild or in gardens. Some wild shrubs grow to be larger than trees. Tall shrubs are planted in gardens to make hedges or borders. Low shrubs are often planted around houses. Shrubs can make a handsome, dense green background for flowers, or they can be planted as windbreaks.

Box, sometimes called *boxwood*, is an evergreen shrub. It grows very slowly so it is not usually very big. If you see large, tall boxwoods, you know they are probably very old.

▲ *The lilac shrub has pale mauve flowers in the wild, but cultivated varieties may be white or deep purple.*

Flowering shrubs, or ornamental shrubs, are very popular. The *azalea* is a middle-size shrub that has beautiful flowers in the spring. Some azaleas will not grow in climates with extremely cold winters. In several eastern and southern states, azalea festivals are held every year. Azaleas are related to *rhododendrons*. In the Appalachian Mountains, wild rhododendrons decorate the hillsides with huge pink and lavender blossoms in the spring.

The *lilac* is a tall shrub that is planted in many gardens. It often grows more than ten feet (3 m) high. It can therefore be used to provide privacy or hide an unattractive wall. The flowers of the lilac are very fragrant.

Forsythia grows with graceful, arching branches. Its bright yellow flowers are among the first signs of spring. *Holly* and *magnolia* can be trees or shrubs. They are both evergreens. Their glossy leaves are especially beautiful in winter when the rest of the garden is bare. The holly often has bright red berries, and its leaves have spiny margins. Its branches or leaves are often used as a traditional Christmas decoration, especially as a front door garland.

ALSO READ: PLANT, PLANT KINGDOM.

SIBELIUS, JEAN (1865–1957)

The Finnish composer Jean Sibelius wrote music that seems to capture the beauty and wilderness of his homeland. Born in Hameenlinna, Finland, he was given the names Johan Julius Christian. He later changed the Johan to Jean.

At the time when Sibelius was born, Finland was not an independent country. It was under Russian rule. At school, however, the young Sibelius was taught in Finnish, and he grew up proud of his country and its traditions. He studied piano and violin as a child. Later, he studied law at college but gave it up to devote himself to music.

He traveled to Germany and Austria to study music. But his heart was in Finland. His first important composition was to write the music for plays based on the Finnish epic poem, the *Kalevala*, which contains many Finnish mythological tales. Many of his other works are based on Finnish legend.

In 1897, Sibelius was given a grant of money by his government so that he could concentrate on music. He wrote seven symphonies, and many people are familiar with his stirring tone poem, *Finlandia*.

ALSO READ: FINLAND, MUSIC, MYTHOLOGY.

SIBERIA see SOVIET UNION.

SIERRA LEONE

The name of the African country of Sierra Leone means "Lion Mountain." One story says that the name came from the shape of the country's mountains. Another tells that in the 1460's, when the Portuguese mariner, Pedro da Cintra, first heard the wind and thunderstorms roaring around the coastal peaks, he gave it the name. Guinea and Liberia border Sierra Leone,

▲ *An evergreen shrub called box. This shrub is found growing wild in parts of Europe, and North Africa.*

▲ *The Finnish composer Jean Sibelius is one of the world's most popular classical composers.*

SIERRA LEONE

Capital City: Freetown (500,000 people).
Area: 27,699 square miles (71,740 sq. km).
Population: 4,300,000.
Government: One-party republic.
Natural Resources: Diamonds, bauxite, gold, rutile.
Export Products: Diamonds, coffee, cocoa.
Unit of Money: Leone.
Official Language: English.

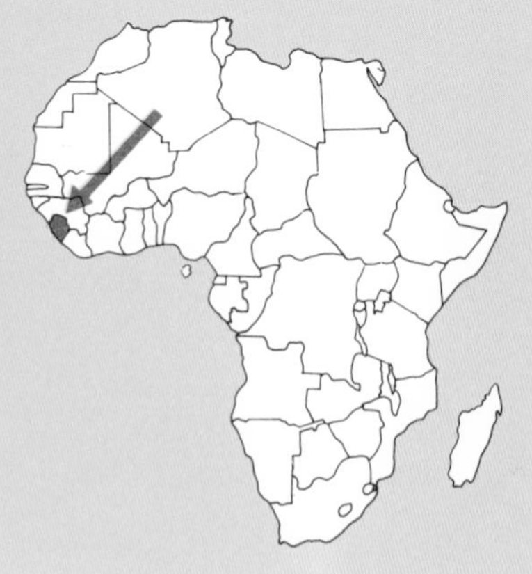

which is on the west coast of Africa. (See the map with the article on AFRICA.)

Freetown, the capital, was founded by the British in 1787 as a haven for freed slaves from Britain, Nova Scotia, and the British West Indies. Their descendants are called Creoles, and for a long time they were the country's political leaders. Because so many missionaries and colonial administrators of the 1800's died of disease in the country, Sierra Leone became known as the "white man's grave." In the vicinity of Freetown, about 150 inches (380 cm) of rain fall each year. The wettest months are from July to September. The average temperature is 80°F (27°C).

Sierra Leone became the 100th member of the United Nations in 1961.

Many of the people are farmers, producing rice, palm kernels, ginger, coffee, and cocoa. Diamonds, bauxite, and iron ore are major resources. The Mende people of the south and the Temne of the north are the two largest tribal groups. About 12 smaller groups have their own language and traditions, passed down through folk tales and proverbs. English is the official language, and there is a "pidgin" (simplified) English dialect called Krio. The life expectancy (the average length of the people's lives) in Sierra Leone is still under 50 years.

The University of Sierra Leone, formerly called Fourah Bay College, was founded in 1827. For more than 100 years this college was the only institution of higher learning in West Africa. The college was affiliated with Durham University in England in 1876, and today the standards are the same as those of the British university. Sierra Leone, formerly a British colony and protectorate, became an independent state within the Commonwealth in 1961 and a republic in 1971. In 1978, a one-party government backed by the Temne was formed.

ALSO READ: AFRICA, SLAVERY.

SIERRA NEVADA The Sierra Nevada mountain range extends about 400 miles (640 km) north and south through eastern California, forming a natural boundary between California and Nevada. A small part of the range is in Nevada. At its northern end, the range merges with the Cascade Range that continues through Oregon and Washington into Canada.

The highest section in the range is called the High Sierra. It includes ten mountains higher than 14,000 feet (4,270 m). The highest, Mount Whitney, is 14,495 feet (4,418 m) high and is the highest peak in the United States outside Alaska. Giant sequoias and redwood trees, among the oldest living things in the world, grow in the Sierra Nevada's three national parks—King's Canyon, Sequoia, and Yosemite. Lake Tahoe is a famous year-round resort area in the High Sierra, which is noted for its magnificent scenery.

Sierra Nevada in Spanish means "snow-covered mountains." In a pass in the Sierra Nevada mountains, 34 pioneers died in the deep snows in the winter of 1846–1847. The pass was later named for their leader and called Donner Pass. Today, skiers in the Sierra find snow in the fall and winter and even in early summer. Snow-fed rivers generate hydroelectricity and supply water. Gold and silver are mined in the mountains.

ALSO READ: YOSEMITE VALLEY.

SIGHT Almost all living things are sensitive to light. The one-celled amoeba's whole body is sensitive to changes in brightness. But an amoeba cannot actually "see"—it can only sense light and dark. More advanced animals, such as the earthworm, have special light-sensitive cells. But, in order to have true sight, an animal must have eyes that form an image.

Many animals without backbones have *simple* or *compound* eyes. Simple eyes (which are not true eyes) are groups of cells that can detect light and dark. Some simple eyes have a clear outer covering, or *lens*. Some animals, such as insects, can use their simple eyes to tell from which direction light is coming. But insects also have compound eyes, and these give them true sight.

A compound eye is somewhat like many simple eyes joined together. A compound eye may be made up of from 12 to 9,000 simple eyes, each having its own lens. Insects, lobsters, and crabs have compound eyes. To them the world looks like a mosaic (picture broken up into blocks) of light and dark spots.

Animals with backbones usually have *camera* eyes. The human eye is a typical camera eye. In a camera eye, all the light is gathered by one lens. The lens focuses (directs) the light to the retina, a layer of light-sensitive cells at the back of the eye. When light strikes a light-sensitive cell, it sets off a chemical reaction that sends a nerve impulse to the brain. The brain puts together all the impulses from all the light-sensitive cells and forms a picture. Despite their name, camera eyes do not focus like a camera—by moving the lens backward and forward. Instead, muscles around the lens make it fatter or thinner, depending on how near or far is the object being looked at. Only in fishes does the lens move backward and forward.

In a way every animal has the eyes it needs. A bee, with its compound eyes, cannot see distant objects or different shades of gray nearly as well as we can. But a bee can see better at distances of less than an inch (2.5 cm), it can detect movement better than we can, and it can see ultraviolet light we cannot see.

Camera eyes have two kinds of light-sensitive cells—rods and cones. Rods are sensitive to black, white, and gray, and respond even in dim light. Cones are sensitive to color and bright light but are not as sensitive. Only if an animal has cones in its retina can it see colors. Some animals

▲ *These amazing rock formations are found at Moon Lake in the Sierra Nevada mountain range, in California.*

▼ *The main features of the human eye.*

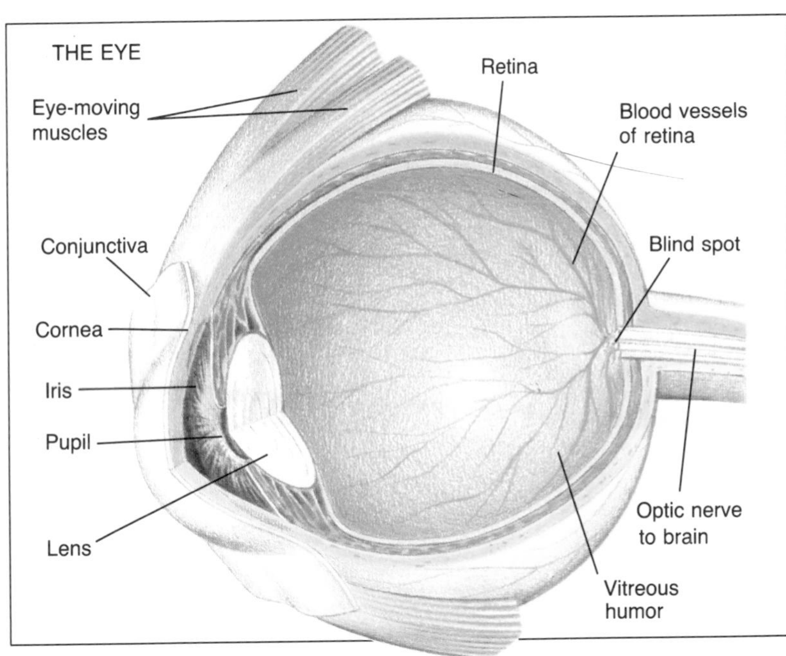

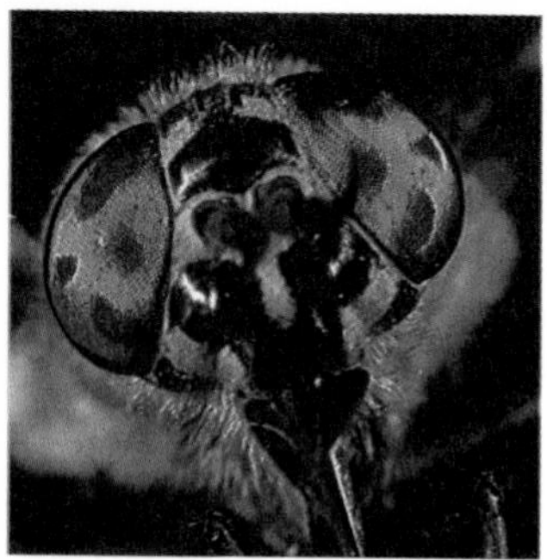

▲ *The head of a horsefly, showing its large compound eyes.*

The shortest light waves that we can see are violet. The longest light waves we can see are red. There are other waves shorter than violet and longer than red that we cannot see but some animals can. Bees and ants see colors beyond violet.

Human beings have a better sense of color than any other animal. We can distinguish 250 different pure colors, from red to violet, and about 17,000 mixed colors. We are also able to distinguish about 300 shades of gray between black and white.

that are active only in the daytime—such as squirrels and certain birds and lizards—have almost all cone cells and only a few rod cells. These animals have excellent daytime and color vision, but they are almost blind at night. On the other hand, animals that are active at night, such as cats, have few cone cells and many rod cells. They cannot usually see much color or see very well in bright light, but they can see quite well in near-darkness.

Animals also differ in their fields of vision—the area they can see. An animal with eyes on the sides of its head, such as horses, fishes, and most insects, can see almost all of its surroundings. Each eye covers a different field of vision. An animal with eyes toward the front of its head, such as monkeys, human beings, and predatory (hunting) birds, can see only about half of its surroundings. But the fields of vision overlap, which means these animals have *binocular* vision. Each eye forms an image of an object, and sends this image to the brain. In the brain the two images are fused into one image.

Binocular vision makes *stereoscopic* vision possible. Stereoscopic vision is the ability to see *depth*. Each eye sees an object from a slightly different angle. Each eye also sees the object at a slightly different place in the field of vision. When the two images are brought together in the brain, these differences are seen as depth—the distance and size of the object.

Depth perception is partly learned. Through experience, we learn how large a certain kind of object usually is. We use this information to judge the distance and size of an actual example of the object. People who live in dense forests, such as the pygmies of Africa, have little experience with distances of more than a few yards, and so they have poor depth perception. When one pygmy was taken on a trip to the plains, he could not believe that the moving dots he saw in the distance were buffaloes, because no buffalo could ever be that small. Up close, he saw that they were, in fact, buffaloes—but he still refused to believe it. With his limited experience of distance, it made more sense to think that the buffalo had grown than that they could ever have looked so small.

ALSO READ: EYE, LIGHT, NERVOUS SYSTEM, SENSE ORGAN.

SIGNAL People have used many kinds of signals or signs to transmit messages across a distance. In early times, people used their own arms and hands, fires, trumpet blasts, or drum rhythms to send messages. Today, mirrors, flags, lights, flares, and electronic equipment are also used.

For centuries, sound and fire have been used to relay a message. A trumpet blast signaled entry into battle. African tribes used drums to "talk" across great distances and relay messages from one village to another. North American Indians used smoke signals as visual ways of sending messages.

A famous signal was sent by Paul Revere at the start of the American Revolution. He arranged to hang lanterns to warn Bostonians of the arrival of British troops. One lantern meant the troops were approaching by land. Two lanterns meant they were coming by sea.

Foghorns sound through dense fog to guide ships safely away from dangerous places. In your school, a ringing bell may be used to signal recess, lunchtime, or the end of the school day.

Semaphore signaling, wigwag signaling, and Morse Code are different ways of transmitting messages. In semaphore signaling, you use two flags, one in each hand. Keeping your arms stiff, you move the flags into various positions to signal letters of the alphabet. Semaphore is the quick-

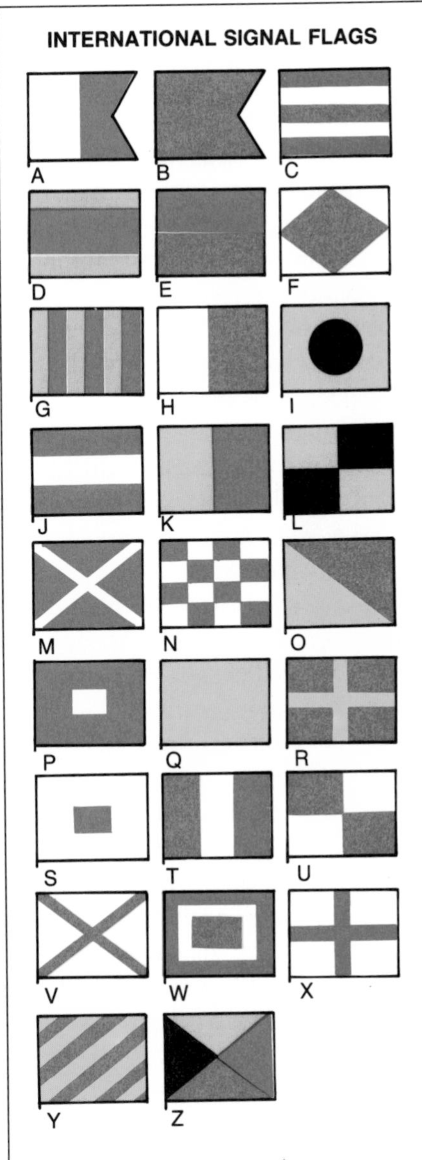

est way to send a flag message, but it can be seen only in the daytime and over short distances. The semaphore code is used by the armed forces and by Boy Scouts everywhere. Boy Scouts also use wigwagging to signal each other. In wigwagging, only one signal flag is used. It is swung to the right and left to send a message by Morse Code.

The Morse Code was invented by Samuel Morse in 1838 to send messages by telegraph. He used combinations of dots and dashes (short and long sounds) to stand for letters of the alphabet. The Morse Code can be used to signal by flag, by sound, by light (using mirrors or flashlights), or by radio.

The International Signal Code is a way of transmitting messages by flag from one ship to another. Most ships carry a set of International Signal flags. Ships fly these flags in groups or alone. Each flag has a distinctive color and design that stands for a letter of the alphabet or for a certain kind of message, such as "help!" or "danger!"

■ LEARN BY DOING

Look around you, both indoors and outdoors. Signals are used every-

An expert can send and receive signals in Morse code at as much as 40 words per minute. This means more than 10 Morse dots or dashes a second.

▼ *Semaphore is a way of signaling over a distance by using flags. What words could you make up from this selection of semaphore signs? Can you recognize "send" or "figure" for example?*

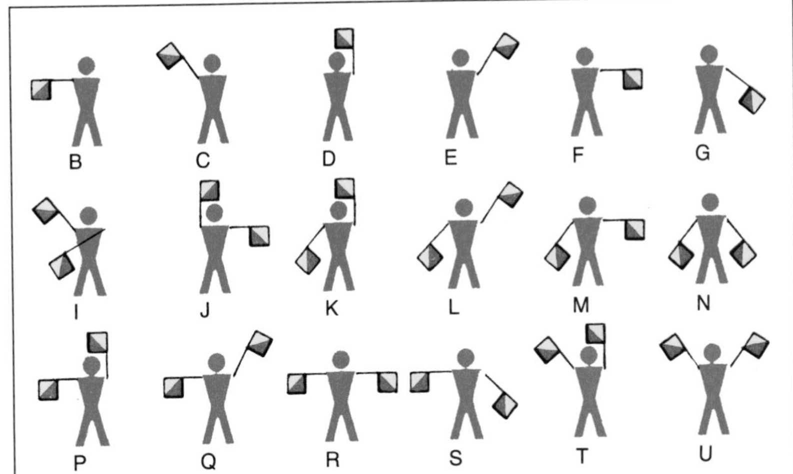

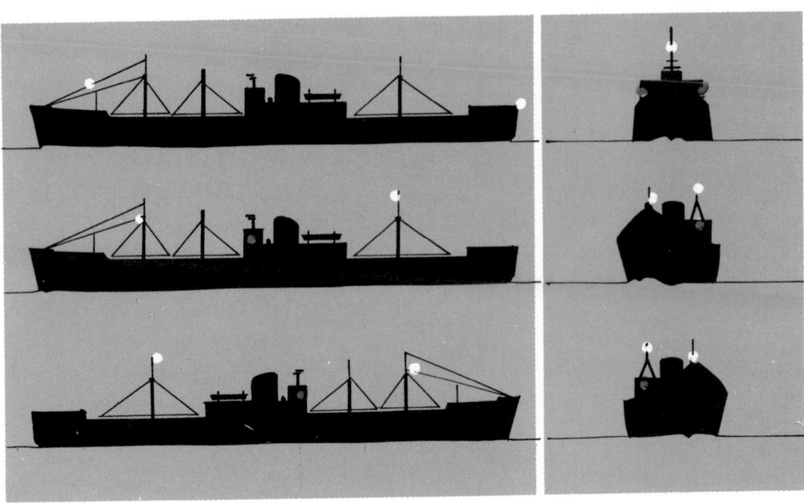

▶ *Signals used by ships. The two white lights are used to indicate a ship is at anchor. The other five pictures show the lights carried by a moving ship—white on the foremast and mainmast (and at the stern), green on the starboard side, and red on the port.*

▲ *Traffic signals control the flow of traffic. They keep it running as smoothly as possible, and so help prevent accidents.*

where to send messages. What messages are being sent by the following signals? (1) A flashing right taillight on a car. (2) A football umpire throwing a yellow cloth on the ground. (3) A ringing telephone. (4) A siren on an ambulance, police car, or fire truck. (5) A ringing alarm clock. (6) A person waving a hand while walking away. (7) Soldiers waving a white flag. (8) A judge pounding a gavel. ■

ALSO READ; CODES AND CIPHERS; COMMUNICATION; MORSE, SAMUEL F. B.; MORSE CODE; RADAR; SIGN LANGUAGE; TELEGRAPH; TELEPHONE.

◀ *Look at these photographs and see if you can work out what is happening from the people's gestures and facial expressions. Even if we are unaware of it, our bodies use sign language, which is also called "body language."*

SIGN LANGUAGE From earliest times until the present, people have used gestures to communicate without spoken words. Sign language may be a simple gesture, such as putting your index finger to your lips to indicate silence. Or sign language may be a complicated series of movements, such as the sign language that deaf people use to talk to each other.

The tribes of North American Plains Indians spoke different languages. When they needed to talk to people of another tribe, they used sign language. They also used sign language in speaking with white fur traders and settlers. Indian sign lan-

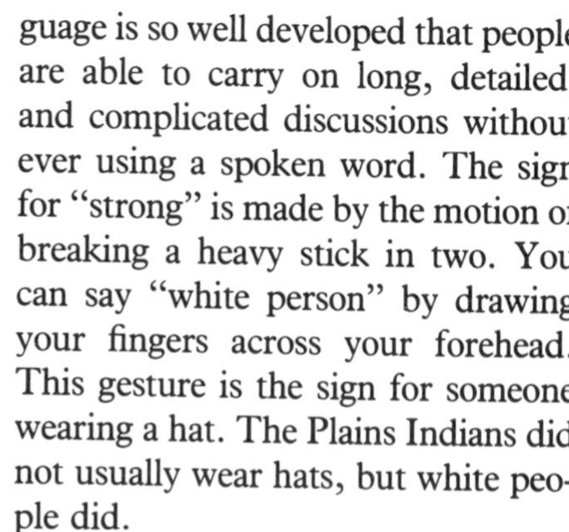

guage is so well developed that people are able to carry on long, detailed, and complicated discussions without ever using a spoken word. The sign for "strong" is made by the motion of breaking a heavy stick in two. You can say "white person" by drawing your fingers across your forehead. This gesture is the sign for someone wearing a hat. The Plains Indians did not usually wear hats, but white people did.

Sign language is an important communication tool of the deaf. In 1760, a French monk, Abbé de l'Épée, invented a way for the deaf to communicate. He developed a hand alphabet. Letters are made by placing the fingers in different positions. By spelling out what they wanted to say, the deaf were able to form sentences that could be seen rather than heard. Abbé Épée's finger alphabet has since become a rapid method of communication. Now there are gestures standing for entire words, phrases, and sentences, as well as letters. The sign language used by the deaf is a powerful tool. The version of it used in the

▼ *Sign language is used by the deaf in order to communicate. Some scientific researchers have taught chimpanzees to use this language, too.*

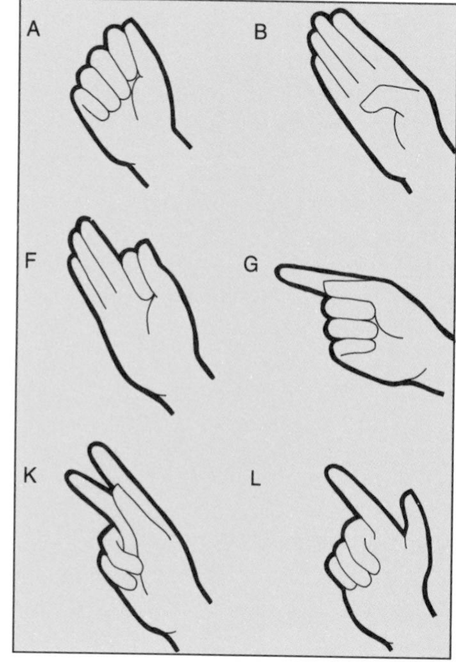

United States is called *Ameslan*. With it one can express complicated ideas. Not only fingers, but hands, arms, and facial expressions are used in communication. If you would like to learn the original finger alphabet, see the illustration with the article on HEARING.

Sign language plays an important part in many sports. In games such as football, basketball, and baseball, referees and umpires use various systems of arm and hand signals to tell spectators, coaches, and scorekeepers what is happening in the game and what the official decisions are.

■ LEARN BY DOING

Try turning off the sound of your television. How well can you follow what's going on? The actors' gestures may tell you a lot. You use sign language every day to communicate certain things. What do these gestures mean? (1) Twirling your index finger around your ear. (2) Shaking your fist. (3) Shrugging your shoulders. (4) Shaking your head. (5) Nodding your head. (6) Running the tip of your index finger under your chin from ear to ear. (7) Raising your hand in class. ■

ALSO READ: COMMUNICATION, HEARING, SIGNAL, SYMBOLISM.

SIKHISM Sikhs are people who live in the Punjab, in India. Their religious faith is known as Sikhism. The founder of Sikhism was a holy man named Nanak (1469–1539). He was the first of a line of ten religious teachers (*gurus*). The people who followed Nanak's teaching were named *sikha*, meaning "disciples."

The Sikh teachings are written in a holy book called *Ádi Granth*. One of their sacred places is the Golden Temple at Amritsar. The Sikhs grew from a religious group into a nation, famed for military prowess. They fought against the Muslim rulers of India, and also against the British in the 1840's.

Today, there are about 10 million Sikhs. Sikh men do not shave or cut their hair, and wear a *turban*, or linen headdress. Many carry a short dagger, or *kirpan*; other marks of a devout Sikh are a bangle, a comb, and short breeches. Some Sikhs now live in Europe, Canada, and the United States.

ALSO READ: INDIA.

SIKKIM The snow-covered Mount Kanchenjunga, soaring up more than 28,000 feet (8,530 m) in the Himalaya Mountains, overlooks the former kingdom of Sikkim. Sikkim lies between India and Tibet. It has no outlet to the sea. (See the map with the article on INDIA.)

More than a dozen peaks in Sikkim are higher than 20,000 feet (6,100 m). From the mountains, the land plunges down into deep valleys and gorges, separated by steep mountain ridges. Streams cascade into clear blue lakes. The lowest land is in the plains and tropical rain forests in the southern river valleys. The snow leopard, Himalayan bear, and lesser panda live in the Sikkim mountains. The yak, buffalo, wild pig, and deer also roam the highland.

Most of the people are of Nepalese descent and speak Gurkhali. Others are Lepchas, the region's first inhabitants, and Bhotias, nomadic herders in the mountains. The Lepchas and Bhotias speak Sikkimese and practice Buddhism. The Nepalese are mainly Hindus, but their religion has been strongly influenced by Buddhism.

Sikkim was established as a kingdom in 1642. For many years, Gurkhas from Nepal invaded the kingdom until the British defeated them in 1816. Sikkim was a dependency of Tibet until a treaty in 1890 between China and Great Britain made it a British protectorate. In

▲ *Sign language is still used by traders in some stock markets. This hand sign means that a trade has been completed.*

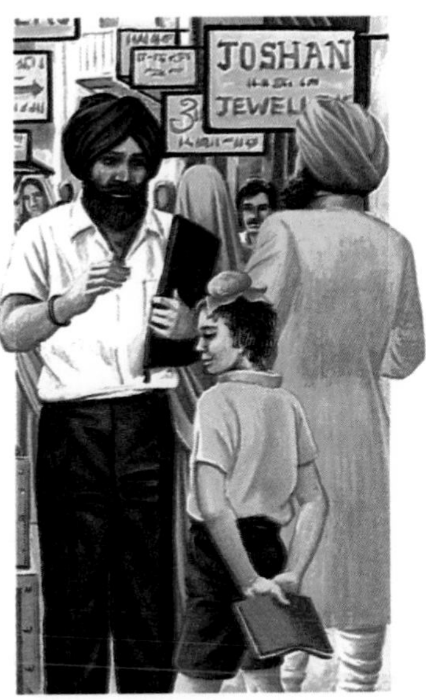

▲ *Male members of the Sikh religion never appear in public unless they are wearing a turban.*

▲ *A Buddhist pilgrim holds his traditional prayer wheel as he passes through Sikkim on his way to Tibet to the north.*

1950, Sikkim became a protectorate of India. Its capital is Gangtok.

In 1963, the chogyal (king) of Sikkim, Prince Namgyal, married a U.S. woman named Hope Cooke. Ten years later, he agreed to a constitutional agreement that gave more democratic rule to Sikkim. However, demonstrations against his rule brought many Indian troops into Sikkim to restore order. India gained greater control over the kingdom's affairs. Sikkim's legislative assembly voted in 1975 to become a state of India. It also voted to abolish the monarchy. The people of Sikkim approved statehood with India that same year. Today, Sikkim is ruled by a chief minister appointed by India.

ALSO READ: INDIA.

SILENT MOVIES see MOTION PICTURES.

It takes 3,000 silkworm cocoons to make a single pound (454 g) of silk thread.

SILICON You have probably heard people talk about "silicon chips." They are referring to tiny components made of silicon that are used in electronic machines. These components are called *semiconductors*, and without them your TV and your calculator would not work.

However, there are many other reasons why the element silicon is important. Of all the elements in the Earth's outer crust, silicon is the second most frequently found (oxygen is first). Ninety percent of the rocks of the Earth's crust are made of compounds of silicon.

Silicon and oxygen combine to produce *silica*. Silica is the commonest mineral of all. It takes many different forms. One of these is quartz—pure sand is made mostly of quartz. Other forms of silica are the mineral chalcedony, and opal, which is a gem. Glass is mostly made of silica.

ALSO READ: ELEMENT, GEM, GLASS, MINERAL, SAND, SEMICONDUCTOR.

▲ *Young silkworms feed on fresh mulberry leaves until they are fully grown and ready to spin their cocoons.*

▲ *A silk moth newly emerged from its cocoon.*

SILK Silk is a protein fiber, or thread, produced by spiders and certain insect larvae. Silk that is used commercially is obtained from the cocoon of the *silkworm*. A silkworm is the caterpillar of a silk moth. The word "silk" also refers to the cloth woven from silk threads. Silkworms have been raised in China and Japan for more than 4,000 years. *Sericulture*—the raising of silkworms—is still an important industry in parts of Asia, Europe, and the Middle East.

Silkworms, which are kept on large trays in hatching rooms, are fed leaves of the mulberry tree. After feeding for about five weeks, the silkworm stops eating and begins to spin itself a cocoon. A silkworm has glands that secrete a liquid that hardens into silk as it comes into contact with air. The glands open through two organs called *spinnerets*, which are beneath the silkworm's mouth. As the two threads of silk are secreted by the spinnerets, another gland secretes a gummy liquid that glues the two threads together. The silkworm keeps turning around, wrapping itself in the silk thread, which forms the cocoon. The gummy liquid also holds the threads of the cocoon together. (If people did not interfere at this stage, an adult silk moth would eventually emerge from the cocoon.)

To obtain the silk threads, factory workers put the cocoons into boiling water. This kills the larva, melts the gum, and loosens the threads. Then the thread is unwound. As much as 3,000 feet (900 m) of thread can be obtained from one cocoon. Several threads are wound together to get a single silk thread large enough for weaving.

Silk threads are woven (often with other kinds of fiber) into several fabrics, such as chiffon, satin, and velvet. Silk is also used in making ribbon, lace, and thread for sewing. Until nylon was invented, silk was used for making women's stockings. In spite of synthetic (man-made) fabrics, silk is still widely used because it is light and very strong.

ALSO READ: LACE, METAMORPHOSIS.

SILVER Silver is a metallic chemical element. It is one of the oldest metals known. Some silver is found in the ground in pure form, but today most silver is separated from ores. The two most important silver ores, *argentite* and *cerargyrite*, contain high percentages of silver. Copper ore often contains a little silver. As copper ore is much more common than silver ore, more silver comes as a by-product of copper mining than from mining silver ores. Silver is usually extracted from copper ore by a process called electrolysis, which uses electricity to separate the metals.

Silver is a fairly soft, white metal. It combines easily with oxygen to form a compound called silver oxide. This process is called tarnishing. The surface of tarnished silver is dark brown, blue-black, or black.

Silver is ductile, which means that it can be easily pulled into wires. It is also malleable, which means that it can be beaten into different shapes and thin sheets. Silver is one of the best conductors of heat and electricity. Beautiful jewelry and tableware are made from silver. For these purposes an alloy called sterling silver is often used. Sterling silver is 92.5 percent silver and 7.5 percent copper. The copper makes sterling harder than pure silver. Much tableware is now made of silver plate instead of sterling silver. Silver plate is much less expensive. By the process of electrolysis, a thin coat of silver alloy is applied to base metals. However, silver plate does not wear nearly as well as sterling silver does. The base metal tends to show through as the silver plate wears off, leaving a soiled appearance.

Silver has been used to make coins since ancient times. But pure silver is both too soft and too valuable, so most modern "silver" coins are made of alloys of silver and copper, or more usually of copper and nickel.

Today, most silver is used in photography. A coating of crystals of a silver compound on the film changes when it is exposed to light, so that it holds a black-and-white image. Silver is used also in high-quality electrical switches and electronic equipment. Tanks that hold chemicals and dyes are sometimes lined with silver.

More than half of the world's supply of silver comes from Canada, Russia, Peru, and Mexico. The United States and Australia also have large silver mines.

ALSO READ: ELEMENT, JEWELRY, METAL, MINES AND MINING, PHOTOGRAPHY.

▲ *Silver is a beautiful, rare, and precious metal. It tarnishes in air, especially air polluted by sulfur.*

▲ *The Egyptian Pharaoh Psusennes, who lived around 1000 B.C., was buried in this silver coffin made in his image. The casket is solid silver except for the gold cobra on the pharaoh's forehead.*

SIMPLE MACHINE see MACHINE.

SINGAPORE Singapore is an independent republic at the tip of the Malay peninsula in Asia. It is an island 27 miles (43 km) long and 14 miles (22.5 km) wide, about one-fifth

The largest silver nugget was found at Sonora in Mexico. It weighed 2,261 pounds (1,026 kg).

SINGAPORE

Capital City: Singapore (2,300,000 people).
Area: 224 square miles (581 sq. km).
Population: 2,670,000.
Government: Republic.
Export Products: Machinery and transport equipment, mineral fuels, chemicals, garments, electronic components.
Unit of Money: Singapore dollar.
Official Languages: Chinese, English, Malay, Tamil.

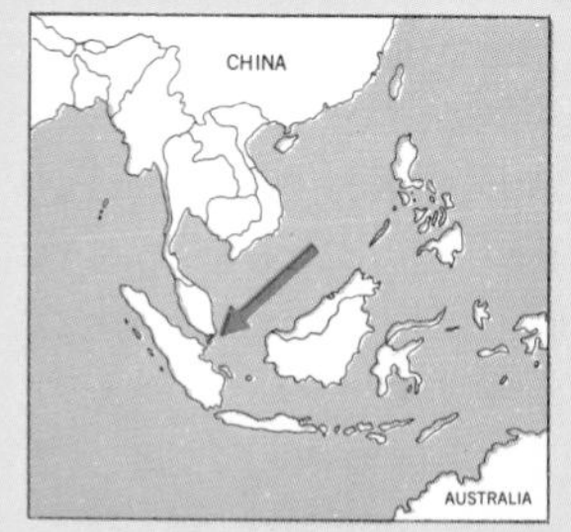

the size of Rhode Island. Singapore is connected to the mainland of Malaysia by a causeway that crosses the Strait of Johore. About 50 small islets are also a part of Singapore. (See the map with the article on ASIA.)

A fascinating mixture of people and cultures, the city of Singapore is located on the southeast end of the island of Singapore. It is one of the busiest seaports in the world, and the most important port in southeast Asia. Rubber, timber, textile, and machinery pass through there.

▲ *Singapore is the name of both a tiny country in Southeast Asia and its capital city.*

Most of Singapore is low. Originally, the island was made up of swamps and tangled jungle. The climate is warm and humid for most of the year. However, the temperature seldom exceeds 95° F (35° C) because of the cool sea breezes.

Singapore is one of the most heavily populated countries in the world, with more than 11,600 persons per square mile (4,480 per sq. km). Most are Chinese. Malay is the national language, but Chinese, English, and Tamil are also official languages. Standards in health, education, and housing are high. Tourism is flourishing, and many modern hotels have been built. Singapore is also growing in importance as a financial center with well-developed worldwide air, sea, and telecommunication links.

A British East Indian administrator named Sir Thomas Stamford Raffles founded the city of Singapore as a trading post in 1819. In 1826, it was made a part of the Straits Settlement, which became a British crown colony in 1867. Great Britain built a big naval base at Singapore. In World War II, Japan captured Singapore. It was returned to Great Britain after the war. In 1959, Singapore became a self-governing state in the Commonwealth of Nations. In 1963, Singapore joined the Federation of Malaysia, but it broke away in 1965 and became an independent republic.

ALSO READ: MALAYSIA.

SINGING Your voice is your own built-in musical instrument. You use it to communicate with others when you speak and to make music when you sing. Some people take voice lessons and become professional singers. But most people sing just for fun, either alone or with a group. If your school has a chorus or your church has a children's choir, you might like to join one of them. By singing with a group, you will learn how to follow a choral director and how to sing music that is performed in parts. You'll also learn many types of music that most people never have a chance to learn.

Vocal Sound When you exhale air, it passes between a pair of muscles, called *vocal cords*, in your throat. When you tighten your vocal cords, the air passing between makes them vibrate. The vibrating cords cause the air to come out in the form of sound waves that can be heard. The faster the vibrations, the higher the pitch of the sound. When your vocal cords are completely relaxed, they do not vibrate and no sound can be heard. You can feel this in action. Sing a tone—any tone—and gently touch your throat. You should be able to feel the vibrations. Now close your mouth and hum a tone. You may be able to feel the vibrations by touching your cheekbones or the bridge of your nose.

When the sound waves leave your throat, they vibrate against the bones of your face and against the inside of your mouth and nose areas. These secondary vibrations are called *resonance*. It is the resonance that determines to a great extent what a person's singing voice sounds like. You can probably recognize people you know just by hearing their voices. This is because the voice quality, or resonance, is different for each person. Each person's mouth and nose area has its own individual shape, and so the resonance is different in each. Some people have heavier bones than others, and this causes differences in resonance. If you watch people's mouths, you'll notice that they all open and close slightly differently.

The pitch (highness or lowness) of a voice depends on the length of the vocal cords. Shorter vocal cords produce higher-pitched voices than do longer vocal cords. Boys' and girls' voices are usually light and high because their vocal cords are short. As boys reach their early teens, their vocal cords lengthen and their voices become lower and deeper. Girls' voices also get somewhat lower when they reach adulthood, but the change is not so obvious as in boys.

▼ *Dame Joan Sutherland is an Australian soprano known throughout the world for her opera singing.*

Types of Singing Voices Adult singing voices are divided into types according to how high or low they can sing. Women's voices are classed as *soprano* and *alto* (also called *contralto*). The alto range is lower than the soprano. Men's voices are classed as *tenor* and *bass*. The bass range is lower than the tenor. *Countertenors* are men with voices higher than tenors. There are two middle ranges for men and women. A *mezzo-soprano* has a pitch range between soprano and alto. A *baritone*'s range is between tenor and bass.

Voices are also classed according to their quality. *Coloratura sopranos* can sing very high notes. Their voices are quite flexible and can move very rapidly and accurately from one note to another. *Lyric sopranos* have a more flowing voice quality and cannot change pitch so rapidly. *Dramatic sopranos* have powerful voices that can be heard clearly over a large orchestra.

Dramatic tenors (also called *heroic tenors*) have big, full voices capable of great power. *Lyric tenors* have softer, more flowing voices. *Basso profundos* (deep basses) can sing extremely low notes and are capable of great power. *Basso contantes* (singing basses) have lighter, flowing voices and are not able to reach the low notes of the basso profundo.

Types of Singers Singers are often classified according to the kinds of music they sing. Folk singers perform folk songs. Often they have had no

▲ *A group of gospel singers, clapping as they sing spiritual songs.*

The longest operatic aria (a song sung by one person) is the one performed by Brünnhilde in Richard Wagner's opera *Götterdämmerung*. It lasts for almost 15 minutes.

▲ *David Bowie, a pop singer who has highlighted many different musical styles in an unusually long career.*

vocal lessons but have pleasing, natural voices that express the feelings or meaning in a song. Singers of popular rock music as well as jazz vocalists use their voices as part of the sound made by the musical group.

Singers in the field of classical music usually go through years of vocal training—learning how to control their voices and perform very complex vocal works. Some specialize in opera or in giving solo concerts. Many sing with professional choirs and choruses.

Singing and Speaking In speaking, you do not use such a wide variety of pitches as in singing. When you sing, you hold the pitches out for a much longer length of time, and there are fewer pauses (or periods of silence) than when speaking. When a singer holds out a pitch, he or she is almost always holding it on a vowel sound. There are very few consonants that can be easily sustained. When you speak, the vowel sounds are usually held about the same length of time as consonant sounds. You do not extend vowels as you do in singing.

There is a great difference in the way you can use your lungs when singing. As you speak, you inhale and exhale about every four seconds. Within that time, you can speak one or two whole sentences in a clear voice without having to gasp or catch your breath. But in singing, you sometimes have to hold a note out for 20 to 25 seconds or more. During that time, you cannot take a breath without breaking the tone, so you have to control carefully the flow of air from your lungs. When singing, you must often control your voice to make it louder or softer while still holding out a single tone. This also requires a special breath control.

ALSO READ: CAROL; CARUSO, ENRICO; CHORAL MUSIC; CHORUSES AND CHOIRS; FOLK SONG; MUSIC; MUSICAL COMEDY; OPERA.

SINGLE-CELLED ANIMAL see PROTOZOAN.

SIOUX INDIANS The Sioux Indians were a large and powerful group of tribes that lived in Minnesota, Wisconsin, and North and South Dakota. The name Sioux is not an Indian word. It is taken from *Nadowessioux*, the name French traders gave to these Indians. The Sioux called themselves the Dakota, which means allies.

Protestant missionaries devised a Sioux alphabet in the 1850's. As a result, the stories and myths of the Sioux have been preserved in writing.

The Sioux were divided into three main divisions—the Santee, the Yankton, and the Teton. The Santee and the Yankton were farmers. The Teton, the largest and best-known division of the Sioux, were warriors and buffalo (bison) hunters. Buffalo meat was their main food. They made clothes, moccasins, and tipis from buffalo hides, and tools from buffalo bones. The Sioux are noted for their fine beadwork and the paintings they made on buffalo hides.

The Sun Dance was one of the chief Sioux rituals. The four-day dance was held on important occasions to honor the Great Spirit or to ensure good hunting.

▲ *An old Sioux Indian woman.*

When gold prospectors began to take over Sioux lands in the Black Hills in the 1870's, the Sioux went to war with the white people. Chiefs Sitting Bull, Crazy Horse, Rain-in-the-Face, and their braves massacred about 260 U.S. Army troops under the leadership of General George Custer at the Battle of Little Big Horn in 1876. The uprising was later crushed by troops of the Federal Government.

In 1890, a band of Sioux belonging to the Ghost Dance cult were captured and brought to Wounded Knee Creek, South Dakota. Some Indians, wearing "bulletproof" ghost shirts, refused to disarm. A battle began, and U.S. troops opened fire, killing about 200 Sioux. In 1973, about 200 Indians, mostly Sioux, seized the village of Wounded Knee, demanding better treatment. An agreement was reached after about 70 days.

About 40,000 Sioux now live on reservations in North and South Dakota and in Minnesota. Many of them are farmers.

ALSO READ: BISON; CUSTER, GEORGE; INDIANS, AMERICAN; INDIAN WARS; SITTING BULL.

SITTING BULL (about 1834–1890) Sitting Bull was a medicine man and chief of the Sioux Indians. He organized Indians to fight in the Battle of Little Big Horn, the last big Indian victory over the whites.

Sitting Bull was born in South Dakota. He was the son of a subchief and was named Jumping Badger. He earned the reputation of being a brave warrior when, at the age of 14, he scalped an enemy in a battle against the Crow Indians. In honor of this feat, he was given the name Sitting Bull, his father's name.

Sitting Bull became a respected leader in his tribe. When white prospectors began to invade Sioux land looking for gold, Sitting Bull organized an alliance of Cheyenne, Sioux, and Arapaho Indians to fight them. The result was the massacre of General George Custer and about 260 U.S. Army troops at the Battle of Little Big Horn in 1876. After the battle, Sitting Bull and some of his followers retreated into Canada. However, Sitting Bull was forced to return to the United States in 1881. He surrendered and was sent to live on a reservation in North Dakota. Several years later, he joined Buffalo Bill's Wild West Show and toured with the show in Europe.

When Sitting Bull returned to the reservation, he helped start the Ghost Dance cult, a kind of religion that promised the Indians a return to their old way of life. Indian guards working for the Federal Government tried to arrest Sitting Bull for his support of the Ghost Dance cult. When he resisted, he and his son were shot dead.

ALSO READ: BUFFALO BILL; CUSTER, GEORGE; INDIANS, AMERICAN; INDIAN WARS; SIOUX INDIANS.

▲ *Sitting Bull, the great Sioux Indian chief.*

SKELETON The bones of your body support the softer parts of your body, and give your body its general shape. The bones also provide anchors for muscles and leverage for the movements of muscles. The long bones of your body contain *marrow* that makes red blood cells and some white blood cells. All the bones together make up a skeleton. Your skeleton is inside your body, so it is called an *endoskeleton*. All animals with backbones—amphibians, birds, fish, reptiles, and mammals—have endoskeletons. So do some simpler animals, such as sponges and echinoderms. Other animals have skeletons on the outside of their bodies called *exoskeletons*. An exoskeleton not only provides support and shape for its owner's body but also acts as a protective armor. Insects have exoskeletons made of a hard, tough material called *chitin*. Crustaceans (crabs, lobsters, crayfish, shrimp, and others) have chitin exoskeletons strengthened with lime. Mollusks (clams, oysters, mussels, and others) have skeletons made of a hard, chalklike material.

Your ribs form a cage that protects your heart and lungs. You should have 12 pairs of ribs in all, though some people have an extra pair.

The Human Skeleton Bones are shaped and connected in many different ways. A bone can be long and tubular, like an arm or leg bone, or it can be a flattish plate, like the bones of the skull. Some bones are connected at movable joints, such as the knee or shoulder. Other bones are joined by connective tissue, or knitted solidly together, like the bones of the skull. A baby may have more than 300 bones. As a child grows older, some bones grow together (knit) to form single bones. Most adults have 206 bones. Some adults may have a

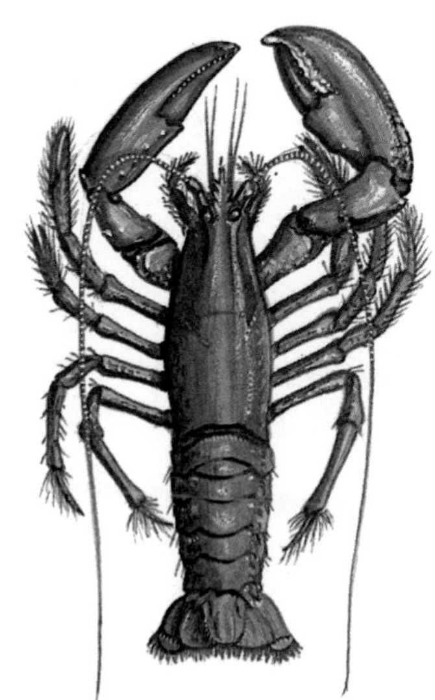

▲ *A lobster has an* exoskeleton—*that is a skeleton on the outside rather than the inside of its body.*

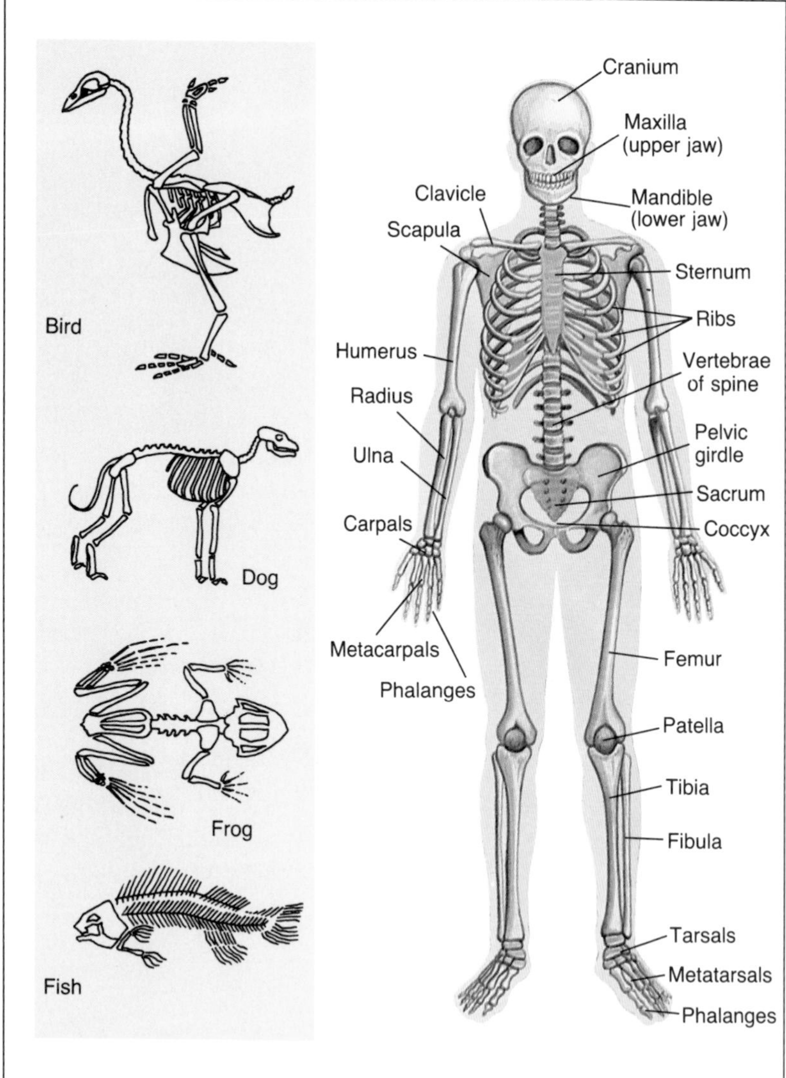

▲ *The skeletons of four quite different vertebrates (animals with backbones)—bird, mammal, amphibian, and fish. On the right is the skeleton of another mammal, a human being.*

The largest bone in your body is the *femur*, or thigh bone. The smallest bone you have is the *stapes*, or stirrup bone in your middle ear. It is about 1/10–1/6 in (2.6–3.4 mm) long.

few more bones, or a few less bones, depending on the number of bones that knitted together.

Your skull is made up of 28 bones, and there are 26 *vertebrae*—rings of bone—in your spine. Your chest consists of 25 bones: one breastbone, called the *sternum*, and 24 ribs.

You have two collarbones and two shoulder bones. Each arm consists of one upper-arm bone and two lower-arm bones. There are eight bones in each one of your wrists. The palm of each hand is made up of five bones, and 14 bones make up the fingers of each hand.

There are two hipbones. Each leg consists of one thighbone, one kneecap, one shinbone, and one bone on the other side of the lower leg.

The ankle of each foot has seven bones. The foot has five, and 14 bones make up the toes of each foot.

Most of the bones in your body are connected to other bones. One that does not meet another bone is the U-shaped *hyoid* bone in the throat. The patella (kneecap) is another.

ALSO READ: BONE, HUMAN BODY.

SKIING Skiing is the art of traveling over snow-covered ground on *skis*—long, narrow runners with upward-curved tips in the front. Skiing is a competitive winter sport and a popular form of recreation, as well as a means of transportation.

Equipment *Ski boots* are among the most important pieces of ski equipment. They are made of plastic or stiff leather, high enough to cover the ankles. The boots provide ankle support and also keep the feet warm. Some ski boots lace up, but most of them have buckles.

▼ *Alpine skiing in Switzerland. Most skiers wear special winter gear, but the hot sun brings out the more comfortable casual wear on this skier.*

Ski bindings and *ski poles* are also important. Ski bindings hold the skier's boots on the skis. When a skier has a jarring fall, a safety mechanism in the bindings releases the skis, preventing serious injury to the skier's feet and legs. Ski poles are used for balance. They are made of fiberglass, aluminum, steel, or bamboo. Ski poles must not be too heavy, but they should be strong. A ski pole has a sharp tip and a circular webbed ring at the bottom to prevent the pole from sinking into the snow when the skier pushes it down.

Most skis today are made of fiberglass or aluminum. These skis are very strong, lightweight, and flexible. Skis are also made of hardwood, such as hickory or spruce.

Experienced skiers use skis that are usually more than one foot (30 cm) longer then their height. Beginners use shorter skis. Usually, a new skier should have skis that are a few inches longer than his or her height. Some beginners start out in a training course with skis that are only three feet (91 cm) long and gradually work their way up through a series of three or four different lengths.

Skiing Competition Skiing is an official Olympic sport and is an important part of the Winter Olympic Games. The two main types of skiing are *Alpine* and *Nordic*. Alpine skiing includes *downhill* racing and an event called the *slalom*. Downhill races are fast races down an open slope. The slalom is a downhill race across a zigzag course marked by a series of *gates*. The gates are sets of stakes with flags on top. The skier must pass through each of the gates in turn. The *giant slalom* is like the slalom, but it is more rugged.

Nordic skiing includes *ski jumping* and *cross-country* skiing. In ski jumping, the contestants are judged on their form (grace and style) as they leave the ramp, fly through the air, and land. Judges also award points for the distance of each ski jump. In cross-country skiing, the skiers must travel a long distance through snowy country, racing uphill and down, and across flat ground. Freestyle, or "hot-dog," skiing involves all sorts of aerial acrobatics and is becoming an increasingly popular competition.

▲ *Cross-country skiing is becoming increasingly popular as both a recreational and a competitive winter sport. The cross-country skier wears trainers which are secured to the long, narrow ski by a toe-hold binding only. This leaves the ankles free for maneuvering and "walking" the skis over the terrain.*

Skiing Technique The techniques used in Alpine skiing are those applied in recreational skiing. Basically, a skier must know how to go down a hill, turn, and stop. It is best to start by zigzagging or *traversing* across the surface of the slope. The simplest way to turn, slow down, or stop is to do the *snowplow*. The back ends of the skis are spread far apart and the tips of the skis are pushed together in a V shape. Both skis are bent slightly inward. To turn to the left, the skier puts weight on the right ski.

Skiing for beginners is not very dangerous so long as the new skiers get the proper instruction and have correctly maintained and adjusted equipment. *Don't* make the mistake of trying to learn to ski or going on difficult slopes without the aid of an expert, such as a ski instructor.

▲ *The slalom involves skiing through a series of "gates" (pairs of flags) placed very close together.*

History of Skiing People have traveled on skis for thousands of years. In the Djugarden Museum in Stockholm, Sweden, a pair of skis said to be

▲ *A traditional style ski resort in the Swiss Alps.*

more than 5,000 years old is on display. Skis were used by soldiers in Scandinavian countries during the Middle Ages. Northern countries still have ski troops. Skiing became widespread in Europe in the late 1500's, and in North America by the early 1800's.

ALSO READ: OLYMPIC GAMES, SPORTS, WATER SKIING.

SKIN The bodies of most animals are covered by an outer layer of skin. The adult human body is covered by about 18 square feet (1.67 sq. m) of skin. Human skin varies in thickness. It is very thin over the eyelids and quite thick on the soles of the feet.

The skin of some simple animals is only one cell thick. The skin of humans and other animals with backbones is made up of two main layers. The outer layer is the *epidermis*. It is made up mostly of dead, flattened cells, which are continually wearing away and being replaced by live cells from beneath.

▼ *Some of the major features of your skin.*

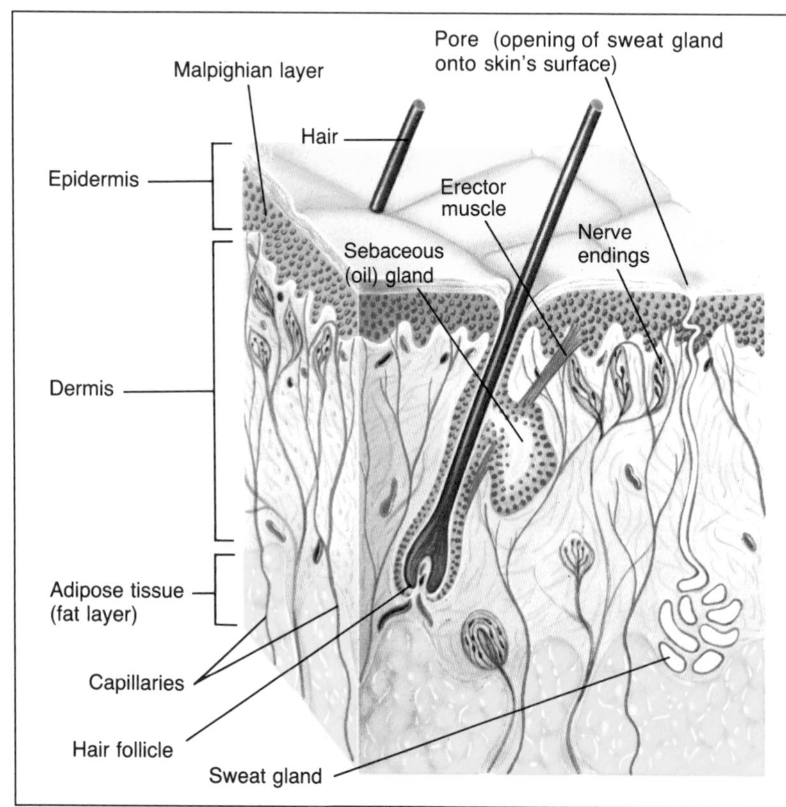

Under the epidermis is the *dermis*. This layer of skin is made up entirely of living cells. Many small blood vessels and nerve endings run through the dermis. Because of these nerve endings, the skin is our organ of the sense of touch. Small, coiled tubes in the dermis lead to the outer surface of the epidermis. These tubes are *sweat glands*, and their openings are *pores*. Hairs grow out of the skin. The roots of the hairs are in the dermis, and the openings in the skin from which hairs grow are called *follicles*.

When the skin is unbroken, it helps keep out harmful bacteria. There is, however, a way bacteria can enter unbroken skin. In the dermis are glands that produce a thick, fatty oil, called *sebum*. These glands ooze sebum into hair follicles. The sebum keeps the skin and hair from becoming too dry. Some people have glands that produce too much sebum. The sebum clogs hair follicles and pores. Certain kinds of bacteria grow in the sebum. When they do, they produce an infection. You see the infection as a pimple or possibly a boil. This infection can develop into a skin disease called *acne*. Adolescent people often have acne, but almost always it disappears as they grow older. Good medical advice can help overcome serious acne.

The skin helps to regulate the temperature of the body. Blood in vessels near the skin surface loses heat by radiation. When the skin becomes cold, the tiny blood vessels in it contract and force blood deeper into the body. This holds heat in. When the body is too warm, the blood vessels in the skin expand and take in more blood. The blood gives off heat by radiation. The sweat glands in the skin pour out water in the form of *perspiration* or *sweat*. The perspiration evaporates. Since evaporation is a cooling process, perspiring cools the skin.

Sometimes, when you are embarrassed, you blush—the blood vessels

▲ *When you tan in the sun, your skin produces a lot of a substance called melanin, which turns your skin brown. Too much tanning can give you skin cancer.*

of the skin fill with extra blood and your skin becomes deep pink.

Skin Color Cells in the lowest layer of the epidermis produce a brown substance called *melanin*. This substance colors the skin. The difference in the skin color of black, brown, and white people is due to varying amounts of melanin in their skins. The more melanin in the skin, the darker it is. The skin of a "white" person is really a light brownish pink. This color results from a sparse scattering of melanin and from the tiny blood vessels just below the epidermis. A very few people, called *albinos*, have no melanin.

Another skin-coloring substance is *carotene*. Carotene gives carrots their color. Human beings with more carotene than melanin are said to be yellow-skinned, as are the people of much of Asia.

When your skin is exposed to sunlight, the melanin-producing cells make an extra amount of melanin. The result is a tanning of your skin. Sometimes the tanning is spotty because the melanin forms clumps. These clumps are *freckles*. Over exposure to the sun can cause skin cancer.

Tattoos A tattoo is a mark or figure that is set on the body by putting dye under the skin or by making scars. For thousands of years, tattooing had religious meaning. It still does among many people of Asia and the islands of the South Pacific Ocean. In the United States today, some people have designs, mottoes, and names tattooed on their skins. Modern tattooing is done with an electric needle that punctures the skin and injects a small amount of red, blue, green, or yellow dye into the dermis. Amateur tattooing can cause serious skin ailments.

Skin Care Too much sunlight can be bad for your skin. You should let your skin tan slowly and gradually, and not too deeply. Excessive tanning can irritate the skin, causing wrinkling and even skin cancer.

Excessive dryness and oiliness are also bad for the skin. Unusually dry skin should be washed with a cleansing cream. Oily skin should be washed with a detergent soap.

ALSO READ: ALBINO, BLOOD, CELL, HAIR, HUMAN BODY, SENSE ORGAN, TOUCH.

SKIN DIVING see SCUBA DIVING.

SKUNK

The world's smelliest mammal, the skunk, can be smelled from as much as half a mile (800 m) away. Several kinds live in North America. The skunk is a black and white animal about the size of a cat and has a very bushy tail. It belongs to the badger family. The smell is a defense against enemies. When frightened, the skunk turns its back, raises its tail, and squirts a foul-smelling liquid from special glands. The stream of liquid can travel up to 12 feet (3.7 m), and it can burn the eyes and skin of the attacker.

Skunks live mainly in woods and grassy places. They hide in burrows

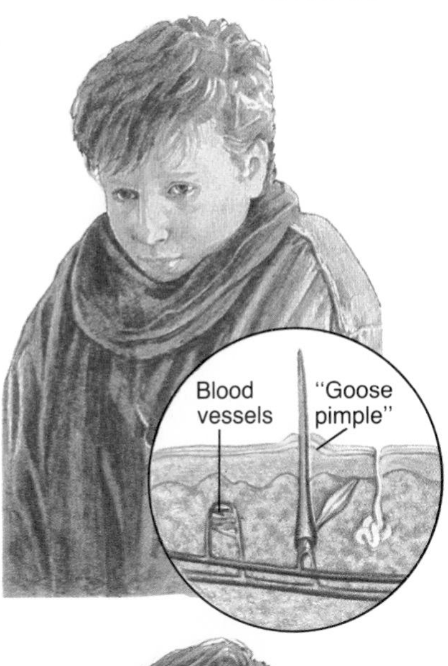

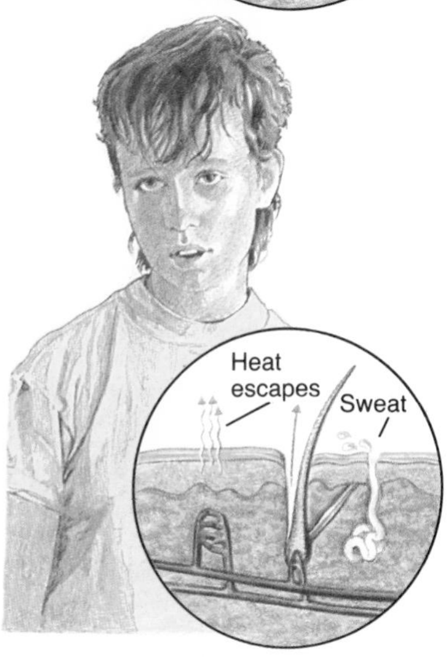

▲ *When you are cold, your skin's blood vessels become narrow, so less heat is lost at the surface. "Goose pimples" help to trap the warm air around hair follicles. In hot weather, though, those blood vessels widen, and sweat evaporates to keep you cool.*

▲ *When a skunk is threatened with attack, it puts on an aggressive display. It stamps its feet and raises its tail over its back to disclose a pair of musk glands. These glands can squirt a foul-smelling liquid a long way! Skunks sometimes live in burrows under outbuildings.*

by day and come out at night to catch various small animals.

ALSO READ: MAMMAL, WEASEL.

SKY When you look at the sky on a clear day, it seems as if the Earth is covered by a blue dome. The sky is blue because of what happens to sunlight as it enters the Earth's atmosphere. Sunlight is made up of light rays of all wavelengths. The longer wavelengths make up red light, and the shorter ones make up blue light. As the light rays enter the Earth's atmosphere they are scattered by tiny molecules and other particles in the atmosphere. The light of shorter wavelength is scattered more than the light of longer wavelength. This means that blue-violet light is scattered all over the sky, while much of the red and yellow light comes straight through the atmosphere. So the sky is blue, while the sun looks more orange than it would if you were looking at it from a spaceship outside the atmosphere.

Sometimes at sunset the sky looks red. The sunlight is coming toward you from a lower angle in the sky. The lower the sun, the longer is the path that the light rays must travel through the atmosphere. Even the longer orange and red rays become scattered. At sunset, the shorter blue rays never get through the atmosphere, so you do not see them. For a while after sunset you can still see the scattered red and orange light in the sky.

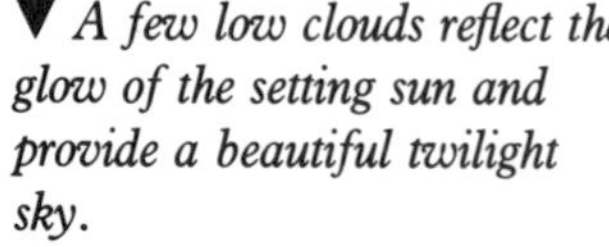

▼ *A few low clouds reflect the glow of the setting sun and provide a beautiful twilight sky.*

If you stand at a place where the surface of the Earth is flat, the sky seems to meet the Earth in any direction you look. The point at which the sky and Earth seem to "meet" is called the *horizon*. From where you are standing, the horizon is at the same distance no matter in what direction you look. If you walk toward the horizon, you do not get closer to it. No matter where you are, the surface of the Earth curves downward and away from you. The distance at which you can no longer see the Earth's surface—because it has curved down too far—is the horizon.

ALSO READ: ATMOSPHERE, COLOR, LIGHT.

SKY DIVING see PARACHUTE.

SKYSCRAPER see CONSTRUCTION.

SLAVERY A slave is a person who is owned by another person as a piece of property. Slaves generally have no rights in society and are often completely at the mercy of their masters, who can treat their slaves as they wish. Slaves work for their masters without pay. But the masters usually provide food, clothing, and shelter to keep their slaves healthy and able to work. Slavery was once common. There are few slaves now, but in some parts of the world slavery has not stopped completely.

Slavery Ancient and Modern Slavery probably began at an early period in human history when conquering people found it profitable to keep prisoners of war instead of killing them. War captives were distributed among the wealthy citizens, who used them to work the land, to build public structures, or for any other task the conquerors decided upon. All ancient Middle East nations had slaves. In the Bible, the laws of Moses state that a Hebrew slave must be freed after six years.

In ancient Greece, slavery was the fate of all prisoners of war. No one considered slavery to be wrong. It was simply the victor's right to take over the lives of conquered people. Slaves could be bought and sold and were considered to be the owner's property—just like a house or a cow. Owners could treat their slaves as they pleased. Slaves in Greek society were used as household servants, field workers, teachers, and as oarsmen for ships.

Roman slavery was a little different from the Greek. Roman law considered all people to be free, and slavery was considered an unnatural way of life. But the Romans considered slavery better than killing a captive. Poor people in both Greece and Rome sometimes sold their children into slavery to get money. Debtors often sold themselves into slavery as repayment for money they owed.

When Christianity became the main religion of Europe, slavery gradually gave way to serfdom. A *serf* was a person who swore faithfulness to an overlord and was required to remain on and work the master's land. Often, the serfs' only payment was the small crops they were able to grow for themselves. By the 1300's, slavery, or complete ownership of people, had nearly died out in Europe. But, in the 1400's, Portuguese explorers and merchants began capturing African blacks and bringing them to Europe as slaves. Spain joined the slave trade when King Charles I allowed colonists and traders to import black slaves into the Spanish colonies.

Slavery quickly became a profitable industry for white Europeans. Traders sent people into the African interior to capture or lure black men and women to the coast. There they dumped the chained blacks into deep pits to await a slave ship. Blacks were beaten, branded, and fed only a starvation diet to keep them frightened and subdued. When a slave ship arrived, the blacks were herded aboard and made to lie side by side on the floors of low-roofed decks with no room even to sit up, much less stand. They were kept in these cramped quarters for an entire voyage, often lasting three or four months. Once a week slaves were allowed to walk on deck for a few minutes of exercise. At these times, slaves often tried to escape the torture by jumping overboard. On reaching the destination, the blacks were put up for sale by auction. Healthy, strong black men brought a higher price than women and children. Sick or injured slaves that could not be sold were usually killed. Besides blacks, Jews, Moors, Turks, and North American Indians were also captured and sold into slavery.

▲ *A picture, painted in 1237, of a slave market in Yemen.*

▲ *Black people were kidnapped from their homes by slave-traders in Africa and then shipped via Europe to be sold as slaves in the Americas.*

Slavery in the United States In 1619, a Dutch ship brought 20 black

▲ *At slave auctions in the South, blacks were sold like work animals. Many whites cared little about the feelings of the slaves and thought nothing of separating parents from their children.*

▼ *Slavery was practiced in many countries besides the United States. European colonial powers used slaves to work the large sugar, and other, plantations in the West Indies and South America.*

men to Jamestown, Virginia. They were treated much the same way as white indentured servants. They served their masters from seven to ten years, then became free men and usually received a grant of land from the colony. But as the colony needed more agricultural workers, planters began to think of slavery as a solution. In 1661, the Virginia colonial legislature—the House of Burgesses—passed a law making black people and their children slaves for life. When the first census was taken in 1790, there were already 757,000 blacks in the United States. Nine out of ten of these were slaves. By 1860, the United States had about four million slaves. This was about one-third the total population of the Southern slave states. Slavery did not spread to the North because most farms there were small. People did not need slaves to help with the work. But the Southern plantation system was based on the use of captive black labor, and Southern prosperity depended on it.

After the invention of the cotton gin in 1793, owning slaves became very profitable because growing cotton was so profitable. Blacks could work for long hours in the cotton fields to grow the cotton that would be processed at the gins.

Ownership of slaves created great class differences in the South. At the top were a few great planters. They owned plantations of 500 to 2,000 acres (200–800 ha) or more, cultivated by 50 to 200 or more slaves. They had beautiful plantation homes where many slaves worked as *house servants*. These plantation owners bought the best land, made the biggest profits, and hired the best *overseers*—people who watched the *field hands* (blacks who worked in the fields). Some plantation owners treated their slaves decently, but others did not. Most planters took care of their blacks so that they could do a good day's work. If a slave died or escaped, replacing him or her was expensive.

Slaves lived in outbuildings, called slave quarters. Slave quarters could be anything from neat little family cottages to prisonlike buildings where all blacks lived in a single large room and were watched over by guards. Working hours for a slave were long—usually from sunrise to sunset. The darker-skinned blacks were usually sent to work in the fields, while the lighter-skinned people were house servants. The field hands worked in groups, called *gangs*, and were watched by a *straw boss* who made sure no one took time to relax. The house servants were less harshly treated and were allowed certain privileges. This created something of a split among blacks. Many came to regard lighter skin as a sign of rank and privilege.

The Northwest Ordinance of 1787 prohibited slavery north of the Ohio River. In 1808, Congress passed a law that forbade bringing any more slaves into the country. But leaders still did not know what would happen if all slaves were freed. They believed blacks would be helpless, especially if not given land, tools, and training for living on their own.

One group of slave owners in Virginia, Maryland, and Kentucky thought they had solved the problem. They founded the American Colonization Society to send slaves back to Africa. In 1822, they established the

▲ *Slaves were forced to work long hours at back-breaking tasks. These field hands had to work all day in the hot sun in the slave-owner's cotton fields.*

Republic of Liberia (meaning "freedom") on the west coast of Africa as a land for U.S. blacks. But the society did not have much money and could send only a few thousand blacks to Liberia. Many blacks did not want to go to Africa. Many were third- and fourth-generation Americans who knew nothing about Africa and had adapted to life in the United States.

Some slaves tried to escape from their masters. Some ran away and became free people in the North. Others were caught and returned to their masters. A few took part in strikes and local uprisings. In 1822 in Charleston, South Carolina, a free black man named Denmark Vesey enlisted slaves in an attempt to capture the city. The revolt was put down and 37 blacks were executed. In Virginia in 1831, a serious rebellion was led by a slave named Nat Turner. He led an uprising that ended in at least 100 deaths before he was captured and hanged. In 1845, about 75 unarmed slaves from Maryland tried to fight their way to freedom in Pennsylvania.

After these uprisings, whites became frightened and placed more controls upon blacks. They were forbidden to assemble or move about after dark. Nighttime road patrols were set up. Whites were forbidden to teach slaves to read or write in every Southern state except Maryland, Kentucky, and Tennessee. Some free blacks could not enter Southern port cities at all. The Fugitive Slave Law was passed by Congress in 1850, in exchange for allowing new U.S. territories to enter the Union as free states (rather than as states where slavery was allowed). This law required all free states to help in hunting down runaway slaves and returning them to their masters.

The Dred Scott Decision further tightened controls on slaves. Dred Scott was a slave who had moved with his master from Missouri to Wisconsin—a territory where slavery was not allowed. After four years, Scott and his master returned to Missouri, a slave state. His master died there, and Scott was sold to another master. Scott had been told that he should be a free man because he had once lived in a free state. Scott's supporters took the case all the way to the Supreme Court. But the court decided that Scott was still a slave. Slaves were not citizens and had no residence rights. The court further stated that slavery could not be prohibited in free states. The announcement of this decision in 1857 caused a violent public reaction and increased the bad feelings that had built up between the North and the South.

Unrest among slaves grew. Support for the abolition of slavery spread in the North. People wanted slavery

▲ *Pierre Dominique Toussaint L'Ouverture, the slave who at the beginning of the 1800's led the revolution in Haiti against the French slave-owners.*

▶ *General Sherman's march from Atlanta to the sea in 1864 helped free the slaves and destroy what was left of the South's economic system based on cotton and slavery. Often books and movies tell you how romantic the days of the old South were, but they were not very romantic if you happened to be a slave.*

In Muslim countries, slaves were sometimes recruited as soldiers and as government officials. In some cases, as with the Mamluks of Egypt, they became so powerful in these posts that they were able to take control from their former masters.

abolished because they believed it was morally wrong for one human being to own another. A strong group of antislavery supporters, called *abolitionists*, wanted drastic steps taken immediately to rid the country of slavery. There were not many abolitionists, but they were very active. William Lloyd Garrison, one of their leaders, put out an antislavery newspaper denouncing slavery. Others formed the Underground Railroad, a system whereby slaves were helped to escape to the North. Members of the Underground Railroad claimed they led more than 40,000 slaves to freedom.

The issue of slavery was not settled until the end of the Civil War. During the war, President Lincoln issued the Emancipation Proclamation, effective January 1, 1863, which ended slavery in the Confederate States. The Proclamation said that slaves "shall be then, thenceforward, and forever free." However, it was not until ratification of the Thirteenth Amendment to the Constitution in 1865 that slavery was completely abolished. But this amendment did not provide safeguards to protect black people. Thus, Congress proposed the Fourteenth Amendment, which guaranteed the rights of citizenship to freed slaves. It declared that no state could take away any of these rights. If any states prevented citizens from voting, then the representation of those states in Congress would be cut.

The custom of slavery was a heavy burden for both the black and the white to bear. The Civil War freed blacks from bondage, but tensions and racial discrimination continued. Civil rights laws passed during the 1960's have gone far to assure black citizens of their legal and constitutional rights. Since then, racialism has been slowly dying out, although it is not yet dead. The story of slavery, and how it affected the succeeding generations of one black family, was vividly portrayed in the novel *Roots* by Alex Haley. It was later made into a popular television series.

▼ *When they heard that they were free, many slaves left their plantations and traveled north under the protection of the victorious Union armies.*

ALSO READ: ABOLITION; BLACK AMERICANS; BROWN, JOHN; CITIZENSHIP; CIVIL RIGHTS; CIVIL WAR; CONFEDERATE STATES OF AMERICA; EMANCIPATION PROCLAMATION; LINCOLN, ABRAHAM; MASON-DIXON LINE; RECONSTRUCTION; SPARTACUS; TUBMAN, HARRIET; UNDERGROUND RAILROAD.